THE EFFICIENT EPICURE

Lisa Yockelson

1817

HARPER & ROW, PUBLISHERS, New York
Cambridge, Philadelphia, San Francisco,
London, Mexico City, São Paulo, Sydney

FIRST EDITION

Designer: C. Linda Dingler

Library of Congress Cataloging in Publication Data

Yockelson, Lisa.
  The efficient epicure.

  Includes index.
  1. Cookery. I. Title.
  TX652.Y6   641.5   81-47681
  ISBN 0-06-038016-0 AACR2

82 83 84 85 86 10 9 8 7 6 5 4 3 2 1

For my great-grandmother, Rebecca,
For my grandmother, Lilly,
For my mother, Irene
—businesswomen all, who had great taste—

And,
I take pleasure in extending cupfuls of
thanks to Patricia Falk Feeley, who continu-
ally nurtured the concept of this book from
the time it was but a germ of an idea.

CONTENTS

1
HOW TO BE
AN EFFICIENT EPICURE

For all of you who care about good food and want to enjoy home-cooked meals, but don't have hours every evening to cook, I have a scheme that shows you how to cook in the time you have for the time you don't, without sacrificing the quality of the food that is served.

How is this scheme accomplished? You set aside a block of time after grocery shopping, or during an open weekend morning or afternoon, for preparing a series of main courses to refrigerate for the upcoming week, or freeze for weeks later.

Basically, you shop for several meals at a time, do all the peeling, chopping, and measuring at once, and then put together the dishes in the order of the time they take to cook. While the slowest-cooking dish is simmering, you're at work on the speedier ones. With a little advance thinking, you can have a week's meals prepared in the time it normally takes you to do one, and can outfit your refrigerator with good food to eat during the week.

THE RECIPES

Most of the recipes in this book call for cuts of meat that improve with reheating—shoulders, shanks, breasts, pot roasts, and briskets. These and the chicken fricassees and the sauce bases for aromatic fish stews may be reheated to piping hot with great success. But to make them truly magical, the recipes direct you to wait until serving day to finish the dish with the additions of fresh vegetables, herbs, and the like. On serving day you might cook up the Brussels sprouts and add them along with a few teaspoons of minced dill to a ragout of lamb, or kernels of summer corn and just-shelled lima beans to complete a chicken dish. The last-minute additions are simple. They make each dish glow and guarantee perfectly cooked vegetables.

On serving day, while the main course reheats, you can also wash some salad greens, set a pot of potatoes to steam or a vegetable gratin to bake, or assemble one of the fresh fruit desserts. For a change, you'll have time on your hands. You'll find the recipes for all sorts of accompaniments in Part Two of the book.

You'll note that the main-course recipes (Part One) are grouped by season in order to take advantage of the glorious fresh fruits and vegetables available at the market.

THE COOKING SESSIONS

The Efficient Epicure is divided into a series of weekly cooking sessions—sixteen in all, each with its own Cook's Plan. To plan for each week's cooking session, decide how many of the main courses you want to prepare. Draw up a master list of ingredients after checking what you have on hand in the pantry, refrigerator, and freezer. Also, glance at the suggested accompaniments mentioned at the base of each recipe and, if you choose to make them, add the necessary ingredients to the shopping list.

When you're ready to cook, consult The Cook's Plan. The Cook's Plan organizes your working time in the most efficient way. First, all of the necessary equipment is collected: there is a list of the casseroles, pots, pans, and the like to be put into service for each dish. Then, you set about to prepare the vegetables, measure out such things as tomato purée, broth, wine, and so on, tie up herb bundles, for all the recipes you've selected. If you are not assembling every main course suggested in the week's plan, be sure to adjust the quantities of the measured ingredients in the Cook's Plan. When everything is chopped and measured, the dishes are ready to assemble following a prescribed cooking order. The dish that needs to cook the longest is put together first, or if there is any preliminary soaking (such as for dried beans), that procedure takes place first. Then the remaining dishes are set to cook.

The first part of each recipe takes the dish through preparation up to the point it can be stored. Instructions for storage and recommended storage times for both refrigeration and freezing are listed in the recipes under the heading "To Store." (These storage times have been established through many elaborate testing sessions.) When you are ready to serve the main course, return to the recipe and follow the second part—"To Serve"—which describes how to finish the dish.

A FINE BALANCE

Because fish and shellfish as well as certain cuts of meat—like chops and scaloppine—are at their very best when prepared just prior to serving, and because they add variety and texture to a week's menu, I've included recipes for them to round out every week. These dishes are really very easy to put together and need no advance preparation. In fact, if you're caught off guard with no meal preplanned and want to cook something elegant, yet fast and easy, look for the symbol (see below), as those main courses can be put together quickly and served right away.

MAIN COURSES OF THE WEEK

Since some prepared entrées hold better than others, they are listed every week in the order in which it makes sense to serve them. A chicken fricassee, for example, should not linger in the refrigerator for too many days, and for that reason the dish appears early in the week. If you find it's not convenient to serve the chicken early in the week, simply freeze it for another time.

When you see this symbol ✳ preceding a recipe title, remember that this is a quick-cooking entrée. It is added to fill out the week, but because it doesn't need ahead-of-time preparation, it's not incorporated into the week's Cook's Plan.

The recipes in this book will feed four adults quite generously and can be stretched to feed five or six by adding a potato dish, rice, or buttered noodles, a nice loaf of bread, and a simple green salad.

A SPECIAL KIND OF COOKBOOK

The Efficient Epicure is designed to save you time in the kitchen by helping you make a series of main courses at one cooking session. By following the Cook's Plan for each week, you save considerably on the duplication of tasks. What's more, you can take advantage of the time when you are waiting for a dish to simmer or bake to get started on another dish. In several hours, as many as five dishes can be cooked through, then readied to store or freeze for future use. If you find you don't need all of the main courses during the week, just pop them into the freezer for later use, or make only as many as you will need. In fact, though *The Efficient Epicure* is designed around making many main courses at once, there's no reason why you can't use it like an ordinary cookbook, flipping through the pages until your eye alights on a recipe you'd love to make, or checking the index for ideas and recipes for new ways to cook favorite meats and vegetables.

The recipes are all my personal favorites, and they're the ones readers of my columns and articles, my cooking students, and friends ask for most. However you use *The Efficient Epicure*, I hope the recipes will delight you as much as they have us. And though good cookery does take time, I hope my methods and menus will save you hours in the kitchen. The only ingredient the book lacks, you'll supply: what to do with all those hours you save every week.

RELIABLES

Good stock and tomato purée are basic preparations worth keeping on hand. They add a special well-rounded flavor to home-cooked food, and are a joy to have all cooked up and in the freezer.

When tomatoes are cheap and plentiful, I turn batches of them into a purée and freeze masses of the stuff. The purée captures the fresh taste of summer's plum tomatoes and stores exquisitely for many months in the freezer when parceled out into individual containers. Though canned plum tomatoes, chopped up with their juice, are a perfectly acceptable substitute for the homemade purée, here is my favorite version of tomato purée:

FRESH TOMATO PURÉE

for each 4 pounds of fresh plum
   tomatoes, washed well:
1 tablespoon coarse salt

1. Cut each tomato in half, and as they are cut, pop them into a large nonmetallic pot. Sprinkle the coarse salt over the tomatoes.

2. Cover the pot and cook the tomatoes over low heat for 15 minutes or until some of the juices begin to well up. Simmer, covered, for another 15 minutes.

3. Uncover the pot and cook the tomatoes at a lively simmer, adjusting the heat properly so that they do not scorch. Stir the pot every so often. Simmer until the tomatoes have thickened up, about 1 hour 30 minutes, or longer as necessary.

4. Pass the tomatoes through a food mill to purée them, leaving skin and seeds behind. Cool and parcel out the tomato purée into containers. Label according to the contents and amount. (I find ½ and 1 cup the handiest quantities in which to freeze the purée.) Refrigerate until quite cold, then freeze.

Stews and other types of casseroles depend on liquid to see them through the long simmering times. The most important of these liquids is stock. Good, characterful home-made stock will enhance any dish, and here are three recipes for beef, chicken, and fish stock. If you do not have homemade stock in the freezer, commercially bottled and canned broth can be substituted.

BEEF STOCK

3 pounds beef bones
2 pounds beef bones with some meat on
them
1 pound veal bones (including a knuckle
or two, if possible)
3 carrots, trimmed, left unpeeled, and
quartered

1 large onion, unpeeled and quartered
2 ribs celery, quartered
1 tablespoon coarse salt
1 imported bay leaf
3 celery leaf sprigs
8 parsley stalks
12 peppercorns

1. Put the beef and veal bones in a 10-quart kettle or stockpot. Pour in enough cold water to cover the bones and set the pot over a medium flame. Bring the water to a simmer, skimming well as the grayish brown scum floats to the top.

2. Place the vegetables into the stockpot, along with the coarse salt. Tie the bay leaf, celery leaf sprigs, and parsley stalks together with a piece of kitchen string and add to the pot. Dump in the peppercorns.

3. Add more water to cover the vegetables, if necessary, partially cover, and cook the stock at a gentle simmer for a minimum for 4 hours, 6 if possible, for best flavor and strength. Simmer the stock, uncovered, for the last hour.

4. Strain the stock into bowls, cool to room temperature, then cover and refrigerate. The next day, remove the layer of fat that has hardened over the top. Portion out the stock into individual containers and freeze.

NOTE: For Brown Beef Stock, put all the bones and root vegetables into a roasting pan and brown them in the upper level of a preheated 425° F oven for 35–40 minutes, until they have taken on a deep brown color. Drain off any fat that may have accumulated and put the bones in the stockpot. Complete the procedure as for beef stock.

CHICKEN STOCK

2 pounds veal bones, including a knuckle
or two
4 pounds chicken bones
1 imported bay leaf
8 parsley stems
1 tablespoon coarse salt

10 peppercorns
2 onions, quartered
2 carrots, trimmed, left unpeeled, and
quartered
2 ribs celery, quartered

1. Put the veal bones in a large pot, cover with cold water, and bring to the boil. Boil slowly for 3 minutes. Drain the bones and rinse thoroughly under cool water to clean off the scum.

2. Place the chicken bones and veal bones in a 10-quart stockpot. Tie the bay leaf with the parsley stems. Add to the bones with the coarse salt and peppercorns. Cover with water; bring the water to the simmer, skimming for the first 10 minutes. Add the vegetables. Simmer the stock, partially covered, for a minimum of 4 hours or as long as 6. Remove the cover from the pot the last hour. Cool, strain, and store as directed in the preceding recipe for Beef Stock.

NOTE: For Brown Chicken Stock, boil the veal bones as instructed. Film a large skillet with vegetable oil and brown the root vegetables and bones in several batches in the hot oil, browning the chicken bones too. Add the bones to the stockpot and continue with the recipe.

FISH STOCK

6 pounds clean lean fish trimmings and
   frames, including some heads
1 onion, peeled and sliced
2 carrots, peeled and sliced
2 ribs celery, sliced

1 imported bay leaf
8 parsley stems
3 sprigs of celery leaves
10 peppercorns
1 tablespoon coarse salt

1. Layer the fish trimmings, frames, and heads with the vegetables in a 10-quart stockpot. Tie the bay leaf together with the parsley stems and celery leaves. Add to the pot along with the peppercorns and salt.

2. Pour on enough cold water to cover the contents of the pot. Bring the liquid to a simmer over moderate heat, skimming off the scum that surfaces. Simmer the stock, uncovered, for 30 minutes. Strain, cool, and store the stock as directed in the recipe for Beef Stock (page 7).

STORING PREPARED FOOD

Storing home-cooked food in the refrigerator or freezer, prepared from ingredients you select, is just like having a luxurious take-out specialty store within reach. However, even the most carefully prepared fine food does not keep forever, and really not nearly as long as those standard freezer charts promise. To keep the main courses fresh and lively, note the storage times recommended for each dish.

When you are freezing food, use heavy-duty plastic storage containers—the kind with the lids that make airtight seals. Fill to within an inch of the top so that there is room for the contents to expand during freezing. Before you cover the container, gently push down the solids so that the liquid covers them. I have found that a small piece of aluminum foil placed directly on top of the food before the storage carton is sealed offers double protection against the top layer of food drying out.

Label everything that is stored with the name of the dish, the date prepared, and the number of servings. If you have ever defrosted a quart of meat sauce thinking that it was some kind of soup, you'll appreciate spending the extra few minutes to label containers properly. Notes on reheating and last-minute additions are quite helpful for family members who may be heating up the main courses on their own. For example:

Name of dish/page number:	Braised Veal Cubes with Mushrooms and Tarragon, page 148
Number of servings/date prepared:	For 4—4/27/82
Information for reheating and serving-day additions:	Covered casserole/low flame/mushrooms, tarragon

EQUIPMENT

Here is a short list of the pots and pans that are called for most frequently in this book. If you are purchasing equipment, buy the best you can afford: durable, professional-quality equipment.

Casseroles: Enameled cast-iron pots hold heat perfectly and simmer food to a succulent finish. Casserole covers should fit well so that moisture isn't lost through evaporation. Ideally, you should equip yourself with a 4-quart round casserole, three 6-quart casseroles, and a 12-inch oval one. These are the most convenient sizes.

Doufeu: A *doufeu* is an unusual type of casserole that works very well for braising foods. The lid of the *doufeu,* all but a large outer band, dips in to form a deep recess which is filled with cool water or ice cubes (I prefer the latter). The cool liquid encourages condensation. The underside of the lid is covered with small raised dots. The steam gathers around the dots and finally drips back onto the food, basting it during cooking. A *doufeu* of 6-quart capacity is a handy size to have in your collection of pots and pans.

Sauté pan: Choose a heavyweight one that's 10 inches in diameter with straight sides about 2½ inches high. It should be sturdy so that it will sit atop a burner without tilting or falling over. The bottom should be thick so it conducts heat evenly. You'll need a lid.

Large soup pot or kettle: Choose a 12- or 16-quart pot (12- or 14-inch diameter) with a lid that fits tightly for a good seal.

Gratin pans: These shallow bake-and-serve dishes are available round and oval. I generally use the oval pans. Eight, 9, 10, and 12 inches are good sizes to have, unless you regularly cook for eight people, in which case you will need the 14-inch size. Ovenproof porcelain gratin dishes are easy to wash up and look pretty on the table. Copper gratin dishes are quite handsome, but do need to be polished.

Also worth having on hand are sharp, well-balanced knives (the recipes don't require a food processor). A sturdy electric hand beater, one with several speeds, is a good investment if you do not own a freestanding electric mixer. In addition to plenty of bowls to handle everything that is chopped, minced, and sliced, you need several measuring cups and sets of measuring spoons, a food mill to purée sauces, and a nest or two of sturdy storage containers with snug lids.

PART ONE

THE SEASONAL MAIN COURSES

2

THE AUTUMN WEEKS

MAIN COURSES

* Shrimp with Mussels in Wine

Sweetbreads with Spinach

Rosemary Chicken with Cauliflower

Ragout of Lamb with Dill

Garlic Sausages and Cabbage

Paprika Veal with Mushrooms and *Crème Fraîche*

* Pork with Sweet Red Peppers

THE COOK'S PLAN

1. Set out 6-quart casserole with lid for the Ragout of Lamb with Dill, 6-quart casserole with lid for the Paprika Veal with Mushrooms and *Crème Fraîche*, 6-quart casserole with lid for starting the cabbage in Garlic Sausages and Cabbage, 4-quart casserole with lid for the Sweetbreads with Spinach, 10-inch sauté pan with lid for the Rosemary Chicken with Cauliflower.

2. Thaw and measure out about 9 cups chicken stock.

3. Wash and dry 3 ribs celery.

4. Peel 6 onions, 5 garlic cloves, 2 carrots.

5. Finely chop 1 garlic clove; chop 2 garlic cloves, 1 onion; roughly chop 2 heaping tablespoons rosemary leaves; slice 2 carrots, 4 onions, 3 celery ribs; thinly slice 1 onion, 2-pound head cabbage; cube ¼-pound piece of bacon.

6. Measure out about 4½ cups white wine; 1½ tablespoons tomato paste; ¾ cup tomato purée or canned plum tomatoes; 1½ tablespoons sweet Hungarian paprika; 2 tablespoons white wine vinegar.

7. Set out olive oil, vegetable oil, butter, salt, pepper, flour.

8. Tie herb bundles: 1 small imported bay leaf with 3 parsley stems and 2 sprigs fresh thyme; 1 imported bay leaf with 8 parsley stems and 3 branches fresh thyme.

9. Trim sweetbreads and soak, Step 1 (page 16).

10. Garlic Sausages and Cabbage: Trim, core, and thinly slice the cabbage; begin to cook, Steps 1–3 (page 17).

11. Ragout of Lamb with Dill: Brown the lamb cubes; add onion, wine, garlic, and herbs; simmer, Steps 1–3 (page 18).

12. Paprika Veal with Mushrooms and *Crème Fraîche:* Brown the veal, season, add wine; simmer with the wine and stock, Steps 1–3 (page 20).

13. Sweetbreads with Spinach: Set the sweetbreads to simmer with the aromatic vegetables, white wine, and stock, Steps 2–3 (page 16).

14. Rosemary Chicken with Cauliflower: Prepare through Step 4 (page 21).

15. Cool all dishes to room temperature; refrigerate or freeze, following the instructions in "To Store" of each recipe.

SWEETBREADS WITH SPINACH

This is a fine, delicate way for doing sweetbreads. After an initial trimming and soaking, the sweetbreads are simmered in a white wine liquid flavored with slices of onion, carrot, and celery. After this stage, the liquid is concentrated and the sweetbreads are stored overnight, awaiting a final reheating in spinach and heavy cream.

2½ pounds sweetbreads
½ teaspoon salt
1 onion, sliced
2 tablespoons butter
1 carrot, sliced
1 rib celery heart, sliced
⅔ cup dry white wine
1⅔ cups chicken stock
1 small imported bay leaf tied with 3 parsley stems and 2 sprigs of fresh thyme

To Serve

½ pound spinach, cooked and finely chopped
2 tablespoons butter
salt and freshly ground pepper
several pinches of freshly ground nutmeg
¾ cup heavy cream, warmed
1 teaspoon lemon juice

1. Wash the sweetbreads under cold running water and peel off the clinging thin outer membrane. Cut away any tubes. Soak the sweetbreads in cold water for 1½ hours, changing the water several times during that period.

2. Drain the sweetbreads, put them in a large saucepan, and pour in enough cold water to cover them by 1½ inches. Add the ½ teaspoon salt. Bring the sweetbreads to a boil, drain, and run cool water over them. Dry the sweetbreads on paper toweling and remove any outer membranes still lurking on the surface.

3. In a 4-quart casserole, soften the onion in the 2 tablespoons butter over moderately low heat. Add the carrot and celery slices; stir to coat with the butter. Cover and cook over low heat for 10 minutes. Pour in the wine and bring to the simmer. Add the sweetbreads, pour the chicken stock over them, and drop in the herb bundle. Bring the liquid to a simmer, cover, and simmer slowly for 40 minutes.

To Store   Cool the sweetbreads in the cooking liquid. When cool, remove the sweetbreads to a storage container. Discard the herb bundle. Strain the liquid (with all the vegetables) through a food mill into a container. Cover both containers and refrigerate when room temperature for up to 1 day.

To Serve   On serving day, cut the sweetbreads into 2-inch clusters. In a skillet, sauté the spinach in the 2 tablespoons of butter until hot. Stir in the strained cooking liquid and the sweetbreads. Bring to a rapid simmer; simmer for 4 minutes, or until the liquid has reduced and the sweetbreads begin to warm up. Pour in the warmed heavy cream and simmer until all the components are piping hot throughout. Season well with salt, pepper, and freshly ground nutmeg. Stir in the lemon juice and serve from a warm platter.

Menu Suggestion   Follow the sweetbreads with Figs in Black-Currant Syrup (page 283).

SHOPPING LIST
Meat: sweetbreads
Vegetables and fruit: spinach, onion, carrot, celery, lemon
Dairy: butter, heavy cream

Staples: chicken stock, dry white wine
Herbs and spice: bay leaf, parsley, thyme, ground nutmeg

GARLIC SAUSAGES AND CABBAGE

A foundation of cabbage for savory sausages: the cabbage shreds simmer lazily in a little white wine, and the whole is flavored with onion and thyme sprigs. The exceptional quality of the cabbage dish makes reheating just as aromatic, if not more so, than it was on the day it was prepared.

4 tablespoons olive oil
1 onion, thinly sliced
1 garlic clove, finely chopped
2-pound head firm, white cabbage, trimmed, cored, and thinly sliced
½ cup dry white wine
salt and freshly ground pepper

2 sprigs thyme

To Serve

3 tablespoons olive oil
8 garlic sausages
⅓ cup white wine
2 tablespoons warm water

1. Heat the 4 tablespoons olive oil in a heavy 6-quart casserole over a moderate flame. Stir in the onion slices and cook for 2 minutes. Add the chopped garlic and continue cooking for another minute.

2. Stir in the sliced cabbage and combine it well with the onion, garlic, and oil. Cook for several minutes, stirring, until the shreds have wilted down slightly. Pour in the wine, season with salt and pepper to taste, and bury the thyme sprigs in the cabbage.

3. Cover the casserole and cook the cabbage very slowly over a low flame for 2½–3 hours or until quite tender. Give the cabbage a few stirs as it cooks.

To Store   Cool the cabbage to room temperature. Remove the branches of thyme and refrigerate the cabbage in a tightly covered storage container for up to 5 days.

(continued)

To Serve   Heat the cabbage in a covered casserole over low heat. Put the 3 tablespoons olive oil in a heavy skillet and place over moderately high heat. Brown the sausages in the oil. Pour off the oil and pour in the wine and warm water. Cover the pan and cook the sausages at a simmer for 25 minutes or until cooked throughout. Make sure that the cover of the pan fits tightly; otherwise the liquid will evaporate faster than the sausages are able to cook. Taste the cabbage and check for additional seasoning, then turn it out onto a warm serving platter. Top with the sausages and any pan juices.

Menu Suggestion   Serve Warm Potato Salad with White Wine (page 250) along with the sausages and sauerkraut; follow with the Gratin of Apples with Brown Sugar and Pecans (page 269).

SHOPPING LIST
Meat: garlic sausages
Vegetables: onion, cabbage, garlic

Staples: olive oil, dry white wine
Herb: fresh thyme

RAGOUT OF LAMB WITH DILL

This dish will be a change for those who are unaccustomed to cooking with fresh herbs. The most important ingredients are a number of garlic cloves, very subtle because they are kept in the outer papery skin, and a shock of fresh dill folded into the dish at the end. Use only the feathery parts of the dill sprigs and cut them from their stems with a pair of sharp scissors.

2¾–3 pounds boneless lamb shoulder, cut into 2-inch cubes, including some of the bones from the piece, if possible
3½ tablespoons vegetable oil
salt and freshly ground pepper
2 tablespoons butter
1 onion, chopped
1 cup dry white wine
12 garlic cloves, left unpeeled and whole

1½ tablespoons tomato paste
2¾ cups chicken stock
1 imported bay leaf tied with 8 parsley stems and 3 branches of fresh thyme

To Serve

2 pints Brussels sprouts, trimmed and boiled gently until tender-crisp
1 small bunch of dill, snipped (about ½ cup loosely packed)

1. Dry the lamb cubes on paper toweling. Heat the oil in a heavy 6-quart casserole and brown the lamb cubes in batches. Remove the cubes to a plate as they brown and season with salt and pepper. Brown the bones, too, if you have any.

2. Pour out the oil from the casserole and add the butter. Stir in the chopped onion and cook over moderate heat for 2 minutes. Pour in the wine and scrape up the bits clinging to the bottom of the casserole. Add the garlic cloves, stir in the tomato paste, and pour in the chicken stock.

3. Add the lamb cubes to the casserole, drop in the herb bundle, and lay the browned bones on top. Bring the contents of the casserole to a simmer, cover tightly, and simmer on the stove top or in the lower third of a preheated 325° F oven for 1¾–2 hours or until the lamb is tender.

To Store   Discard the lamb bones and remove the lamb cubes to a storage container. Degrease the cooking liquid and purée it , along with all the solids, in a food mill. Pour the puréed liquid over the cubes. Cool the lamb to room temperature; then cover and refrigerate for up to 5 days or freeze for up to 1 month.

To Serve   Reheat the lamb in a covered casserole. If the sauce is thin, remove the lamb from the pot and boil down the liquid until syrupy. Add the cooked Brussels sprouts (simmered on serving day and not in advance) and snipped dill to the lamb, adjust the seasoning, and simmer for a few minutes longer to combine the flavors. Spoon the lamb and Brussels sprouts onto a warm serving platter.

Menu Suggestion   Serve Buttered Noodles (page 253), steamed potatoes, or rice along with the ragout; follow with a Watercress and Walnut Salad (page 263); for dessert a fruit salad of apples, bananas, and oranges steeped in orange and lemon juice with enough honey to sweeten and a little dark rum.

SHOPPING LIST
Meat: lamb shoulder
Vegetables: Brussels sprouts, onions, garlic
Dairy: butter

Staples: vegetable oil, dry white wine, tomato paste, chicken stock
Herbs: bay leaf, parsley, thyme, dill

PAPRIKA VEAL WITH MUSHROOMS
AND *CRÈME FRAÎCHE*

This veal dish has a smooth and vibrant paprika taste and creamy quality, owing to the dense character of *crème fraîche.* The paprika cooks with the veal in the braising liquid. On serving day, the *crème fraîche* enriches the sauce, mildens it, and changes the color to a soft rose-red.

2¾–3 pounds boneless veal shoulder, cut into 2-inch cubes
3½ tablespoons vegetable oil
salt and freshly ground pepper
2 onions, sliced
2 garlic cloves, peeled and halved
1 carrot, sliced
2 small ribs celery heart, sliced
1½ tablespoons sweet Hungarian paprika
1¼ cups dry white wine

¾ cup tomato purée (homemade) or chopped canned plum tomatoes
1 small imported bay leaf
2½ cups chicken stock

To Serve

1 pound small fresh mushrooms
2 tablespoons butter
2 teaspoons lemon juice
¾ cup *crème fraîche* or sour cream
1½ tablespoons finely chopped parsley

1. Dry the veal cubes on paper toweling. Heat the oil in a heavy 6-quart casserole and brown the veal cubes, a batch at a time. Remove the cubes to a plate as they are browned and season them with salt and pepper.

2. Drain all but 2 tablespoons oil from the casserole (or add more oil, if necessary) and sauté the onions for 2 minutes. Stir in the garlic clove halves and carrot and celery slices. Sauté for 2 minutes. Stir in the paprika and cook for 1 minute; it should darken a bit and release a pungent aroma.

3. Pour the wine into the casserole. Stir in the tomato purée or canned tomatoes, bay leaf, and chicken stock. Season with salt and freshly ground pepper. Replace the meat, stir, and bring the contents of the casserole to a simmer. Cover the casserole securely and cook the veal in the lower third of a preheated 325° F oven for 1¾–2 hours or on the stove top at a gentle simmer, until the veal is tender when pierced with a fork.

To Store Remove the meat to a storage bowl. Discard the bay leaf and strain the liquid and vegetables through a food mill. Pour the sauce over the meat, cool, cover, and store in the refrigerator for up to 5 days or freeze for up to 1 month.

To Serve Heat the veal in a casserole with the cover slightly askew. While the veal is heating, trim the mushroom stems level with the caps. (Store the stems, packed in a plastic bag, in the freezer for use in making up a pot of stock.) Melt the butter in a saucepan, and stir in the mushrooms and lemon juice. Season the mushrooms with salt and pepper, cover, and cook over moderate heat for 3 minutes.

If the sauce in the casserole is not lightly condensed, remove the meat and boil down the liquid rapidly. Add the mushrooms and bring to a rapid simmer. Simmer for 5 minutes and adjust the seasoning with additional salt and pepper, to taste.

Blend ½ cup of the cooking liquid with the *crème fraîche* in a small mixing bowl. Remove the casserole from the heat and return the *crème fraîche* mixture to the casserole, stirring well. Put the casserole back over moderate heat, bring to a simmer, and stir and cook a few moments longer to blend the flavors. Fold in the chopped parsley and serve.

Menu Suggestion   Serve Buttered Noodles (page 253) or steamed potatoes along with the veal; follow with a homey dessert such as whole, tart cooking apples baked with honey, heavy cream, raisins, and a little sweet butter and served warm.

SHOPPING LIST
Meat: veal shoulder
Vegetables and fruit: onions, garlic, carrot, celery, mushrooms, lemon
Dairy: butter, *crème fraîche*

Staples: tomato purée or canned plum tomatoes, dry white wine, chicken stock
Herbs and spice: parsley, bay leaf, paprika

ROSEMARY CHICKEN WITH CAULIFLOWER

This dish depends on a branch or two of fresh rosemary. The dried herb won't work here —the taste would be too harsh and less authentic.

¼-pound piece of bacon, trimmed of rind and cut into cubes
1 tablespoon butter
3 tablespoons vegetable oil
2¾–3-pound chicken, cut into serving pieces
½ cup all-purpose flour, in a shallow bowl
salt and freshly ground pepper
1 onion, chopped
2 garlic cloves, chopped

2 tablespoons white wine vinegar
2 heaping teaspoons fresh rosemary leaves, roughly chopped
1 cup dry white wine
2 cups chicken stock

To Serve

1 head cauliflower
⅓ cup milk
2 teaspoons butter, softened
1 tablespoon finely chopped parsley

1. Drop the bacon cubes into a pot of boiling water, simmer for 10 minutes, drain, and dry on paper towels.

2. Heat the butter and oil in a 10-inch sauté pan over moderately high heat. Lightly dredge the chicken parts, a few at a time, in the flour and brown the pieces on both sides

in the oil and butter. Remove the chicken pieces to a plate as they are browned and season with salt and pepper.

3. Remove all but 2 tablespoons of the oil-butter (or, if the oil-butter has burned, rinse out the pan and add a fresh chunk of butter). Stir in the bacon cubes and sauté until just golden. Stir in the chopped onion and cook for 3 minutes over moderately low heat. Add the garlic and continue cooking for 2 minutes. Sprinkle on the vinegar and rosemary, stir, and cook for 1 minute.

4. Pour the white wine and chicken stock into the pan. Add the chicken parts and baste with the liquid. Bring the contents of the pan to a simmer, cover, and simmer for 30 minutes or until the chicken is tender. Turn the chicken in the liquid once or twice while cooking.

To Store   Cool the chicken in the liquid, then transfer to a storage container. Cover and refrigerate for up to 2 days or freeze for up to 2 weeks.

To Serve   Divide the head of cauliflower into flowerets and place them in a large pot. Pour in the milk and add enough cold water to cover. Add a few pinches of salt and bring to the boil. Simmer the cauliflower until tender, about 10–12 minutes. Drain.

While the cauliflower is cooking, reheat the chicken in a covered pan. Add the cauliflower, season with salt and pepper as necessary, and simmer until piping hot throughout. If the sauce seems too thin, remove the chicken and cauliflower and keep warm while you boil down the cooking liquid until it has taken on body; replace the chicken and simmer for a few moments longer. Remove the pan from the heat. Swirl in the butter and fold in the chopped parsley.

Menu Suggestion   Follow the chicken with Bread Pudding with Dates and Walnuts (page 276). Begin the preparation of the pudding before you cook the cauliflower or heat up the chicken.

SHOPPING LIST
Meat and poultry: bacon, chicken
Vegetables: onion, garlic, cauliflower
Dairy: butter, milk

Staples: vegetable oil, flour, white wine vinegar, dry white wine, chicken stock
Herbs: rosemary, parsley

✻ SHRIMP WITH MUSSELS IN WINE

The best part of this dish is when you mop up the "gravy" from the mussel-shrimp-tomato combination (spicy with garlic and hot pepper) with slices from a sturdy loaf of bread. Indeed, this is a simple and straightforward dish to prepare, one that easily adapts to first-course status if the amount of shrimp is slightly reduced. Follow with a simple sauté of fish to preserve the tone of the meal.

3 tablespoons olive oil
3 shallots, finely chopped
3 garlic cloves, finely chopped
3 tablespoons finely chopped parsley
1 small fresh hot pepper, cored, seeded, and finely chopped, or ¼ teaspoon crushed red pepper

¾ cup dry white wine
1¼ cups tomato purée (homemade) or chopped canned plum tomatoes
salt
3 dozen mussels, well scrubbed
1 pound shrimp, shelled, with the tails left intact, and deveined

1. Heat the olive oil in a heavy pot large enough to contain the bulk of the mussels and shrimp. (One of your 6-quart casseroles will work well here.) Stir in the shallots and cook for 3 minutes over moderately low heat.

2. Stir in the chopped garlic and cook for 2 minutes. Add the chopped parsley and hot pepper. Pour in the wine and let it bubble up gently for a few seconds.

3. Stir in the tomato purée or plum tomatoes and season lightly with salt. Simmer this mixture, uncovered, for 20 minutes.

4. Put in the mussels, toss them around in the garlic-tomato liquid, cover the pan, and raise the heat to moderately high. Cook the mussels until they *just* begin to open. Toss in the shrimp and cook for 2–3 minutes longer—the mussels should be fully opened and the shrimp should turn opaque. Do not overcook.

5. Serve the mussels and shrimp from wide, deep plates or bowls, and be sure to include spoonfuls of the good wine, tomato, and garlic "gravy."

Menu Suggestion   Follow with a simple mixed green salad that includes a healthy amount of watercress.

Shopping List
Shellfish: mussels, shrimp
Vegetables: shallots, garlic, hot pepper

Staples: olive oil, dry white wine, tomato purée or canned plum tomatoes
Herb: parsley

✳ PORK WITH SWEET RED PEPPERS

The appeal of the red peppers and anchovies in this dish is the way they play against the flavor of the pork. You could marinate the pork chops briefly before cooking in 2 teaspoons of lemon juice, 2 tablespoons of olive oil, and a turn or two of freshly ground pepper to point up the flavor of the meat, then pat dry on paper toweling before browning. To do this and not waste time, marinate the chops right away, then set the soup to reheat (if you are serving soup), cut up and sauté the red peppers (Step 3) for later on, and finally chop, slice, and measure all the remaining ingredients the recipe calls for before browning the chops.

3 tablespoons vegetable oil
4 loin pork chops cut 1 inch thick
3½ tablespoons olive oil
1½ tablespoons butter
2 onions, thinly sliced
2 garlic cloves, chopped

2 anchovy fillets, chopped
1 tablespoon finely chopped parsley
⅓ cup dry white wine
salt and freshly ground pepper
3 firm sweet red peppers, cored, seeded,
  and cut into strips

1. Heat the vegetable oil in a skillet over moderately high heat and brown the pork chops on both sides.

2. In a 10-inch casserole, heat 1½ tablespoons of the olive oil and butter over moderately low heat. Soften the onions in the butter and oil. Stir in the chopped garlic and cook for 2 minutes. Add the anchovy fillets, mashing them in with the back of a spoon until dissolved into the onions and garlic. Stir in the chopped parsley. Pour in the wine, arrange the pork chops in it, and season with salt (remember the anchovies lend their own saltiness) and pepper. Baste the tops of the pork chops with a little of the pan juices. Bring the contents of the casserole to a rapid simmer, cover tightly, and bake in a preheated 325° F oven for 15 minutes.

3. While the chops are cooking, prepare the red pepper strips. Heat the remaining 2 tablespoons olive oil in a skillet and sauté the peppers until barely tender. Season lightly with freshly ground pepper.

4. After the pork has cooked for 15 minutes, add the peppers and moisten everything with the pan juices. Cover and continue to cook for another 15 minutes or until the chops are cooked through. Adjust the seasoning and transfer the pork along with the peppers (and all the pan juices) to a warm serving platter, spooning the peppers and sauce over and around the chops.

Menu Suggestion   Begin with Broccoli and Celery Soup (page 210); for dessert, any kind of poached pear arrangement served with a puréed fresh fruit sauce or a fruit preserve sauce.

Meat: pork chops
Vegetables: garlic, onions, sweet red peppers
Dairy: butter

Staples: vegetable oil, olive oil, anchovies, dry white wine
Herb: parsley

MAIN COURSES

* Scallops and Oysters with New Potatoes

Sausages and Eggplant

Chicken with Fennel

Kettle of Beef with Cabbage and Beets

Chestnut-Stuffed Breast of Veal

Lamb with Fresh Figs

* Pork Stuffed with Prunes

THE COOK'S PLAN

1. Set out: soup kettle with lid for the Kettle of Beef with Cabbage and Beets, 4-quart casserole with lid for the Lamb with Fresh Figs, 12-inch oval casserole with lid for the Chestnut-Stuffed Breast of Veal, 10-inch sauté pan with lid for the Chicken with Fennel, 10-inch sauté pan with lid for the Sausages and Eggplant.

2. Thaw and measure out 1¾ cups beef stock, about 4½ cups chicken stock.

3. Wash and dry a bunch of parsley, 4 ribs celery heart, 3 leeks.

4. Peel ⅓ pound chestnuts, 4 onions, 8 garlic cloves, 2 carrots, 6 beets, 2 eggplants.

5. Finely chop 8 garlic cloves, 1 onion, 2 ribs celery heart, 2 tablespoons parsley; chop 2 onions, 1 tablespoon parsley; slice 3 leeks, 1 onion, 2 ribs celery heart; cube 6 beets; dice 2 carrots, ⅓ pound chestnuts; shred 1 head cabbage.

6. Measure out 4 cups dry white wine, 1½ cups tomato purée, 1½ cups canned plum tomatoes, 1½ tablespoons vinegar, 1½ tablespoons sugar, ¾ cup bread crumbs, ⅓ cup milk, ¼ teaspoon ground allspice, 3 allspice berries, 3 cloves, 3 garlic cloves.

7. Set out vegetable oil, olive oil, butter, salt, pepper, flour.

8. Tie herb bundles: 2 bundles, each containing 1 bay leaf and 6 parsley stems; 1 bundle of 1 bay leaf tied with 6 parsley stems and 2 pieces dried orange peel.

9. Kettle of Beef with Cabbage and Beets: Cook the vegetables; add the beef, tomato purée, seasonings, stock; simmer, Steps 1–3 (page 28).

10. Chestnut-Stuffed Breast of Veal: Prepare the chestnut stuffing, stuff the veal breast, sew it up with kitchen string, brown the stuffed breast in the butter and oil, simmer with the vegetables, wine, and stock, Steps 1–3 (page 29).

11. Lamb with Fresh Figs: Brown the lamb; add garlic, parsley, wine, beef stock, orange-scented herb bundle, spices; simmer, Steps 1–2 (page 31).

12. Salt the eggplant for Sausages and Eggplant, Step 1 (page 32).

13. Chicken with Fennel: Prepare through Step 2 (page 33).

14. Sausages and Eggplant: Sauté the eggplant; brown the sausages; cook the onion, garlic, and tomatoes; combine all; simmer, Steps 2–4 (page 32).

15. Cool all dishes to room temperature; refrigerate or freeze, following the instructions in "To Store" of each recipe.

KETTLE OF BEEF WITH CABBAGE AND BEETS

This is a lusty, solidly built brew, in the same category as round loaves of rye and pots of lentil soup, sturdy and filling. It's fun to serve this "kettle" in two courses, the soup with the cabbage and beets, a boiled potato nested in. To this you would stir in some sour cream. Next, take out the beef (keep the cubes warm in some of the soup to this point) and offer some strong horseradish on the side.

3½ tablespoons vegetable oil
1 onion, chopped
3 leeks, white part only, thinly sliced
2 garlic cloves, finely chopped
2 carrots, diced
1-pound head of cabbage, trimmed, cored, and sliced into thin shreds
6 fresh beets, trimmed, peeled, and cubed
1 pound beef bones, blanched and rinsed in cold water (optional)
2 pounds rump pot roast or chuck pot roast, cut into 2-inch cubes
1½ cups tomato purée (homemade) or chopped canned plum tomatoes

1½ quarts beef stock
salt and freshly ground pepper
1 imported bay leaf tied with 6 parsley stems
1½ tablespoons vinegar
1½ tablespoons granulated sugar
¼ teaspoon ground allspice

To Serve

4 sprigs of dill, feathery parts only, snipped
4 small potatoes, boiled until tender and peeled
1 cup sour cream (optional)
strong horseradish (optional)

1. Heat the oil in a heavy soup kettle. Stir in the onions and leeks, and cook over moderate heat for 2 minutes. Add the garlic and carrots, and cook 2 minutes. Stir in the cabbage and cook for a few minutes or until the bulk of it has reduced slightly.

2. Stir in the beets, beef bones (if you have them), beef cubes, and tomato purée or canned tomatoes. Pour on the beef stock, add salt and pepper to taste, and add the bay leaf and parsley package.

3. Bring the contents of the casserole to a simmer, and simmer for several minutes, skimming the top of any scum that rises to the surface. Stir in the vinegar, sugar, and allspice. Cover the pot and simmer for 3 hours; the meat should be very tender.

To Store   Discard beef bones and herb package. Skim off fat and cool contents of the pot. Transfer the "kettle" to a storage container, cover, and refrigerate for up to 4 days.

To Serve   Heat the "kettle" until very hot. Stir in the snipped dill, heat for 5 minutes longer, and readjust the seasoning with more salt and pepper as necessary. Divide the boiled potatoes into quarters, put each divided potato into a deep soup plate, and pour over a healthy serving of meat, plus vegetables and the soupy liquid. Or, serve the soup separately with a spoonful or two of sour cream, followed by the meat and horseradish on the side.

SHOPPING LIST
Meat: pot roast, beef bones (optional)
Vegetables: onion, leeks, garlic, carrots, cabbage, beets, potatoes
Dairy: sour cream (optional)

Staples: vegetable oil, tomatoe purée or canned plum tomatoes, beef stock, vinegar, sugar
Herbs and spice: bay leaf, parsley, horseradish (optional), dill, allspice

CHESTNUT-STUFFED BREAST OF VEAL

The pocket cut into a boned veal breast can be an inspiring container for all manner of stuffings. In summer, I often combine just-picked vegetables, sautéed and bound with ricotta cheese and eggs, and pile that into the cavity. Or I might cook up an extra pair of sweetbreads (while I am preparing them for another dish) and add some ground veal and herbs along with freshly grated cheese to make a filling. I also like the flavor of chestnuts in a stuffing for this cut of veal that includes bread crumbs, celery, and ground veal; here are the proportions and method for that treatment.

The Stuffing
1 onion, finely chopped
4 tablespoons butter
2 ribs celery heart, finely chopped
1 garlic clove, finely chopped
⅓ pound fresh chestnuts, peeled and diced, or the equivalent of whole roasted chestnuts available in jars and imported from France, diced
⅓ cup chicken stock
¾ cup fresh bread crumbs
⅓ cup milk
12 ounces ground veal
1 egg yolk

1 tablespoon chopped parsley
salt and freshly ground pepper

The Veal Breast
3-pound veal breast (boned weight), with a large pocket cut for stuffing
1 tablespoon butter
1 tablespoon olive oil
1 onion, sliced
2 ribs celery heart, sliced
1 imported bay leaf tied with 6 parsley stems
1¼ cups dry white wine
2¼ cups chicken stock
salt and freshly ground pepper

1. First prepare the stuffing. In a small saucepan, soften the onion in the butter over moderately low heat. Stir in the celery, cover, and cook for 4 minutes. Stir in the garlic and diced raw chestnuts. Pour in the chicken stock, cover, and simmer for 15 minutes. If you are using the jarred chestnuts add them now. Cool this mixture completely. Combine the bread crumbs and milk in a large mixing bowl and soak for 5 minutes. Add cooled chestnut mixture. Beat in ground veal, egg yolk, and parsley, and season with salt and pepper.

2. Pack the stuffing into the pocket of the veal breast, making sure that the stuffing settles in a neat layer. Tie up the open side with a piece of heavy-duty kitchen string.

3. Heat the 1 tablespoon butter and 1 tablespoon olive oil in a heavy 12-inch oval casserole (or a similar cooking vessel which will hold the veal in one flat layer). Dry the veal breast on paper toweling, brown it on both sides, then remove it to a plate. Put the onion in the casserole, and sauté for 2 minutes. Stir in the celery and sauté for another minute. Put back the veal breast, toss in the bay leaf and parsley package, and pour in the wine and stock. Season with salt and pepper. Bring the liquid to a simmer, cover the pot tightly, and simmer for 2–2½ hours (or until tender) on the stove top or in the lower third of a preheated 325° F oven. Carefully turn the veal breast over once or twice during the cooking.

To Store When the veal breast is tender, cool it in the cooking liquid, then transfer to a storage container. Boil the cooling liquid for 3 minutes, discard the bay leaf and parsley package, then pass the liquid and vegetables through a food mill. Pour this over the veal, cool completely, cover tightly, and refrigerate for up to 5 days.

To Serve Heat the veal in a covered casserole until quite hot all through. Keep the veal warm while you boil down the liquid until syrupy and lightly thickened. Remove the strings from the veal breast, carve into long slices, and assemble them on a serving dish. Moisten the slices with some of the sauce and serve.

Menu Suggestion Start off with Cream of Sorrel Soup (page 218); for dessert, a poached fruit compote of apples and pears with grapes added at the last few moments, using any of the plain syrups for fruit in this book.

SHOPPING LIST
Meat: veal breast, ground veal
Vegetables and nuts: onions, celery, garlic, chestnuts
Dairy: butter, milk, egg

Staples: chicken stock, bread crumbs, olive oil, dry white wine
Herbs: parsley, bay leaf

LAMB WITH FRESH FIGS

Fruit and meat, when put together with care, are a delectable combination. It is not uncommon to find supple dates and soft raisins or fresh orange wedges in a dish of lamb, chicken, or duck. Late autumn bears some of the sweetest pear-shaped figs, oftentimes bigger and plumper than earlier seasonal yields, so good with lamb (as are the dried variety).

It is then that I want to make this special dish. It is not complicated, but it does depend on the choicest fresh figs you can garner.

2½ pounds boneless lamb shoulder, cut
    into large cubes
3 tablespoons vegetable oil
¾ tablespoon butter
salt and freshly ground pepper
1½ tablespoons butter
3 garlic cloves, left whole and unpeeled
2 tablespoons finely chopped parsley
1¾ cups dry white wine

2 cups beef stock
1 bay leaf tied with 6 parsley stems and
    2 pieces of dried orange peel
3 whole allspice berries
3 whole cloves

To Serve

4–6 medium-large ripe figs, trimmed and
    quartered

1. Dry the lamb cubes on paper toweling. Heat the vegetable oil and ¾ tablespoon of butter in a heavy 4-quart casserole. On moderately high heat, brown the meat cubes in several batches. Remove the cubes to a plate and season with salt and pepper.

2. Pour out all of the oil-butter combination and put in the 1½ tablespoons butter. Over moderate heat, stir in the garlic cloves and parsley. Pour in the wine and beef stock. Drop in the bundle of bay leaf, parsley and orange peel, the allspice berries, and cloves. Add the browned meat and baste with liquid. Bring the liquid to a simmer, cover, and cook at a steady simmer in the lower third of a preheated 325° F oven or on the stove top for 2 hours, until tender.

To Store   Transfer the meat with a slotted spoon to a storage container. Boil the cooking liquid for 3 minutes, then pass through a food mill, and pour the resulting light puréed mixture over the lamb. When completely cool, cover and refrigerate for up to 5 days or freeze for up to 1 month.

To Serve   Reheat the lamb in a heavy casserole until hot. Check the seasoning. Put the quartered figs on top of the lamb cubes, baste with a little of the liquid, cover, and simmer for 5 minutes longer or until the figs have heated through but still keep their shape. Carefully spoon the meat and figs plus liquid onto a warm serving platter.

Menu Suggestion   Follow the lamb with Bibb Lettuce Salad (page 257); for dessert, a do-ahead vanilla Bavarian cream, or Frozen Vanilla Cream (page 319).

SHOPPING LIST
Meat: boneless lamb shoulder
Vegetable and fruit: garlic, figs
Dairy: butter

Staples: vegetable oil, dry white wine, beef stock
Herbs and spices: dried orange peel, parsley, bay leaf, allspice berries, whole cloves

SAUSAGES AND EGGPLANT

Eggplants flood my kitchen on a regular basis. I am always intrigued by their versatility—baked and fried, stuffed and sautéed—equally good as a vegetable on their own in nuggetlike cubes or supporting such goods as sausages, where the combination is intoxicating.

2 firm, shiny eggplants, about ¾ pound each
salt
5 tablespoons olive oil
2 tablespoons vegetable oil
8 sweet or hot sausages

1 onion, chopped
2 garlic cloves, finely chopped
1½ cups canned plum tomatoes, measured along with the juice, chopped
freshly ground pepper
finely chopped parsley (optional)

1. Peel each eggplant and cut into 1½–2 inch cubes. Sprinkle salt on the cubes and let them drain in a colander for 30 minutes. After 30 minutes, dry the cubes on paper toweling.

2. Heat 2½ tablespoons of the olive oil in a heavy skillet and lightly brown half the eggplant cubes in the oil, stirring frequently. Repeat with remaining 2½ tablespoons olive oil and eggplant cubes. Transfer cubes to a plate lined with paper toweling as they brown.

3. Film the bottom of a 10-inch sauté pan with the vegetable oil and brown the sausages. Remove them to a plate. If there is an excessive amount of fat in the pan, spoon out all but 2 tablespoons. Add the onion to the pan and cook over moderately low heat until wilted and translucent. Stir in the garlic and cook for 2 minutes.

4. Add the tomatoes to the onions and garlic. Season with salt and pepper to taste. Bring the tomato mixture to a simmer and let it bubble gently for 5 minutes. Add the sausages, and baste and stir with the tomato mixture. Cover the pan and simmer everything for 25 minutes—the sausages should be cooked through and the eggplant tender.

To Store   Cool the sausages and eggplant to room temperature, then store in a covered container in the refrigerator for up to 2 days.

To Serve   Rewarm the sausages in a tightly covered casserole over moderately low heat until piping hot throughout. Add a tablespoon of water on reheating if the tomato mixture seems too thick. Spoon the sausages and eggplant onto a warm platter and sprinkle over some finely chopped parsley, if you like.

Menu Suggestion   Follow with a Salad of Red Leaf Lettuce with Herbs (page 260).

SHOPPING LIST
Meat: sausages
Vegetables: eggplants, onion, garlic
Staples: olive oil, vegetable oil,

canned plum tomatoes
Herb: parsley (optional)

CHICKEN WITH FENNEL

Crisp raw fennel has a decidedly anise flavor. But as the vegetable cooks in this recipe, it absorbs the olive oil and some of the liquid in which the chicken has cooked. Then the fennel flavor becomes tempered.

This recipe, which comes from a family of superb Old World cooks, introduced me to cooking fennel. I am presenting it in a slightly different form, preparing the fennel independently of the chicken so that at least one part of the recipe can be prepared in advance. It is a magnificent dish that I urge you to try.

3 tablespoons vegetable oil
2¾–3-pound chicken, cut into 8 serving
   pieces
½ cup all-purpose flour, in a shallow
   bowl
salt and freshly ground pepper
1 tablespoon olive oil
3 garlic cloves, finely chopped
1 cup dry white wine

2 cups chicken stock

To Serve

4 tablespoons olive oil
2 fennel bulbs, trimmed and cut into
   ⅓-inch-thick slices
¼ pound prosciutto, sliced ⅛ inch thick
   and cut into narrow strips
2 teaspoons butter, softened

1. Heat the vegetable oil in a 10-inch sauté pan. Dust the chicken pieces in the flour and brown them a few at a time, in the hot oil. Transfer to a plate and season with salt and pepper.

2. When you have browned all of the chicken pieces, pour out the vegetable oil and add 1 tablespoon of olive oil. Sauté the garlic in the oil for 1 minute. Pour in the wine and

scrape the bottom of the sauté pan to release any of the clinging bits. Add the chicken stock, arrange the chicken parts in the pan in one layer, and bring to a rapid simmer. Cover the pan and simmer for 30 minutes or until the chicken is tender.

To Store   Place the chicken with all the cooking liquid in a storage container. Cool completely, then cover and store in the refrigerator for up to 2 days or freeze for up to 2 weeks.

To Serve   Reheat the chicken in a covered pan. Heat the 4 tablespoons olive oil in a large saucepan. Stir in the fennel and ½ cup of the liquid from the chicken. Season with salt and pepper, stir once, and cover the pan closely. Simmer the fennel about 25 minutes until it is tender.

   If, as the chicken reheats, you see that the remaining liquid is thin and not so syrupy, keep the chicken warm while you boil down the pan juices. Add the fennel and prosciutto strips and heat, uncovered, to combine the flavors. Off the heat, swirl in the 2 teaspoons softened butter and serve from a warm platter.

Menu Suggestion   Follow the chicken with a Gratin of Pears with Maple Syrup and Nutmeg (page 300).

SHOPPING LIST
Meat and poultry: prosciutto, chicken
Vegetables: garlic, fennel
Dairy: butter

Staples: vegetable oil, olive oil, flour, dry white wine, chicken stock

❋ SCALLOPS AND OYSTERS WITH NEW POTATOES

This light stew, fragrant with leeks and thyme, is especially warming on a chilly evening. I often put this dish together at the end of a long day because it is relatively quick, or serve it as a first course, reducing the amounts of scallops and oysters proportionately.

3 tablespoons butter
3 leeks, white part only, thinly sliced
½ pound new potatoes, peeled and cubed
1¼ cups light cream and ¾ cup heavy cream, heated together
1 teaspoon fresh thyme leaves

1 pound scallops, preferably bay scallops
1 pint freshly shucked oysters
salt and freshly ground pepper
cayenne pepper
1 tablespoon butter, softened
1 tablespoon finely chopped parsley

1. Melt the 3 tablespoons butter in 4-quart casserole. Stir in the sliced leeks and cook for 2 minutes over moderately low heat. Stir in the potatoes. Tightly cover the pot and cook about 15 minutes until the potatoes are tender.

2. Pour the heated creams into the pot and bring just to the simmer. Stir in the fresh thyme. Add the scallops and oysters; season with salt and pepper to taste. Stir. Heat all the components together until the scallops and oysters are cooked. The edges of the oysters will flute slightly and the scallops will turn opaque. Do not overcook.

3. Remove the pot from the heat, dust in a little cayenne pepper, and swirl in the butter and parsley. Serve from deep plates or wide bowls.

Menu Suggestion   Follow this gentle and lovely soup-stew with a tossed green salad or a cooked green vegetable steamed and fashioned into a salad.

SHOPPING LIST
Shellfish: scallops, oysters
Vegetables: leeks, new potatoes
Dairy: light cream, heavy cream, butter

Herbs and spice: fresh thyme, parsley, cayenne pepper

* PORK STUFFED WITH PRUNES

You will need to prepare one phase of this dish the night before cooking the pork: marinating the meat in lemon juice and spices, the prunes in port. Although this demands a small amount of extra time, the remaining work is minimal: stuffing the pork loin takes a few minutes, and browning the piece a few minutes longer. Yes, you must wait for the pork to cook (in late spring and summer you could make this ahead and serve it cool—

delicious), but in that time a wonderful soup could be readied for a first course or apéritifs enjoyed with friends.

For Marinating

½ pound dried prunes

½ cup port

2¾–3 pounds boned loin of pork, with a pocket cut through the middle of the loin

2 garlic cloves, peeled and quartered

2 large pinches of ground allspice

½ teaspoon salt

freshly ground pepper

juice of 1 lemon

2 sprigs fresh thyme, if available, or 2 pinches of dried thyme

For Cooking and Serving the Pork

2½ tablespoons vegetable oil

5 shallots, chopped

1 small carrot, sliced

1 bay leaf tied with 6 parsley stems

⅓ cup port, taken from the drained prunes, or enough extra port to fill up this measure

½ cup beef stock

salt and freshly ground pepper, to taste

watercress (optional)

1. The night before serving the pork, soak the prunes in the port. Put the pork loin in a nonmetallic baking dish that holds the loin in snugly. Rub the pieces of garlic, allspice, salt, and several grinds of pepper over the pork. Pour on the lemon juice, rub it in, and lay the thyme sprigs on top (or sprinkle the dried thyme on top). Cover the pork with a tight, airproof sheet of plastic wrap and refrigerate. The next morning, turn the pork over and lay the thyme sprigs on top. Cover again and refrigerate until cooking time.

2. First thing on cooking day, remove the pork from the refrigerator. Drain the prunes from the port and reserve the leftover port. Remove the pork from the marinating ingredients, brush off all the spices, and dry thoroughly on paper toweling. Fill the pocket of the loin with the marinated prunes.

3. Heat the oil in a 12-inch oval casserole. Brown the pork on all sides and remove it to a side dish. Add the shallots, stir them around, and cook over moderately low heat for 3 minutes. Add the carrot and cook for 2 minutes. Add the herb bundle, port, and beef stock and season with salt and pepper. Return the pork to the casserole and bring the liquid to a simmer.

4. Cover the casserole and cook the pork in a preheated 325° F oven for 1 hour 55 minutes, basting it once or twice as it cooks. Remove the pork from the casserole and keep warm while you boil down the liquid until lightly condensed. Season with salt and pepper, if necessary. Put the liquid and vegetables through a food mill or just mash the vegetables against the side of the pan.

5. Cut the pork into slices and spoon over some of the reduced pan juices to moisten the slices. Garnish the pork with a bold bunch of crisp watercress, if you like.

Menu Suggestion Start with Autumn Garden Soup (page 209) and finish with a cold, citrus-based soufflé, such as lemon, or another lemony dessert, such as Hot Lemon Sponge Pudding (page 290).

<small>SHOPPING LIST</small>
Meat: boned loin of pork
Vegetables and fruit: prunes, lemon, garlic, shallots, carrot, watercress (optional)

Staples: port, vegetable oil, beef stock
Herbs and Spice: ground allspice, bay leaf, thyme, parsley

MAIN COURSES

*Calves' Liver with Apple Wedges

Country Fricassee of Chicken

Brisket of Beef with White Beans

Pork with Red Cabbage and Chesnuts

*Mélange of Halibut, Scallops, and Striped Bass in
Fennel-Saffron Sauce (sauce can be prepared in advance)

Lamb with Garlic and Coriander

*Veal Chops with Mushrooms and Cream

THE COOK'S PLAN

1. Set out: 6-quart casserole with lid for the cabbage preparation of Pork with Red Cabbage and Chestnuts, 6-quart casserole with lid for Lamb with Garlic and Coriander, 12-inch oval casserole with lid for the Brisket of Beef with White Beans, 10-inch sauté pan with lid for the Country Fricassee of Chicken.

2. Thaw and measure out 4 cups beef stock, 4½ cups chicken stock, 5 whole cloves.

3. Wash and dry 4 ribs celery heart.

4. Peel 1 apple, ½ pound chestnuts, 4 onions, 2 red onions, ¾ pound pearl onions, 3 garlic cloves.

5. Finely chop 1 garlic clove; chop 2 garlic cloves; slice 1 apple, 1 head red cabbage, 4 onions, 2 red onions, 2 carrots, 4 ribs celery heart; cube about ½ pound bacon.

6. Measure out 4¼ cups dry red wine, 1½ cups dry white wine, 1 tablespoon dark-brown sugar, 1 tablespoon molasses, 1½ teaspoons prepared mustard, ¼ teaspoon cumin seed, 1 tablespoon tomato paste.

7. Set out vegetable oil, olive oil, butter, salt, pepper, flour.

8. Tie 1 bay leaf with 6 parsley stems and 2 sprigs thyme.

9. Pork with Red Cabbage and Chestnuts: Sauté bacon, onions, garlic, apple; add sugar, cabbage, spices, wine, beef stock; simmer the cabbage, Steps 1–2 (page 40).

10. Brisket of Beef with White Beans: Brown the meat; sauté the vegetables; add molasses, mustard, herb bundle, and liquid; season the brisket; simmer, Steps 1–2 (page 41).

11. Lamb with Garlic and Coriander: Brown the lamb cubes; prepare vegetables and add spices; pour on wine, stock, and tomato paste; simmer, Steps 1–3 (page 43).

12. Country Fricassee of Chicken: Brown the chicken pieces in the butter-oil; sauté bacon and onions; add wine and stock; simmer, Steps 1–3 (page 44).

13. Cool all dishes to room temperature; refrigerate or freeze, following the instructions in "To Store" of each recipe.

PORK WITH RED CABBAGE AND CHESTNUTS

Here is one way to arrive at one of the more celebrated compositions: pork with red cabbage (and chestnuts, too). Deep-red cabbage shreds cook slowly in red wine with apples and spices. The cabbage simmers away lazily while all the flavors blend and deepen; it stores perfectly for a few days until you slip several pork chops in the center to cook. Serve this, piping hot, from a beautiful earthenware platter.

¼-pound piece of bacon, cubed
1 tablespoon olive oil
2 tablespoons butter
2 red onions, sliced
1 garlic clove, finely chopped
1 apple, peeled and sliced
1 tablespoon dark-brown sugar
1¾–2-pound firm head of red cabbage, quartered, cored, and and finely sliced
2 pinches ground cloves
1 pinch ground mace
1½ cups dry red wine

1 cup beef stock
salt and freshly ground pepper
½ pound fresh chestnuts, peeled, or the equivalent of whole roasted chestnuts, available in jars and imported from France

To Serve

4 pork chops, cut 1 inch thick, taken from the rib loin
3–4 tablespoons vegetable oil

1. Simmer the bacon cubes in a large pot of water for 10 minutes, then drain and dry well on a sheet of paper toweling. Put the oil and butter in a heavy 6-quart casserole, add the cubed bacon, and sauté until lightly golden. Add the onions and sauté for 3 minutes. Stir in the chopped garlic and apple slices and stir-cook for 2 minutes.

2. Add the brown sugar to the casserole, stir once, then add the cabbage. Cook and stir until the cabbage reduces in bulk slightly and absorbs some of the oil and butter, about 3 or 4 minutes. Stir in the cloves, mace, wine, and beef stock. Season with salt and pepper. Bring the contents of the casserole to a simmer. Cover the casserole and cook over a low flame on the stove top or in the lower third of a preheated 325° F oven for 2½ hours. Add the fresh, raw chestnuts to the casserole, stir, cover, and cook until the chestnuts are tender, 45 minutes to 1 hour.

To Store   Cool the cabbage to room temperature, then refrigerate in a covered container for up to 5 days.

To Serve   Reheat the cabbage to a simmer along with the roasted chestnuts, if you are using them, in a covered casserole. While the cabbage is heating, brown the pork chops in the vegetable oil in a heavy skillet, season with salt and pepper, and bury them in the cabbage. Cover the casserole and transfer to a preheated 325° F oven for about 25 minutes, or until the chops are cooked through. Serve the pork and cabbage from a warm serving platter.

Menu Suggestion End the meal with Hot Lemon Sponge Pudding (page 290).

Shopping List
Meat: bacon, pork chops
Vegetables, fruit, and nuts: red onions, garlic, red cabbage, apple, chestnuts
Dairy: butter

Staples: olive oil, vegetable oil, dark-brown sugar, dry red wine, beef stock
Spices: ground cloves, ground mace

BRISKET OF BEEF WITH WHITE BEANS

This is a savory, warming dish of brisket and Great Northern white beans—short ribs, by the way, could replace the brisket for an equally delicious variation. The sauce is strengthened by a collection of onion, carrot, and celery slices, a veal knuckle—which lends characterful body—and some fresh thyme. The meat may be kept in one piece, for long thin slices, or cubed. The latter is more time-consuming to brown but easier on serving day because the meat is already cut.

3 tablespoons vegetable oil
1 tablespoon butter
3-pound piece brisket of beef, preferably taken from the first cut
salt and freshly ground pepper
2 onions, sliced
2 carrots, sliced
2 ribs celery heart, sliced
1 tablespoon dark unsulfured molasses
1½ teaspoons sharp prepared mustard
1 small imported bay leaf tied with 6 parsley stems and 2 sprigs of fresh thyme
1½ cups dry red wine

3 cups beef stock
1 veal knuckle or a few cracked veal bones (optional, but highly recommended to enrich the cooking liquid)
5 whole cloves

To Serve

1½ cups dried Great Northern white beans
½ onion, halved
1 rib celery heart, halved
1 small carrot, halved
1 small imported bay leaf
2 tablespoons finely chopped parsley

1. Heat the vegetable oil and butter in a heavy 12-inch oval casserole. Brown the brisket on both sides in the hot oil-butter, then remove the meat to a large plate and season with

salt and pepper. Sauté the onions in the oil-butter for 2 minutes. Stir in the sliced carrots and celery and sauté another 2 minutes.

2. Stir the molasses and mustard into the vegetables. Drop in the bay leaf bundle and pour in the wine and stock. Add the veal knuckle or bones and the cloves. Put in the brisket and bring the content of the casserole to a vigorous simmer. Cover the casserole and cook the meat in the lower third of a preheated 325° F oven for 2½–3 hours, or until very tender.

To Store   Place the meat in a storage container large enough to accommodate the whole piece without bending the meat. Discard the herb bundle and veal knuckle or bones. Rapidly boil down the liquid in the casserole for 5 minutes, or until it just begins to take on body. Put the vegetables, along with the liquid, through a food mill to purée, then pour over the meat. Cool the meat completely, then cover tightly and refrigerate for up to 4 days.

To Serve   The night before serving the meat, put the beans into a large bowl and cover with at least 3 inches of water. On serving day, drain the beans, put them in a large pot, and cover with cold water. Add the onion, celery, and carrot slices along with the bay leaf. Bring the beans to a simmer, cover, and simmer slowly until tender (about 40 minutes).

As the beans cook, reheat the meat in a covered casserole. When the beans are tender, drain in a colander and discard the vegetables and bay leaf. Put the beans in a saucepan, season with salt and pepper, and add a generous cup of the liquid in which the brisket is simmering. Heat the beans in the liquid over a low flame, covered.

When the meat is hot, slice against the grain and arrange the slices on a platter. Moisten the slices with the "sauce." Stir the parsley into the beans, spoon the beans around the slices, and serve.

Menu Suggestion   Start with, as a first course, Gratin of Fennel and Leeks (page 239) or serve the gratin as a vegetable course; for dessert, a gratin of sautéed apple slices moistened with heavy cream and sweetened, all enhanced with spices and jam, then baked with a topping of crushed macaroons and butter.

Shopping List

Meat: brisket of beef, veal knuckle or veal bones (optional)
Vegetables: onions, carrots, celery
Dairy: butter

Staples: vegetable oil, molasses, mustard, dry red wine, beef stock, Great Northern white beans
Herbs and spice: bay leaves, parsley, thyme, whole cloves

LAMB WITH GARLIC AND CORIANDER

One whole head of garlic and the leaves from a small bunch of coriander are featured as the flavors in this dish. The garlic taste is softly submissive because the cloves are left unpeeled. As for the lamb, my first choice would be to use meat from the shoulder and the breast for a pleasing set of textures. After the lamb cooks slowly, the liquid and vegetables are puréed through a food mill. The papery coverings of the garlic cloves remain behind and the soft, subdued flesh goes into the sauce. Cubes cut from slender zucchini finish off the dish, cooked until just tender in the garlic-coriander sauce.

1½ pounds boneless lamb breast and 1½ pounds boneless lamb shoulder (3 pounds boneless shoulder may be substituted; ask for the bones from the shoulder and breast—they will add great flavor to the dish), cut into 2-inch cubes
3 tablespoons vegetable oil
1 tablespoon butter
salt and freshly ground pepper
2 onions, sliced
2 ribs celery heart, sliced

1 whole head of garlic, broken into individual cloves but left unpeeled
¼ teaspoon whole cumin seed
1 small imported bay leaf
1½ cups dry white wine
2½ cups chicken stock
1 tablespoon tomato paste

To Serve

3 zucchini, cut into wedges or cubes
¼ cup coriander leaves, about 1 small bunch

1. Blot the lamb cubes of any excess moisture on paper toweling. Heat the vegetable oil and butter over moderately high heat in a 6-quart casserole. Brown the lamb cubes, in several batches, in the oil-butter. Remove the lamb cubes to a side plate as they are browned and season with salt and pepper. Brown the bones.

2. If the oil-butter has burned, rinse out the casserole and add another 2 tablespoons butter. If not, continue on to add the onions and sauté for 2 minutes. Add the celery and sauté 1 minute longer. Stir in the garlic cloves, cumin seed, and bay leaf. Pour in the wine and stock, and stir in the tomato paste. Add the lamb cubes and bones, and bring the contents of the casserole to a rapid simmer.

3. Cover the casserole and cook the lamb at a simmer on the stove top or in the lower third of a preheated 325° F oven for 2–2½ hours or until the lamb is tender.

To Store   Place the lamb cubes in a storage container. Discard the bay leaf and bones and degrease the cooking liquid. Boil the liquid for 3 minutes, then strain through a food mill. Pour this puréed vegetable and liquid mixture over the lamb. Cool to room temperature, cover, and refrigerate for up to 5 days or freeze for up to 1 month.

(*continued*)

To Serve   Reheat the lamb in a covered casserole. If the liquid seems too thin, remove the meat and boil down the liquid until lightly syrupy. Add the zucchini cubes and coriander to the lamb, cover, and simmer until the zucchini is tender. Correct the seasoning with additional salt and pepper. Serve from a deep platter.

Menu Suggestion   Follow the lamb with Watercress Salad with Lemon Vinaigrette (page 261).

<small>Shopping List</small>
Meat: boneless lamb breast, boneless lamb shoulder
Vegetables: onions, celery, garlic, zucchini
Dairy: butter
Staples: vegetable oil, dry white wine, chicken stock, tomato paste
Herbs and spice: bay leaf, fresh coriander, whole cumin seed

COUNTRY FRICASSEE OF CHICKEN

This is one of those dishes I return to again and again, changing the ingredients to suit my mood and the offerings at the market. My standing constants are the mushrooms and bacon cubes. Otherwise, I might do all dark meat, using legs and thighs, in place of the whole chicken which has been cut up into parts. Or, I may add half a pound of the very smallest new potatoes and increase the cooking liquid with another ¼ cup of wine and ½ cup of stock so that I can cook the potatoes along with the chicken.

⅓-pound piece of bacon, cubed
2 tablespoons butter
2 tablespoons vegetable oil
2¾–3-pound whole chicken, cut into 8 serving pieces
½ cup all-purpose flour, in a shallow bowl
salt and freshly ground pepper, to taste
¾ pound pearl onions, peeled and trimmed

2 garlic cloves, chopped
1¼ cups dry red wine
2 cups chicken stock

To Serve

1 pound small fresh white mushrooms
1 tablespoon butter, softened
1 tablespoon finely chopped parsley

1. Drop the bacon cubes in a pot of boiling water and reduce the heat so that they simmer. Simmer for 10 minutes, drain, and dry.

2. Heat the butter and oil in a 10-inch sauté pan. Dust the chicken pieces in the flour,

a few at a time, and brown them in the hot butter-oil. Remove the chicken parts to a plate as they brown and season them with salt and pepper. Pour out all but 1 tablespoon of the butter-oil combination, but if it has burned, rinse out the skillet and add a fresh lump of butter.

3. Add the bacon cubes to the skillet and sauté for 2 minutes, stirring often. Add the onions and sauté them until lightly browned. Add the garlic and stir-cook for a minute. Pour in the wine and chicken stock. Add the chicken pieces and bring the contents of the pan to a simmer. Cover the pan and simmer the chicken for 30 minutes, basting a few times with the cooking liquid.

To Store   Cool the chicken in the liquid, then store in a covered container in the refrigerator for up to 2 days or freeze for up to 2 weeks.

To Serve   Put the fricassee in a casserole, cover, and reheat. While the chicken heats, cut the mushroom stems level with the caps (reserve the stems in the freezer and use for stock). Add the mushroom caps to the chicken and simmer for 10 minutes longer or until the caps are tender-crisp. Carefully stir the casserole once or twice as everything heats up. Adjust the seasoning. If the liquid seems too thin, keep the chicken and vegetables warm while you cook down the sauce over moderately high heat. Off the heat, swirl in the butter and fold in the parsley.

Menu Suggestion   For dessert, Frozen Vanilla Cream (page 319).

SHOPPING LIST
Meat and poultry: bacon, chicken
Vegetables: pearl onions, garlic, mushrooms
Dairy: butter

Staples: vegetable oil, flour, dry red wine, chicken stock
Herb: parsley

* CALVES' LIVER WITH APPLE WEDGES

Autumn turns apples, especially the brightly tart ones, into first-rate accompaniments for main dishes. Apple slices are awfully good with pork chops in white wine and with chicken in a sauce made up of cream and a little apple brandy or cider. If you cook liver to a tender rosiness and add apple wedges and the more customary sautéed onions, you will have produced a very elegant quick main course. A taste of apple, a taste of liver. Both play well against each other.

7 tablespoons butter	1 teaspoon granulated sugar
2 onions, thinly sliced	1 tablespoon vegetable oil
salt and freshly ground pepper	1 pound calves' liver, very thinly sliced
2 tart cooking apples, cored, cut into ¾-inch-thick slices, and tossed in the juice of 1 small lemon	and cut into narrow strips
	¼ cup Madeira
	1 tablespoon finely chopped parsley

1. Put 2 tablespoons of the butter in a skillet and add the sliced onions. Sauté the onions, stirring often, until they are soft and golden-colored. Season the onions with salt and pepper; keep warm while you prepare the liver and apples.

2. Rinse out the skillet, add 2 tablespoons butter, and heat over a moderate flame. Add the apple slices, sprinkle with sugar, and cook, stirring occasionally, until the apple slices are lightly glazed and cooked through.

3. As the apple slices sauté, heat remaining 3 tablespoons butter and the vegetable oil in another skillet. When very hot, add the calves' liver strips and sauté quickly, for about a minute, tossing the strips about with a flat spatula. Season the liver with salt and freshly ground pepper. Remove liver. Quickly pour the Madeira into the pan that held the liver and let it boil. When it is syrupy and reduced by half, and this should happen very fast, pour the Madeira over the apples and liver.

4. Combine the onions, liver, and apples in one skillet and fold all together with the chopped parsley. Turn out the liver onto a warm serving platter.

Menu Suggestion   Follow with one of my simple green salads, such as Bibb Lettuce Salad (page 257).

SHOPPING LIST
Meat: calves' liver
Vegetables and fruit: onions, cooking apples, lemon
Dairy: butter

Staples: granulated sugar, vegetable oil, Madeira
Herb: parsley

✳ MÉLANGE OF HALIBUT, SCALLOPS, AND STRIPED BASS IN FENNEL-SAFFRON SAUCE

In this recipe the fish base is touched with saffron and fennel, and simmers for a little while in white wine and fish stock. Remember that the base may be made up in advance, but be sure that the fish fillets and scallops are impeccably fresh, purchased from a reliable and knowledgeable fishmonger.

1 onion, chopped
¼ cup olive oil
2 shallots, chopped
1 garlic clove, chopped
1 fennel bulb, trimmed and cut into ½-inch chunks
¾ cup tomato purée (homemade) or chopped canned plum tomatoes
1 tablespoon finely chopped parsley
½ cup dry white wine
1½ cups fish stock
⅛ teaspoon saffron
salt and freshly ground pepper

To Serve

1½ pounds halibut fillets, cut into 2-inch pieces
1½ pounds striped bass fillets, cut into 2-inch pieces
½ pound scallops, preferably bay scallops
¾ pound small new potatoes, well scrubbed
1½ tablespoons butter
1 tablespoon finely chopped parsley

First prepare the fennel-saffron base. Sauté the onion in the olive oil until translucent. Stir in the shallots and chopped garlic. Sauté for 2 minutes. Add the chunks of fennel, stir, cover the pot, and cook for 5 minutes over moderately low heat. Stir in the tomato purée (or chopped canned tomatoes), 1 tablespoon chopped parsley, wine, fish stock, and saffron. Season with salt and pepper. Bring to a rapid simmer, cover, and cook 30 minutes.

To Store   Put the liquid and vegetables through a food mill to purée. Cool to room temperature, then store in a covered container for up to 1 day in the refrigerator or freeze for up to 1 week.

To Serve   Remove the halibut, bass, and scallops from the wrappings and pat dry. Put the potatoes in a large deep saucepan. Cover with cold water and add ½ teaspoon salt. Bring the water to a boil, then simmer until the potatoes are tender. Drain the potatoes, peel them or not as you like, and return them to the saucepan. Add the butter, season with salt and pepper, and toss until piping hot. Off the heat, fold in the chopped parsley and serve with the fish mélange.

While the potatoes are simmering, bring the fennel-saffron base to a steady simmer in a casserole. Add the fish fillet pieces, baste with the fennel sauce, and simmer for 4 minutes. Add the scallops and simmer uncovered for another 3 minutes or until the scallops and fillets are just cooked. Do not overcook. Serve from a deep platter with the buttered, parsleyed potatoes.

Menu Suggestion Follow with Bibb Lettuce Salad (page 257); for dessert, oranges glazed in a simple syrup sharpened with orange rind and allspice berries.

✳ VEAL CHOPS WITH MUSHROOMS AND CREAM

This is a dish of veal chops simmered in chicken stock, tomato purée, a little onion, and a few shredded basil leaves. Mushrooms are added to cook along with the veal near the end (mushrooms are so good with veal) and, lastly, all the contents are enrobed in a sauce made pale rose by the addition of heavy cream.

3 tablespoons vegetable oil	chopped canned plum tomatoes
4 rib veal chops, cut 1-inch thick	¾ cup chicken stock
salt and freshly ground pepper	5 fresh basil leaves, shredded
1 onion, chopped	¾ pound button mushrooms, caps only
3 tablespoons butter	½ cup heavy cream, warmed
¼ cup dry white wine	1 tablespoon butter, softened
¾ cup tomato purée (homemade) or	1 tablespoon finely chopped parsley

1. Heat the vegetable oil in a skillet over moderately high heat and brown the veal chops on both sides. Remove the chops to a plate and season with salt and pepper.

2. In a casserole (a heavy 10-inch one works best here), soften the chopped onion in the 3 tablespoons butter. Raise the heat slightly and pour in the white wine. Let the wine bubble up for a few seconds. Stir in the tomato purée or canned tomatoes, chicken stock, and basil leaves. Season lightly with salt and pepper.

3. Put the browned veal chops in the casserole, overlapping slightly as necessary. Baste the chops with some of the tomato-wine-stock liquid and bring to the simmer. Cover and

cook in the lower third of a preheated 325° F oven for 40 minutes. Uncover the casserole, add the mushrooms, baste with some of the liquid, cover, and continue cooking for 15 minutes longer.

4. Keep the mushrooms and chops warm while you finish the sauce. Boil down the liquid in the casserole until lightly thickened and reduced. Pour in the warmed cream, correct the seasoning, and heat for a minute or two to blend the flavors. Replace the chops and mushrooms, baste with the creamy sauce, and off the heat swirl in the butter and fold in the chopped parsley.

Menu Suggestion Accompany the veal chops with Buttered Noodles (page 253), and follow with Endive and Beet Salad (page 257); for dessert, Whole Seckel Pears in Spiced Wine (page 303).

SHOPPING LIST
Meat: veal chops
Vegetables: onion, mushrooms
Dairy: butter, heavy cream

Staples: vegetable oil, dry white wine, tomato purée or canned plum tomatoes, chicken stock
Herbs: fresh basil, parsley

MAIN COURSES

* Mussel and Bass Stew

Veal-Stuffed Cabbage Leaves,
Sweet-and-Sour Style, with Grapes

Chicken with Brussels Sprouts and Tarragon

Lamb Shanks with Tiny Glazed Onions

Sausages with Red Peppers and Onions

Beef with Acorn Squash and Spices

* Swordfish with Olives

THE COOK'S PLAN

1. Set out: 6-quart casserole with lid for the Beef with Acorn Squash and Spices, 6-quart casserole with lid for the Veal-Stuffed Cabbage Leaves, Sweet-and-Sour Style, with Grapes, 12-inch casserole with lid for the Lamb Shanks with Tiny Glazed Onions, 10-inch sauté pan with lid for the Sausages with Red Peppers and Onions, 10-inch sauté pan with lid for the Chicken with Brussels Sprouts and Tarragon.

2. Thaw and measure out 2½ cups beef stock, 4 cups chicken stock.

3. Wash and dry 1 small bunch parsley, 5 sweet red peppers.

4. Peel 7 onions, 4 shallots, 6 garlic cloves, 4 carrots, 2 tart apples.

5. Finely chop 4 garlic cloves, ½ onion, 3 tablespoons parsley; chop 2 carrots, 1 onion, 4 shallots; slice 5 onions, 2 carrots, 2 tart apples.

6. Measure out 1½ cups dry red wine, 3 cups dry white wine, ½ cup soft bread crumbs, 1 tablespoon dark-brown sugar, 3½ tablespoons honey, 4-inch cinnamon stick, 4 cloves, 4 allspice berries, ⅓ cup milk, juice of 1 lemon, 2½ cups tomato purée or canned plum tomatoes.

7. Set out olive oil, vegetable oil, butter, salt, pepper, flour.

8. Tie 2 bundles of 6 parsley stems each.

9. Trim and peel off the cabbage leaves, Step 1 (page 53).

10. Beef with Acorn Squash and Spices: Brown the beef; cook the vegetables; add spices, season, pour in wine and stock; simmer, Steps 1–3 (page 52).

11. Veal-Stuffed Cabbage Leaves, Sweet-and-Sour Style, with Grapes: Prepare the veal stuffing and fill the cabbage leaves; prepare the tomato-apple sauce; add the rolled cabbages; simmer, Steps 2–5 (page 54).

12. Lamb Shanks with Tiny Glazed Onions: Brown the lamb shanks; cook the vegetables; add wine and stock; simmer, Steps 1–2 (page 55).

13. Chicken with Brussels Sprouts and Tarragon: Brown the chicken, season, add wine and stock; simmer, Steps 1–2 (page 56).

14. Sausages with Red Peppers and Onions: Roast the peppers, peel, and cut into strips; brown the sausages; add onions, garlic, white wine; simmer; after 20 minutes add pepper strips and continue simmering, Steps 1–4 (page 58).

15. Cool all dishes to room temperature; refrigerate or freeze, following the instructions in "To Store" of each recipe.

BEEF WITH ACORN SQUASH AND SPICES

A dish of beef redolent of whole cinnamon stick, cloves, and allspice berries, all bathed in red wine. To bring out the fullest flavor in the spices, just don't dump them in the casserole, but sauté them until they turn dark, a sign that the intense flavor has opened up. If you were to cook two pots of the same beef, one in which the spices were left "raw" and not sautéed, and one which contained cooked spices, you would notice that the dish with the cooked spices tasted much more pungently aromatic. The process for "cooking" the spices is outlined in Step 2 below and is worth observing.

2¾–3 pounds rump pot roast, cut into 2-inch cubes
3–4 tablespoons vegetable oil
salt and freshly ground pepper
2 onions, sliced
2 carrots, sliced
2 garlic cloves, peeled and left whole
1 tart cooking apple, peeled, cored, and roughly cubed or sliced
1 tablespoon dark-brown sugar
4-inch piece of cinnamon stick

4 whole cloves
4 allspice berries
1 bay leaf
1½ cups dry red wine
2½ cups beef stock

To Serve

¾-pound acorn squash, cut into cubes
2 tablespoons dark raisins
2 tablespoons finely chopped parsley

1. Dry the beef cubes on paper toweling so that they will brown properly. Heat the vegetable oil in a 6-quart casserole over moderately high heat. Brown the cubes, a small amount at a time, without crowding the pan. Transfer the browned cubes to a plate and season with salt and pepper.

2. When all of the beef has been browned, pour out all but 2 tablespoons of oil. Reduce the heat to moderately low, stir in the onions, and cook for 2 minutes. Stir in the carrots, garlic, and apples, and stir-cook for 2 minutes. Add the cinnamon stick, cloves, and allspice berries, raise the heat to moderate, and stir-cook for a few minutes, or until you can really smell the intense flavor of the spices and the spices darken. Drop in the bay leaf.

3. Pour the red wine and beef stock into the casserole. Put in the beef cubes and bring the contents to a simmer. Cover the casserole and simmer for 3–3½ hours on the stove top or in the lower third of a preheated 325° F oven.

To Store   When the meat is tender, remove the beef to a storage bowl. Degrease the cooking liquid. If the liquid has not condensed slightly, boil it down for a few minutes. Purée liquid with the vegetables through a food mill and add to bowl containing the meat. Cool to room temperature, cover, and refrigerate for up to 5 days or freeze for up to 1 month.

To Serve   Boil the acorn squash until tender. Drain. While the squash is cooking, reheat the meat in a covered casserole. When the meat is hot, add the squash and raisins. Cover the casserole and simmer for a few minutes longer, until the raisins plump up in the sauce and the squash is permeated with the flavors of the beef dish. Baste the meat and squash once or twice as it simmers. Fold in the chopped parsley and serve.

Menu Suggestion Accompany the beef with Buttered Noodles (page 253), and follow with Watercress Salad with Lemon Vinaigrette (page 261); for dessert, any kind of fruit baked custard, such as fresh prune plums, would make a fitting end.

Shopping List
Meat: rump pot roast
Vegetables and fruit: onions, carrots, garlic, acorn squash, apple
Staples: vegetable oil, dark-brown sugar, dry red wine,

beef stock, dark raisins
Herbs and spices: cinnamon stick, whole cloves, all-spice berries, bay leaf, parsley

VEAL-STUFFED CABBAGE LEAVES, SWEET-AND-SOUR STYLE, WITH GRAPES

The design of this recipe combines portions of a light veal stuffing wrapped up in cabbage leaves, all cooked slowly in a sauce of tomatoes and apples. After the stuffed leaves have cooked, the liquid is puréed and poured back over the cabbage cylinders, and the dish is ready to be stored. It is on serving day that plump, fresh grapes and supple currants are added, a good and charming set of contrasts.

The Cabbage and Filling
1 large head of cabbage or 2 medium ones, enough for 16 leaves
½ cup soft bread crumbs
⅓ cup milk
1 pound ground veal
2 small garlic cloves, finely chopped
½ small onion, finely chopped
3 tablespoons finely chopped parsley
1 teaspoon salt
freshly ground pepper
1 egg
1 tablespoon vegetable oil

For Cooking the Stuffed Cabbage Leaves
4 tablespoons butter
1 onion, thinly sliced
1 tart apple, peeled, cored, and thinly sliced
juice of 1 lemon
3½ tablespoons honey
2½ cups tomato purée (homemade), or an equal quantity of chopped canned plum tomatoes plus ½ tablespoon tomato paste

To Serve
½ pound fat, juicy black grapes
2 tablespoons moist, dried currants

1. Bring a large kettle of water to the boil. With a sharp knife, cut several slits at the base of the cabbage where the leaves join together, close to the core. Drop the cabbage,

base side down, into the boiling water. As the water boils and the leaves begin to loosen, peel them off. An easy way to detach the leaves is to lift up the cabbage with two slotted spoons and set the head into a large bowl near the stove top. Pick off as many leaves as will easily detach without tearing them. Return the cabbage to the boiling water to loosen more of the leaves. Place 16 detached leaves on paper toweling to drain.

2. To prepare the filling, put the bread crumbs and milk in a large mixing bowl and leave to soak for 5 minutes. Break up the ground veal, and add to the bread crumbs along with the chopped garlic, onion, and parsley. Season with salt and pepper, and mix. Break on the egg and pour over the vegetable oil. Blend all of the ingredients together.

3. Place a heaping tablespoon of filling on the lower third of each leaf and fold into a neat, tight cylinder, tucking in the sides to secure.

4. For cooking the cabbages, melt the butter in a 6-quart casserole and sauté the onion for 3 minutes. Add the apple slices and lemon juice, stir, and cook for 2 minutes. Blend in the honey and tomato purée or canned tomatoes and paste. Season with salt and pepper. Bring to a simmer and simmer steadily for 5 minutes.

5. Layer the cabbage rolls in the sauce, spooning some of it over the top of each roll. Cover the casserole, bring to a simmer, then cook in the lower third of a preheated 325° F oven for 2½ hours.

To Store Transfer the cabbage rolls to a storage container. Rapidly cook the sauce over moderately high heat for 4 minutes, then put all of it through a food mill. Pour the puréed sauce over the cabbage rolls. Cool completely, cover, and refrigerate for up to 5 days.

To Serve Reheat the cabbage rolls along with the sauce in a covered casserole until very hot. Uncover, scatter over the grapes and currants, baste with some of the sauce, and cover the casserole. Simmer an additional 5–8 minutes or until the grapes are heated through but still keep their shape.

Menu Suggestion Accompany the stuffed cabbage leaves with Cracked Wheat with Pecans (page 252).

SHOPPING LIST
Meat: ground veal
Vegetables and fruit: cabbage, garlic, onions, apple, lemon, black grapes
Dairy: milk, egg, butter

Staples: bread crumbs, vegetable oil, honey, tomato purée or canned plum tomatoes plus tomato paste, currants
Herb: parsley

LAMB SHANKS WITH TINY GLAZED ONIONS

You have probably discovered that I like to use otherwise neglected cuts of meat, such as shanks and shoulders. My romance with these is likely borne out of the end product, since the pieces cook up meltingly tender and are capable of infinite seasonal variations of vegetables, stuffings, and so on. The old culinary saw was never truer: meat close to the bone is sweet and flavorful. This is one of my favorite lamb shank recipes, as long as the very smallest white pearl onions are available—those which, ideally, are only slightly bigger than your thumbnail. The onions, turned in butter, blend well in the light, lively rosemary-scented sauce.

2–3 lamb shanks, enough to provide eight 1-inch-thick pieces
3 tablespoons vegetable oil, or more as needed
salt and freshly ground pepper
2 carrots, chopped
1½ teaspoons fresh rosemary leaves
3 garlic cloves, left whole and unpeeled

1 cup dry white wine
1½ cups chicken stock
6 parsley stems, tied with a piece of kitchen string

To Serve

2½ dozen pearl onions
3 tablespoons butter

1. Dry the lamb shanks on paper toweling. Put the vegetable oil in a heavy 12-inch casserole, heat, and brown the shanks a few at a time, without crowding the pan. As the lamb pieces brown, remove them to a plate, and season with salt and pepper.

2. Add the chopped carrots and stir-cook for 2 minutes. Add the rosemary leaves, garlic, wine, and chicken stock. Stir well to loosen any bits clinging to the bottom of the casserole. Add the parsley stems and put in the lamb shanks in one layer. Bring the contents of the casserole to a simmer, cover, and simmer on the stove top for 2 hours, or until the lamb is tender, turning the shanks a few times while they cook.

To Store   When the shanks are tender, remove them from the liquid in the casserole to a storage container. Discard the parsley stems. Boil the liquid for 3–4 minutes if it is not already lightly condensed, then purée through a food mill. Pour the puréed liquid over the shanks, cool completely, then cover and refrigerate for up to 5 days or freeze for up to 1 month.

To Serve   Reheat the lamb shanks in a covered casserole until piping hot. In the meantime, heat the butter in a skillet. Add the onions, toss them in the butter, and sauté until lightly browned.

Add the browned onions to the lamb shanks, baste with some of the sauce, cover, and simmer until the onions are tender. Transfer the shanks, onions, and sauce onto a warm platter and serve.

Menu Suggestion   Start with Artichokes with Caper and Fennel Sauce (page 231), and end with Apple Fool (page 268).

SHOPPING LIST
Meat: lamb shanks
Vegetables: carrots, garlic, pearl onions
Dairy: butter

Staples: vegetable oil, dry white wine, chicken stock
Herbs: fresh rosemary, parsley

CHICKEN WITH BRUSSELS SPROUTS AND TARRAGON

This is a nice recipe for using several luxurious branches of fresh tarragon that will simmer in with the chicken and Brussels sprouts. Dried tarragon simply won't do here. As far as I'm concerned, the fresh green sprigs bear little resemblance to the dried. If necessary, substitute another dish with different herbs, as available.

3 tablespoons vegetable oil
1 tablespoon butter
½ cup all-purpose flour, in a shallow bowl
2¾–3-pound whole chicken, cut into 8 serving pieces
salt and freshly ground pepper
1 onion, chopped
4 shallots, chopped
1¼ cups dry white wine

2¼ cups chicken stock
6 parsley stems, tied with a piece of kitchen string

To Serve

1½ pints Brussels sprouts
2 full sprigs fresh tarragon, leaves only, roughly chopped, about 2 tablespoons
½ cup heavy cream, warmed

1. While heating the vegetable oil and butter in a heavy 10-inch sauté pan over moderately high heat, flour a few of the chicken pieces. Brown the pieces in the hot oil-butter, remove them to a plate, and season with salt and pepper. When all of the chicken has been browned, spoon out all but 1 tablespoon of the oil-butter (or add a fresh chunk of butter to the rinsed-out pan if the oil-butter has burned). Stir in the onions and sauté them for 2 minutes. Stir in the shallots and sauté 2 minutes longer.

2. Pour in the wine and chicken stock. Toss in the parsley stem bundle. Add the chicken pieces to the pan and bring the contents to a rapid simmer. Cover and simmer for 30 minutes, regulating the heat so that the liquid bubbles steadily. Baste the chicken with the liquid several times.

To Store   Cool the chicken to room temperature. Discard the parsley stems. Refrigerate the chicken (with all the savory liquid) in a tightly covered storage container for up to 2 days or freeze for up to 2 weeks.

To Serve   Cook the trimmed Brussels sprouts in simmering salted water until tender. Drain, pour over a few cups of cold water, and reserve. While the Brussels sprouts are cooking, reheat the chicken in a covered pan until hot throughout. Keep the chicken warm while you boil down the cooking liquid until it has reduced a bit and gains body. Return the chicken to the pan, and add the Brussels sprouts and tarragon. Simmer for 5 minutes. Pour in the heavy cream and simmer for a few minutes longer. Correct the seasoning and spoon out onto a warm platter.

Menu Suggestion   Serve Leeks, Glazed and Baked (page 240) as a vegetable course; for dessert, Persimmon Ice Cream (page 305).

SHOPPING LIST
Poultry: chicken
Vegetables: onion, shallots, Brussels sprouts
Dairy: butter, heavy cream

Staples: vegetable oil, flour, dry white wine, chicken stock
Herbs: parsley, fresh tarragon

SAUSAGES WITH RED PEPPERS AND ONIONS

There are some dishes that never fail to be agreeable each time you put the ingredients together or warm up the dish. This is one of those dishes that are always sound and satisfying. I frequently use spicy-hot links, but you can exchange sweeter, milder sausages as preferred. Every so often I like to turn out a batch of sausages; the endless free-form combinations intrigue me, and I find the whole procedure relaxing, even therapeutic. Many specialty markets and well-stocked grocery stores carry excellent types of sausages, making home sausagemaking relatively obsolete. Red peppers are a must for this dish, even if you use only part red peppers and part green peppers.

5 firm, meaty sweet red peppers, or a mixture of red and green peppers	2 onions, sliced
	2 garlic cloves, finely chopped
3 tablespoons olive oil	¾ cup dry white wine
8 sweet or hot sausages	salt and freshly ground pepper

1. Roast the peppers under a hot broiler or directly over a gas flame until charred on all sides, then wrap them in a large sheet of aluminum foil. When the peppers are cool, unwrap them and remove the peel and the core. Cut the flesh into ½-inch-wide strips.

2. While the peppers are cooling, heat the olive oil in a skillet and brown the sausages slowly in the oil. Remove the sausages and spoon off all but 2 tablespoons of oil.

3. Add the onions to the skillet and sauté for 3 minutes. Stir in the chopped garlic and sauté for an additional 2 minutes. Pour on the white wine, return the sausages to the pan, and bring the contents to a simmer. Season lightly with salt and pepper, cover the pan closely, and cook at a gentle simmer for 20 minutes.

4. After 20 minutes, add the pepper strips, stir to combine, cover, and simmer another 15 minutes.

To Store   Cool completely, turn into a storage container, and refrigerate for up to 2 days.

To Serve   Heat the sausages, peppers, and onions in a covered casserole until hot throughout. Then spoon onto a warm serving dish.

Menu Suggestion   Begin with Cauliflower and Potato Soup with Chives (page 211).

SHOPPING LIST
Meat: sweet or hot sausages
Vegetables: sweet red peppers, onions, garlic

Staples: olive oil, dry white wine

* MUSSEL AND BASS STEW

I can still remember the taste of a simple stew containing one firm-fleshed fish and mussels served in a French country home. The stew was enhanced by *crème fraîche* and thyme leaves plus the feathery parts of fresh dill. The fish stock, I know, was made up from at least thirty different kinds of fish and shellfish that swim in European waters alone. This good, strong stock can only be approximated (sadly) by using many fish heads, frames, and even some small whole fish. Here's my rendition of the stew.

4 tablespoons butter
1 onion, chopped
2 ribs celery heart, diced
2 carrots, diced
½ cup white wine
1½ cups full-bodied fish stock
leaves from 2 sprigs of fresh thyme, to measure 1 teaspoon
6 parsley stems, tied with a piece of

kitchen string
salt and freshly ground pepper
2 dozen mussels, well scrubbed
2 pounds sea bass fillets, cut into large chunks
½ cup *crème fraîche,* blended with 2 egg yolks
3 tablespoons snipped fresh dill

1. Melt the butter in a large casserole, stir in the onions, and soften them over moderately low heat.

2. Add the diced celery and carrots, cover, and cook 10 minutes over low heat until tender. Uncover the casserole and pour in the white wine and fish stock. Add the thyme and parsley stems. Season with salt and pepper. Bring the contents of the casserole to a boil and boil gently for 10 minutes.

3. Add the bass chunks and mussels, cover, and cook for 5 minutes, until the bass is just cooked through and the mussels have opened. Discard the parsley stem package.

4. Take up 1 cup of the cooking liquid and slowly pour it into the *crème fraîche* and egg yolks, beating thoroughly as you pour. Off the heat, stir the *crème fraîche* mixture back into the fish, taking care not to mash the bass. Fold in the dill, correct the seasoning, and bring to the simmer to blend all the flavors. Serve the stew from deep plates or wide bowls.

Menu Suggestion Leeks, Glazed and Baked (page 240) would make a pleasant first course, or serve a vinaigrette of cooked leeks first, with plenty of chopped herbs.

Shopping List
Fish and shellfish: sea bass, mussels
Vegetables: onion, celery, carrots
Dairy: butter, *crème fraîche,* eggs

Staples: dry white wine, fish stock
Herbs: parsley, fresh dill, fresh thyme

✷ SWORDFISH WITH OLIVES

Swordfish, in various guises, is good raw material for main-course fare that is chic and fast. I like to combine this firm-textured fish with anchovy sauce, with a combination of chopped basil, oil, garlic, lemon juice, and walnuts, and, as in this treatment, with tomatoes, hot pepper, tiny new potatoes, and olives. Start the potatoes before you do the tomato base preparation, and if you are serving the clam soup (see Menu Suggestion), put that on along with the potatoes: begin boiling the potatoes as the clams steam open, and dice all the vegetables for both dishes at once.

3 tablespoons olive oil
1 onion, diced
1 garlic clove, chopped
1 small hot pepper, cored, seeded, and
 chopped
salt
1 cup tomato purée (homemade) or
 chopped canned plum tomatoes

3 tablespoons chopped parsley
2-pound piece swordfish steak, cut into
 1½-inch cubes
8 very small new potatoes, cooked until
 just tender, peeled or not, as you like
12 pimento-stuffed olives, each sliced
 into thirds
freshly ground pepper (optional)

1. Heat the olive oil in a heavy skillet. Sauté the onions in the oil until tender and translucent. Stir in the chopped garlic, hot pepper, salt to taste, tomato purée or canned tomatoes, and chopped parsley. Bring to the simmer and simmer slowly for 10 minutes.

2. Put the swordfish cubes, potatoes, and olive slices into the skillet. Moisten all with the tomato sauce, cover, and cook for 8–10 minutes or until the swordfish is tender. Correct the seasoning, adding salt and a little freshly ground pepper, if needed. Transfer to a warm serving platter.

Menu Suggestion   Start with Clam Soup with Shallots and White Wine (page 213). Slices of end-of-autumn figs in a citrus syrup of lemon and orange juice added to a not too sweet sugar syrup would make a lovely, refreshing dessert—sprinkle the figs with thin, toasted almond slices just before serving.

SHOPPING LIST
Fish: swordfish
Vegetables: onion, garlic, hot pepper, new potatoes
Staples: olive oil, tomato purée or canned plum

tomatoes, pimento-stuffed olives
Herb: parsley

3
THE WINTER WEEKS

MAIN COURSES

* Shellfish with Peppers and Saffron

Chicken with Jerusalem Artichokes

Pork with Braised Sauerkraut

Brisket of Beef, Pot Roast Style

* Hot Veal Terrine or Garlic Sausages with Sauerkraut

Lamb Shoulder with Lentils

* Veal Chops with Mushrooms (or replace the chops
with the garlic sausages, if you are also doing
the terrine this week)

THE COOK'S PLAN

1. Set out: 6-quart casserole with lid for the Lamb Shoulder with Lentils, 6-quart casserole with lid for the braised sauerkraut for the Pork with Braised Sauerkraut or Garlic Sausages with Sauerkraut, 12-inch oval casserole with lid for the Brisket of Beef, Pot Roast Style, 10-inch sauté pan with lid for the Chicken with Jerusalem Artichokes.

2. Thaw and measure out 6¼ cups chicken stock, 2¼ cups beef stock.

3. Wash and dry 2 ribs celery heart.

4. Peel 3 onions, 4 shallots, 2 garlic cloves, 3 carrots.

5. Finely chop 1 onion, 2 garlic cloves; chop 4 shallots; slice 2 onions, 3 carrots, 2 ribs celery heart.

6. Measure out 2¾ cups dry white wine, 1¼ cups dry red wine, 1 cup tomato purée or canned plum tomatoes, 2 teaspoons tomato paste, 2 teaspoons fresh thyme leaves, 8 peppercorns, 6 juniper berries, ¼ teaspoon caraway seeds.

7. Set out vegetable oil, butter, salt, pepper, flour.

8. Tie two bundles, each containing 6 parsley stems and 1 bay leaf.

9. Braised Sauerkraut with Juniper Berries and Caraway Seeds (or Pork with Braised Sauerkraut, or Garlic Sausages with Sauerkraut): Wash the sauerkraut; sauté vegetables; add herb bundle and spices; pour in wine and stock; simmer, Steps 1–3 (page 64).

10. Brisket of Beef, Pot Roast Style: Brown the brisket; sauté vegetables; season and add liquid; simmer, Steps 1–3 (page 66).

11. Lamb Shoulder with Lentils: Brown the lamb cubes; cook onions and garlic; add tomato purée, wine, tomato paste, herbs, and stock; simmer, Steps 1–3 (page 68).

12. Chicken with Jerusalem Artichokes: Brown the chicken in the oil-butter; sauté shallots; add liquid and seasonings; simmer, Steps 1–3 (page 69).

13. Cool all dishes to room temperature; refrigerate or freeze, following the instructions in "To Store" of each recipe.

BRAISED SAUERKRAUT WITH JUNIPER BERRIES
AND CARAWAY SEEDS

Double this recipe if you are preparing both the Pork with Braised Sauerkraut (page 65) and Garlic Sausages with Sauerkraut (page 65) this week.

2½ pounds sauerkraut	8 peppercorns
3 tablespoons vegetable oil	6 juniper berries
1 onion, sliced	¼ teaspoon caraway seeds
1 carrot, sliced	1 cup dry white wine
6 parsley stems tied with 1 imported bay leaf	2¾ cups chicken stock
	salt

1. Put the sauerkraut in a colander and rinse thoroughly with cold water to remove any harsh, briny liquid. Drain well.

2. In a 4–5-quart casserole (use a larger casserole if doubling the recipe), heat the vegetable oil and stir in the onion slices. Sauté the onion for 3 minutes. Stir in the sliced carrot and sauté another 2 minutes. Add the sauerkraut, parsley stem bundle, peppercorns, juniper berries, and caraway seeds. Stir and cook for 1 minute.

3. Pour in the wine and chicken stock. Season with salt to taste. Bring the contents of the casserole to a simmer, stir once, cover, and simmer on the stove top for 3 hours. Alternately, cook the sauerkraut in the lower third of a preheated 325° F oven.

4. Remove the peppercorns and juniper berries. Discard the parsley bundle.

To Store   Cool the sauerkraut to room temperature, then refrigerate in a covered container for up to 6 days.

To Serve   Heat up the sauerkraut to serve along with Garlic Sausages with Sauerkraut (p. 65) or Pork with Braised Sauerkraut (p. 65).

NOTE: A ⅓-pound piece of bacon, cut into cubes or thick strips, may be added to the sauerkraut for extra flavor; to do this, simmer the strips in water for 8 minutes, drain, dry, and sauté them along with the onions.

If you think you would like a gentler flavor of spice, tie the peppercorns, juniper berries, and caraway seeds in a clean piece of cheesecloth before pouring in the wine and chicken stock. Discard the spice package after the sauerkraut has cooled.

SHOPPING LIST
Vegetables: sauerkraut, onion, carrot
Staples: vegetable oil, dry white wine, chicken stock

Herbs and spices: parsley, bay leaf, peppercorns, caraway seeds, juniper berries

PORK WITH BRAISED SAUERKRAUT

Briny sauerkraut, taken straight from the delicatessen barrel, is seasoned and cooked very slowly. Once cooked, the sauerkraut becomes a naturally moist baster that conceals an interior of pork chops or sausages on cooking day.

> 1 recipe Braised Sauerkraut with Juniper
> Berries and Caraway Seeds (page 64)
>
> *To Serve*
>
> 3 tablespoons vegetable oil
> 4 pork chops, cut 1 inch thick
> salt and freshly ground pepper

To Serve   Bring one quantity of braised sauerkraut (if a double recipe was made) to a simmer in a covered casserole.

Heat the vegetable oil in a skillet and brown the pork chops on each side. Season the pork chops with salt and pepper. Bury the pork chops in the center of the simmering sauerkraut, cover, and bring to a full simmer. Transfer the casserole to the middle of a preheated 325° F oven and bake for 22–25 minutes or until the chops are cooked through. Transfer the pork chops and sauerkraut to a warm platter and serve.

Menu Suggestion   For dessert, Warm Apple-Spice Pudding (page 270).

SHOPPING LIST
Meat: pork chops   *Staple:* vegetable oil
Vegetable: Braised Sauerkraut (see recipe)

GARLIC SAUSAGES WITH SAUERKRAUT

Serve these sausages very hot, with plenty of crusty bread and a jar or two of interesting mustard.

> 1 recipe Braised Sauerkraut with Juniper
>   Berries and Caraway Seeds (page 64)
>
> *To Serve*
>
> 8 garlic sausages

To Serve   Bring the braised sauerkraut to a simmer in a 6-quart casserole. Poach the garlic sausages in simmering water for 10 minutes, and drain. Place the sausages in the middle of the sauerkraut. Cover and simmer for 20–25 minutes, or until the sausages are cooked through.

Menu Suggestion   Follow the same suggestion for Pork with Braised Sauerkraut (preceding recipe).

SHOPPING LIST
Vegetable: Braised Sauerkraut (see recipe)
Meat: garlic sausages

BRISKET OF BEEF, POT ROAST STYLE

The long, slow cooking of brisket in red wine and beef stock produces a very tender piece of meat that, later on, will be enhanced with the addition of wild mushrooms. The brisket sits on a layer of sliced onions, celery, and carrot, the vegetables which make a light and flavorful sauce when the meat has finished cooking.

3 tablespoons vegetable oil
3-pound piece brisket of beef, preferably taken from the first cut
salt and freshly ground pepper
1 onion, sliced
2 ribs celery heart, sliced
2 carrots, sliced
6 parsley stems tied with 1 imported bay leaf

1¼ cups dry red wine
2¼ cups beef stock

To Serve

1 ounce dried wild mushrooms
2 tablespoons butter
3 shallots, finely chopped
1 tablespoon finely chopped parsley

1. Heat the vegetable oil in a 12-inch casserole and brown the brisket on both sides in the hot oil. Remove the meat to a large plate and season with salt and pepper.

2. Sauté the sliced onion in the remaining oil for 2 minutes. Stir in the sliced celery and carrots and sauté for another 2 minutes. Add the parsley stem bundle, wine, and beef stock. Bring the contents of the casserole to a simmer, stirring, and simmer for several minutes. Put the piece of brisket back into the casserole, bring to the simmer again, and cover the pot.

3. Cook the brisket in the lower third of a preheated 325° F oven for 3 hours, or until the meat is tender when pierced with a pronged fork. Carefully remove the meat to a large storage container.

To Store   Degrease the cooking liquid and discard the parsley and bay leaf. Boil down the liquid until lightly thickened, then pass the liquid and vegetables through a food mill. Pour this vegetable-based sauce on top of the meat. When the meat is completely cool, cover tightly and refrigerate for up to 4 days.

To Serve   Soak the wild mushrooms in warm water for 15 minutes. Rinse them thoroughly, drain, and dry. Chop the mushrooms coarsely.

While the mushrooms soak, reheat the brisket in a covered casserole. Melt the butter in a small skillet and sauté the shallots in the butter until they are golden. Stir in the mushrooms and parsley. Stir the mushroom mixture into the meat and simmer until the mushrooms are tender, their flavor deepening the meat and sauce. Remove the meat and cut into long slices against the grain. Serve the meat from a warm platter and spoon over enough of the sauce to moisten well. Serve the remaining sauce separately.

Menu Suggestion   Accompany the brisket with a Gratin of Braised Onions (page 241); follow with Watercress Salad with Mustard and Herbs (page 262); for dessert, Hot Lemon Sponge Pudding (page 290).

SHOPPING LIST
Meat: brisket of beef
Vegetables: onion, celery, carrots, dried wild mushrooms, shallots

Dairy: butter
Staples: vegetable oil, dry red wine, beef stock
Herbs: parsley, bay leaf

LAMB SHOULDER WITH LENTILS

Lentils, cooked slowly with white wine, tomatoes, and thyme, are a good bed for lamb cubes. It is a substantial dish, as is any that uses the tiny, round, flat seeds, such as characterful winter soups and those delicious vinaigrette-based summer salads made up of cooked lentils and chopped onions.

4 tablespoons vegetable oil
2¾–3 pounds boneless lamb shoulder, cut into 2-inch cubes
salt and freshly ground pepper
1 onion, finely chopped
2 garlic cloves, finely chopped
1 cup tomato purée (homemade) or chopped canned plum tomatoes
1 cup dry white wine
2 teaspoons tomato paste
2 teaspoons fresh thyme leaves

1 small imported bay leaf
2 cups chicken stock

To Serve

2 cups lentils
1 small imported bay leaf
1 small onion, peeled and stuck with 2 cloves
½ small carrot, peeled
1 tablespoon finely chopped parsley

1. Heat the vegetable oil in a heavy 6-quart casserole, and brown the lamb cubes, a batch at a time, in the hot oil. Remove the cubes to a plate as they are browned and season them with salt and pepper.

2. In the remaining oil, sauté the chopped onions over moderate heat. Stir in the chopped garlic and cook for 1 minute. Pour in the tomato purée or canned tomatoes and wine, and bring to a boil, stirring all the while. Blend in the tomato paste, thyme leaves, bay leaf, and chicken stock.

3. Return the lamb cubes to the casserole and bring the contents to a simmer. Cover the casserole and cook the lamb at a simmer on the stove top or in the lower third of a preheated 325° F oven for 2 hours or until the lamb is tender.

To Store Remove the lamb with a slotted spoon to a storage bowl. Discard the bay leaf. Concentrate the cooking liquid by boiling it over high heat for 3–4 minutes. Pour the cooking liquid over the lamb cubes, and when completely cool, cover and refrigerate for up to 5 days or freeze for up to 1 month.

To Serve Put the lentils in a deep saucepan. Pour in enough water to cover; add the bay leaf, onion with cloves, and carrot. Bring to a rapid simmer, stirring once or twice, then cover and simmer slowly until the lentils are tender, about 30 minutes, but still hold their shape.

As the lentils cook, heat the lamb in a covered casserole. Drain the cooked lentils and remove the bay leaf, onion, and carrot. Return the lentils to the saucepan, add enough of the cooking liquid from the lamb to moisten, and season with salt and pepper. Heat the lentils for a few minutes. Adjust the seasoning of the lamb and fold in the chopped parsley. Spoon the lentils onto a warm serving platter and top with the lamb cubes.

Menu Suggestion   Follow the lamb with a crisp and tart green salad. For dessert, Oranges and Kiwis in Orange Custard Sauce (page 295).

SHOPPING LIST
Meat: boneless lamb shoulder
Vegetables: onions, garlic, carrot
Staples: vegetable oil, tomato purée or canned plum tomatoes, dry white wine, tomato paste, chicken stock, lentils
Herbs and spice: fresh thyme, parsley, bay leaves, whole cloves

CHICKEN WITH JERUSALEM ARTICHOKES

While Jerusalem artichokes taste reminiscent of artichoke hearts, the similarity ends there. These gnarled roots, which should be used immediately after peeling (or tossed in lemon juice to guard against a brown-gray discoloration), hail from a sunflower plant. This vegetable is now marketed in plastic bags as sunchokes, a helpful bit of merchandising for the shopper, because the skinnier pieces of the vegetable are often mistaken for fresh ginger root. You can make a delicious cream soup with this tuber by substituting the same amount of Jerusalem artichokes for one of the more standard vegetables in any trustworthy soup recipe, like spinach or mushrooms, or as in this recipe, pair it with chicken.

3 tablespoons vegetable oil
1 tablespoon butter
2¾–3-pound whole chicken, cut into 8 serving pieces
½ cup all-purpose flour, in a shallow bowl
4 shallots, chopped
¾ cup dry white wine
1½ cups chicken stock
1 small imported bay leaf
salt and freshly ground pepper

To Serve

1 onion, chopped
3 tablespoons olive oil
2 garlic cloves, chopped
¾ cup tomato purée (homemade) or chopped canned plum tomatoes
1 pound Jerusalem artichokes, peeled and cut into chunks
1 tablespoon finely chopped parsley

1. Heat the vegetable oil and butter in a 10-inch sauté pan. As the chicken pieces are to be browned, dredge them in the flour. Sauté the chicken on both sides until golden, then remove to a plate.

2. Sauté the shallots in the remaining oil-butter for 2 minutes. Pour in the wine and chicken stock; bring the liquid to a boil, stirring the bottom of the pan to dislodge any clinging bits. Add the bay leaf and season with salt and pepper.

3. Put the browned chicken back into the pan, baste with the liquid, cover, and simmer for 30 minutes.

To Store   Cool completely, cover, and refrigerate for up to 2 days or freeze up to 2 weeks.

To Serve   Reheat the chicken. In the meantime, soften the chopped onion in the olive oil in a saucepan large enough to accommodate all of the Jerusalem artichokes. Stir in the chopped garlic and sauté for 2 minutes. Stir in the tomato purée or canned tomatoes, Jerusalem artichokes, and chopped parsley. Season with salt and pepper. Cover the pot closely and simmer the artichokes about 25 minutes until tender but with a bit of crispness still left.

Into the chicken, stir the cooked artichoke mixture, simmer for 2 minutes, then turn out onto a warm platter. Remove the bay leaf and serve.

Menu Suggestion   For dessert, Pears in Sweet Wine with Vanilla (page 302).

SHOPPING LIST
Poultry: chicken
Vegetables: onion, shallots, garlic, Jerusalem artichokes
Dairy: butter

Staples: vegetable oil, olive oil, flour, dry white wine, tomato purée or canned plum tomatoes, chicken stock
Herb: bay leaf

✳ SHELLFISH WITH PEPPERS AND SAFFRON

Garlic and peppers underscore this mosaic of shellfish, and saffron threads tint the savory cooking liquid.

1 onion, chopped
2 tablespoons olive oil
3 garlic cloves, finely chopped
2 green peppers, cored, seeded, and cubed
1½ tablespoons finely chopped parsley
scant ¼ teaspoon saffron threads
½ cup fish stock

½ cup dry white wine
salt and freshly ground pepper
2 dozen mussels, well scrubbed
2 dozen littleneck clams, well scrubbed
1½ dozen shrimp, shelled, with tails left intact, and deveined
1 recipe Crisp Bread Slices (page 154)

1. Soften the chopped onion in the olive oil in a 6-quart casserole. Stir in the chopped garlic and cook for 1 minute, or until it colors to a pale gold.

2. Add the cubed peppers, and stir and cook for 4–5 minutes until they turn tender-crisp. Sprinkle on the parsley and saffron; stir both in. Pour in the fish stock and wine and bring the liquid to a boil, stirring all the while. Season the liquid with salt and pepper to taste. Cook the contents at a lively simmer for 3–4 minutes longer.

3. Add the mussels and clams to the casserole, hinge side down, raise the heat to high, cover, and cook for 3 minutes, or until the mussels and clams are not quite fully opened. Add the shrimp, reduce the heat slightly, and cook until the shrimp have just turned opaque and the clams and mussels have opened all the way.

4. Serve the shellfish in wide bowls with a few bread slices secured amid the shellfish in each bowl.

Menu Suggestion   Follow the shellfish with a plain green salad, such as Bibb Lettuce Salad (page 257).

SHOPPING LIST
Shellfish: mussels, clams, shrimp
Vegetables: onion, garlic, green peppers
Staples: olive oil, dry white wine, fish stock

Herbs: parsley, saffron
For serving: Crisp Bread Slices (see recipe)

∗ HOT VEAL TERRINE

This mostly-veal terrine is no more complicated than putting together any other meatloaf. The mixture is seasoned with Madeira, thyme, and garlic, and speckled with plum tomato bits. Very thin strips of carrot wind through the veal mixture, dotting each slice as it is cut from the terrine.

2 carrots, peeled and cut into thin strips
8 thin slices bacon
2 tablespoons butter
3 leeks, white part only, thinly sliced
2 garlic cloves, finely chopped
4 canned plum tomatoes, chopped
2 teaspoons fresh thyme leaves
1 tablespoon finely chopped parsley
⅓ cup Madeira
1 pound ground veal

⅔ pound pork ground with 5 ounces pork fat
1 tablespoon vegetable oil
1½ teaspoons salt, or to taste
freshly ground black pepper, to taste
2 eggs, beaten
½ cup bread crumbs soaked in ¼ cup milk
1 small imported bay leaf
a few sprigs of fresh thyme (optional)

1. Bring a large saucepan of water to the boil. Simmer the carrot strips in the water until barely tender, about 6 minutes. Remove the carrot strips with a slotted spoon. Add the bacon, simmer for 5 minutes, drain, and dry on a sheet of paper toweling.

2. Line the bottom of a 6-cup terrine with half the bacon slices and set aside.

3. In a skillet, melt the butter, stir in the leeks, and cook them over moderately low heat until soft. In a large mixing bowl, place all of the remaining ingredients except the bay leaf, thyme, carrot strips, and bacon slices, and mix well to combine them. Beat in the softened leeks.

4. Pack one-third of the mixture into the prepared terrine. Lay on half the carrot sticks. Pack on another third of the veal mixture and cover with the rest of the carrot sticks. Layer on the rest of the veal mixture, smooth the top, and press the bay leaf on the surface. Cover with a few sprigs of fresh thyme, if possible.

5. Put the last 4 strips of bacon on top of the mixture. Cover the top of the terrine with a sheet of aluminum foil and the lid to the terrine.

6. Place the terrine in a larger baking dish and fill with enough hot water to rise at least one-third up the sides of the terrine. Bake the terrine in a preheated 350° F oven for 1½ hours. Uncover, and remove the foil and top layer of bacon. Serve in slices, cut directly from the terrine.

Menu Suggestion   Follow the terrine with a Salad of Endive and Celery Heart (page 258) and end with a bread pudding or fruit pudding.

SHOPPING LIST
Meat: ground veal, ground pork, ground pork fat, bacon
Vegetables: carrots, leeks, garlic
Dairy: butter, eggs, milk

Staples: canned plum tomatoes, Madeira, vegetable oil, bread crumbs
Herbs: fresh thyme, parsley, bay leaf

⁜ VEAL CHOPS WITH MUSHROOMS

This is a relaxed, homey sort of dish. The veal chops turn out tender and juicy from cooking slowly in a little white wine and stock. You could further round out the composition of the recipe with chunks of potatoes or browned pearl onions, adding them to the casserole along with the chops.

3 tablespoons vegetable oil

4 shoulder veal chops, cut 1-inch thick

¼-pound piece of bacon, cut into cubes, simmered in water for 8 minutes, drained, and dried

4 tablespoons butter

1 onion, chopped

½ cup dry white wine

1 cup chicken stock

6 parsley stems tied with 1 imported bay leaf

salt and freshly ground pepper

¾ pound firm white mushrooms, caps only

1 tablespoon finely chopped parsley

1. Heat the vegetable oil in a heavy skillet and brown the chops on both sides. Remove the chops to a dish. Add the bacon cubes to the skillet and sauté them in the remaining oil until lightly browned, then set aside along with the veal chops.

2. Melt 2 tablespoons of the butter in a 10-inch casserole. Stir in the chopped onion and sauté for several minutes, until soft and lightly golden. Stir in the wine and chicken stock and drop in the parsley bundle. Season the contents with salt and pepper. Bring the contents of the casserole to a simmer; let the liquid bubble for 1 minute.

3. Add the veal chops and bacon cubes to the casserole and spoon some of the liquid over everything. Cover the casserole and place it in the lower third of a preheated 325° F oven for 55 minutes or until the chops are tender.

4. While the veal is cooking, sauté the mushroom caps in the remaining 2 tablespoons butter until lightly browned. Remove from the heat and season with salt and pepper.

5. When the veal is cooked, check the cooking liquid to see if it has reduced a bit. If not, remove the chops and bacon cubes and keep them warm while you boil down the liquid until it takes on some body. Discard the herb bundle, and add the chops and the mushrooms. Correct the seasoning and simmer all together for a minute longer to combine flavors. Stir in the chopped parsley and serve from a warm platter.

Menu Suggestion   Serve Endives, Glazed and Baked (page 238) as a vegetable course or along with the veal; for dessert, Compote of Spiced Figs (page 284).

SHOPPING LIST

Meat: veal chops, bacon

Vegetables: onion, mushrooms

Dairy: butter

Staples: vegetable oil, dry white wine, chicken stock

Herbs: parsley, bay leaf

MAIN COURSES

✳ Sautéed Chicken Livers with Orange Wedges

✳ Striped Bass with Broccoli

Chicken with Celery Root

Stuffed Cabbage Leaves in Pine Nut Sauce

Veal with Anchovies

✳ Halibut and Swordfish Stew

✳ Pork with Glazed Turnips

THE COOK'S PLAN

1. Set out: 6-quart casserole with lid for the Stuffed Cabbage Leaves in Pine Nut Sauce, 6-quart casserole with lid for the Veal with Anchovies, 10-inch sauté pan with lid for the Chicken with Celery Root.

2. Thaw and measure out ½ cup beef stock, 3¾ cups chicken stock.

3. Wash and dry a small bunch of parsley, 2 leeks.

4. Peel 3 onions, 4 shallots, 1 garlic clove.

5. Finely chop 4 shallots, 1 garlic clove, 4 tablespoons parsley; chop 3 onions, 5 anchovy fillets; slice 2 leeks; cube ¼ pound bacon.

6. Measure out 2 cups dry white wine, ½ cup soft bread crumbs, ⅓ cup milk, 2¼ cups tomato purée or canned plum tomatoes, 2 tablespoons honey.

7. Set out vegetable oil, butter, salt, pepper, flour.

8. Tie 2 herb bundles, each combining 6 parsley stems and 1 bay leaf.

9. Trim and peel off cabbage leaves, Step 1 (page 76).

10. Stuffed Cabbage Leaves in Pine Nut Sauce: Prepare filling for cabbage; stuff the leaves; prepare the sauce for the cabbage rolls; layer in the cabbage rolls; simmer, Steps 2–4 (page 76).

11. Veal with Anchovies: Brown the veal; sauté the vegetables; season; simmer in the wine, tomatoes, and stock, Steps 1–3 (page 77).

12. Chicken with Celery Root: Brown the floured chicken in the oil-butter; sauté the bacon and onion; add wine and stock; set the chicken to simmer, Steps 1–3 (page 78).

13. Cool all dishes to room temperature; refrigerate or freeze, following the instructions in "To Store" of each recipe.

STUFFED CABBAGE LEAVES IN PINE NUT SAUCE

Cabbage leaves are perfect wrappers for this seasoned ground beef blend: the vegetable holds a cylinder of meat in one neat package which reheats very well in a sauce punctuated with tiny currants and slender pine nuts. It is also a good savory, do-ahead main dish for one of those relaxed dinner parties.

1 large or 2 small heads of cabbage, to yield 16 large leaves
½ cup soft bread crumbs
⅓ cup cold milk
1 pound ground beef
4 shallots, finely chopped
1 garlic clove, finely chopped
3 tablespoons finely chopped parsley
1¼ teaspoons salt
freshly ground pepper
1 egg, lightly beaten

1 tablespoon vegetable oil
2 leeks, white part only, thinly sliced
2 tablespoons butter
1½ cups tomato purée (homemade) or chopped canned plum tomatoes
2 tablespoons honey
½ cup beef stock

To Serve

2 tablespoons moist, dried currants
3 tablespoons pine nuts, lightly toasted

1. Cut several slits at the base of the cabbage where the leaves join the core. Drop the cabbage(s) in a large pot of boiling water and begin to peel off the leaves as the water loosens them. Drain 16 leaves on paper toweling.

2. Prepare the filling: In a large mixing bowl, combine the bread crumbs and milk. Break up the ground beef and add it to the bowl. Beat in the shallots, garlic, parsley, salt, pepper, egg, and oil. Blend well. Place a good 2 tablespoons of filling on the lower third of each cabbage leaf and roll into a cylinder.

3. In a heavy 6-quart casserole, soften the leeks in the butter over moderately low heat. Stir in the tomato purée or canned tomatoes, honey, and beef stock. Bring to the simmer and cook steadily for 5 minutes.

4. Arrange the stuffed cabbage leaves in two layers in the casserole, basting with some of the tomato-leek sauce as you go along and sprinkling with a little salt and pepper. Bring the contents of the casserole to a simmer on the stove top, cover, then transfer to the lower third of a preheated 325° F oven to cook for 2½ hours.

To Store   Transfer the cabbage rolls to a storage container and strain the cooking liquid over them. Cool completely, cover, and refrigerate for up to 5 days.

To Serve   Reheat the cabbage leaves in a covered casserole. Stir in the currants and toasted pine nuts; simmer uncovered for 7–8 minutes, then serve.

Menu Suggestion   Serve Buckwheat Kernels with Sautéed Onions (page 251) along with the cabbage rolls; follow with Oranges and Grapes in Hot Orange Sauce (page 293).

SHOPPING LIST
Meat: ground beef
Vegetables: cabbage, shallots, garlic, leeks
Dairy: milk, egg, butter
Staples: bread crumbs, vegetable oil, tomato purée or

canned plum tomatoes, honey, beef stock, currants, pine nuts
Herb: parsley

VEAL WITH ANCHOVIES

In this dish, anchovies add a balanced pungency to the veal shoulder, and a few cured olives lend their own keen flavor.

2¾–3 pounds boneless veal shoulder, cut into 2-inch cubes
3 tablespoons vegetable oil
1 tablespoon butter
salt and freshly ground pepper
2 onions, chopped
4 garlic cloves, left whole and unpeeled
5 anchovy fillets, coarsely chopped
1 cup dry white wine

¾ cup tomato purée (homemade) or chopped canned plum tomatoes
2 cups chicken stock
6 parsley stems tied with 1 small imported bay leaf

To Serve

1 dozen cured black olives

1. Dry the veal cubes on paper toweling. Heat the vegetable oil and butter in a 6-quart casserole. Brown the veal cubes in the hot oil-butter, several batches at a time. Remove the cubes to a plate as they are browned and season with salt and pepper.

2. When all the cubes have been browned, stir in the chopped onions and sauté them for 3 minutes. Add the garlic cloves, anchovy fillets, and wine. Raise the heat to boil the wine and boil for 30 seconds, stirring the pot as the wine bubbles.

3. Stir in the tomato purée or canned tomatoes and chicken stock. Add the parsley stem bundle. Put the veal cubes back into the casserole and bring the contents to a lively simmer. Cover the casserole and cook at a gentle simmer for 2 hours on the stove top, or until the veal tests fork-tender. Alternately, cook the veal in the lower third of a preheated 325° F oven until tender.

(continued)

To Store Transfer the cubes to a storage container with a slotted spoon. Boil the cooking liquid for 4 minutes, just to condense and bind it lightly. Strain the liquid through a food mill, puréeing the solid matter as well, and pour that over the veal. Cool the veal to room temperature, then cover and refrigerate for up to 5 days or freeze for up to 1 month.

To Serve Reheat the veal in a covered casserole. Scatter the olives over the meat and continue to simmer, uncovered, for a few minutes longer until the olives are hot. Correct the seasoning and serve.

Menu Suggestion Follow with a Salad of Watercress and Endive (page 261).

SHOPPING LIST
Meat: boneless veal shoulder
Vegetables: onions, garlic
Dairy: butter
Staples: vegetable oil, anchovies, dry white wine, to-mato purée or canned plum tomatoes, chicken stock, cured black olives
Herbs: parsley, bay leaf

CHICKEN WITH CELERY ROOT

Celery root is a vegetable often found shredded and dressed in mayonnaise. It also works well, once the scraggly brown skin is pared away, when combined with chicken in a light wine sauce.

3 tablespoons vegetable oil
1 tablespoon butter
2¾–3-pound whole chicken, cut into 8 serving pieces
½ cup all-purpose flour, in a shallow bowl
¼ pound piece of bacon, cubed, simmered in water for 8 minutes, drained, and dried
1 onion, chopped
1 cup dry white wine

1¾ cups chicken stock
6 parsley stems tied with 1 small imported bay leaf
salt and freshly ground pepper

To Serve

1 pound celery root, peeled and cubed
1 tablespoon lemon juice
1½ tablespoons butter
½ cup chicken stock
1 tablespoon finely chopped parsley

1. Put the vegetable oil and 1 tablespoon butter in a 10-inch sauté pan and place it over medium-high heat. While the butter is melting, dredge a few pieces of chicken in the

flour and brown them on both sides in the hot oil-butter. As the pieces brown, remove them to a plate.

2. When all 8 pieces have been browned, stir the bacon into the pan and sauté the cubes in the remaining oil-butter until a light golden color. Stir in the chopped onion and sauté for 3 minutes. Pour in the wine, raise the heat to high, and boil for 30 seconds, scraping the bottom of the pan as the wine boils.

3. Pour the chicken stock into the sauté pan, toss in the parsley stem package, and season the liquid with salt and pepper. Replace the chicken, baste with some of the winy liquid, and bring the contents of the pan to the simmer. Cover and simmer for 30 minutes or until the chicken is tender.

To Store   Discard the parsley package. Transfer the chicken to a storage container. Boil the pan liquid for 5 minutes to reduce it slightly, then pour it over the chicken. Cool completely, cover, and refrigerate for up to 2 days or freeze for up to 2 weeks.

To Serve   Combine the celery root, lemon juice, 1½ tablespoons butter, and stock in a saucepan. Season with salt and pepper, cover, and bring the contents to a simmer. Simmer until the celery root is just tender, about 20 minutes, and the liquid reduces to a light glaze. Reheat the chicken in a covered casserole until piping hot. Add the celery root, carefully combine it with the chicken, and simmer everything for a few minutes. Fold in the chopped parsley and serve.

Menu Suggestion   Start with Mushroom and Barley Soup (page 222); for dessert, Pear and Ginger Bread Pudding (page 299).

SHOPPING LIST
Meat and poultry: bacon, chicken
Vegetables and fruit: onion, celery root, lemon
Dairy: butter

Staples: vegetable oil, flour, dry white wine, chicken stock
Herbs: parsley, bay leaf

✳ PORK WITH GLAZED TURNIPS

Turnips are good traveling companions for pork, and here they take on a light shiny glaze from simmering in beef stock and butter. This recipe uses chops, which makes it a kind of dish you can comfortably do on serving day, but you can use another pork recipe from this book, double it, and use half of that recipe as a part of this dish. If you should like to do this, prepare a double recipe of Pork in Red Wine with Pearl Barley (page 87—minus, of course, the pearl barley) and freeze half for the following week. Cook the turnips as directed in this recipe, and when you reheat the pork, add them to simmer for a final blend of flavors.

4 pork chops, cut 1-inch thick	1½ cups beef stock
4 tablespoons vegetable oil	1 small imported bay leaf
4½ tablespoons butter	salt and freshly ground pepper
1 onion, chopped	1 pound turnips, trimmed, peeled, and
2 garlic cloves, finely chopped	quartered
½ cup dry white wine	1 tablespoon finely chopped parsley

1. Dry the pork chops on paper toweling. Heat the vegetable oil in a heavy skillet and brown the pork chops on both sides in the hot oil.

2. In a 10-inch casserole, heat 2 tablespoons of the butter. Soften the onions in the butter. Stir in the chopped garlic and cook for 2 minutes. Pour in the wine and bring to the boil. Add ½ cup of the beef stock and the bay leaf; season the liquid with salt and pepper.

3. Put in the pork chops, overlapping them slightly, and baste with some of the liquid. Bring to the simmer on the stove top, baste again, and cover. Cook the chops in the lower third of a preheated 325° F oven for 20–22 minutes, turning the chops over once or twice as they cook.

4. While the pork chops are cooking, prepare the turnips. Put the quartered turnips, remaining 2½ tablespoons butter, remaining cup of beef stock, and salt and pepper to taste in a saucepan. Bring to a low boil, then cover and simmer the turnips in the stock until they are tender and glazed over, about 15–20 minutes. If you start out with small turnips which have been quartered, the turnips should be ready as soon as the chops have cooked. If the turnips are not small, reduce the quarters to small wedges to facilitate cooking.

5. Discard the bay leaf from the cooked pork chops. Add the glazed turnips to the casserole and fold in the chopped parsley. Serve from a warm platter.

Menu Suggestion   Accompany the pork with Buttered Noodles (page 253); follow with a Bibb Lettuce Salad (page 257); for dessert, Deep-Dish Rhubarb Pie (page 312).

SHOPPING LIST
Meat: pork chops
Vegetables: onion, garlic, turnips
Dairy: butter

Staples: vegetable oil, dry white wine, beef stock
Herbs: bay leaf, parsley

✻ STRIPED BASS WITH BROCCOLI

Sometimes the best, most pleasing way to cook fish steaks is in a simple wine and garlic bath with a fresh vegetable and unexpected herb. Here, the fish is bass, and the tender, mild flowerets of broccoli absorb a rush of fresh coriander and lemon.

1 bunch broccoli, trimmed and divided
    into flowerets
2 tablespoons olive oil
1 tablespoon butter
3 garlic cloves, finely chopped
2 tablespoons finely chopped parsley
½ cup dry white wine

6 striped bass steaks, cut 1-inch thick
salt and freshly ground pepper
½ tablespoon lemon juice
¼ cup loosely packed chopped fresh cor-
    iander leaves
lemon wedges

1. Cook the broccoli flowerets in simmering salted water until tender, about 10 minutes. Drain in a colander and pour a few cups of cool water over to stop the cooking process and turn the vegetable's color back to a bright green. Dry the flowerets on paper toweling.

2. Put the olive oil and butter in a 10-inch sauté pan. Place over moderate heat and, when the butter has melted, stir in the chopped garlic and cook for 3 minutes. Stir in the parsley. Cook for 1 minute.

3. Raise the heat to moderately high. Pour in the wine and let it bubble away for 1 minute. Put in the fish steaks, season lightly with salt and pepper, and baste with some of the garlic and wine liquid. Reduce the heat so that the liquid simmers and cover the pan. Cook for 5 minutes.

4. Turn the steaks and baste with some of the liquid. Intersperse the broccoli flowerets between the steaks and lightly season everything with salt and pepper. Cover and simmer 5 minutes.

5. Remove the fish and vegetable to a serving platter. Add the lemon juice and coriander leaves to the pan, stir, and bring to a rapid boil. Pour this over the broccoli and fish steaks, then serve with lemon wedges.

Menu Suggestion   Finish with Pineapple in Port with Pecans (page 306).

SHOPPING LIST
Fish: striped bass steaks
Vegetables and fruit: broccoli, garlic, lemons
Dairy: butter

Staples: olive oil, dry white wine
Herbs: parsley, fresh coriander

✱ HALIBUT AND SWORDFISH STEW

Chunks of fish are delicious when cooked in different types of savory bases, with or without tomatoes, with a predominant herb at times, and occasionally bound very lightly with potatoes—which is the kind of treatment you will be dealing with here.

2 small white onions, chopped
2 tablespoons butter
2 carrots, diced
2 small boiling potatoes, peeled and diced
6 parsley stems tied with 1 small imported bay leaf
½ cup dry white wine
1½ cups fish stock
salt and freshly ground pepper

To Serve

¾ pound fresh white mushrooms, caps only
1 tablespoon butter
1 teaspoon lemon juice
1¼ pounds fillet of halibut, cut into large chunks
1¼ pounds swordfish steak, cut into large chunks
½ cup heavy cream, warmed
cayenne pepper
1 tablespoon butter, softened

1. Soften the onions in the 2 tablespoons butter in a heavy 1-quart saucepan (if preparing the fish base in advance) or in a small casserole (if preparing the base on serving day).

2. Stir in the diced carrots and cook for 2 minutes; stir in the diced potatoes and cook 1 minute longer. Add the parsley stem bundle, wine, and fish stock. Season with salt and pepper. Bring the contents of the pan to a rapid boil, then reduce the heat so that the liquid simmers. Simmer, covered, for 30 minutes.

To Store   Pass the fish base through a food mill. Cool to room temperature, then refrigerate in a covered container for up to 1 day or freeze for up to 1 week, if you are preparing this part in advance. If not, continue on with the recipe.

To Serve   To complete the stew, bring the base to a simmer. In the meantime, put the mushroom caps, 1 tablespoon butter, and lemon juice in a saucepan, cover, and cook over moderate heat, shaking the pan occasionally, until the mushrooms begin to stew in their own steam and turn tender.

Add the fish chunks to the base, baste with the liquid, cover, and simmer for 10 minutes or until just tender. Keep the chunks warm while you finish the rest of the dish. Bring the base to a low boil, and add the mushrooms and warmed cream. Simmer for a minute; season with salt as necessary, and a sprinkling of cayenne pepper. Fold in the fish chunks and swirl in the softened butter. Serve from a deep platter.

Menu Suggestion   Follow the stew with a Salad of Red Leaf Lettuce with Herbs (page 260).

SHOPPING LIST
Fish: halibut fillet, swordfish steak
Vegetables and fruit: white onions, carrots, boiling potatoes, mushrooms, lemon

Dairy: butter, heavy cream
Staples: dry white wine, fish stock
Herbs and spice: parsley, bay leaf, cayenne pepper

✷ SAUTÉED CHICKEN LIVERS WITH ORANGE WEDGES

A field of chicken livers served up with an accent of tangy orange wedges.

1⅓ pounds chicken livers, trimmed
5 tablespoons butter
2 tablespoons vegetable oil
salt and freshly ground pepper
4 large shallots, finely chopped

2 juicy seedless oranges, peeled and cut into wedges
3 tablespoons Madeira
1 tablespoon finely chopped parsley

1. Cut each chicken liver in half along the natural separation. Heat 3 tablespoons of the butter and all of the vegetable oil in a skillet. When the butter has melted, add the livers and sauté them, turning once and seasoning with salt and pepper.

2. As the livers cook, heat the remaining 2 tablespoons of butter in another skillet, stir in the chopped shallots, and sauté them until tender. Add the orange sections and stir-cook until they are hot throughout but still keep their shape. Pour on the Madeira and let it bubble away quickly until reduced by half.

3. Add the livers to the orange wedges and shallots. Stir. Fold in the chopped parsley and serve.

Menu Suggestion   Follow with Watercress and Walnut Salad (page 263).

SHOPPING LIST
Meat: chicken livers
Vegetable and fruit: shallots, seedless oranges
Dairy: butter

Staples: vegetable oil, Madeira
Herb: parsley

MAIN COURSES

*Oysters with Spinach and Pernod

Kettle of Garlic Sausages
with White Beans and Vegetables

Chicken with Green Olives

Lamb with Grapefruit

Veal Shanks with Wild Mushrooms

*Scallops with Leeks and Fennel

Pork in Red Wine with Pearl Barley

THE COOK'S PLAN

    1. Set out: 6-quart casserole with lid for the Lamb with Grapefruit, 6-quart casserole with lid for the Pork in Red Wine with Pearl Barley, 12-inch oval casserole with lid for the Veal Shanks with Wild Mushrooms, 10-inch sauté pan with lid for the Chicken with Green Olives, soup pot or kettle for the Kettle of Garlic Sausages with White Beans and Vegetables.

    2. Thaw and measure out 10¾ cups beef stock, 3½ cups chicken stock.

    3. Wash and dry 8 ribs celery heart.

    4. Peel 8 onions, 8 garlic cloves, 6 carrots, 1 turnip, 4 boiling potatoes.

    5. Finely chop 2 garlic cloves; chop 8 onions, 4 ribs celery heart, 6 garlic cloves, 2 carrots, 2 teaspoons rosemary leaves; slice 1 head cabbage; dice 4 carrots, 4 ribs celery heart, 1 turnip; cube 4 boiling potatoes.

    6. Measure out 1½ cups dry red wine, about 2½ cups dry white wine.

    7. Set out vegetable oil, olive oil, butter, salt, pepper.

    8. Tie 3 herb bundles, each containing 6 parsley stems and 1 bay leaf.

    9. Soak the white beans, Step 1 (page 86).

    10. Kettle of Garlic Sausages with White Beans and Vegetables: Sauté the vegetables; add tomatoes; season and add beef stock; simmer, Steps 2–3 (page 86).

    11. Pork in Red Wine with Pearl Barley: Brown the pork cubes; sauté onion and garlic; add wine, stock, and season; set to simmer, Steps 1–3 (page 87).

    12. Lamb with Grapefruit: Brown the lamb and bones; sauté vegetables; add liquid, season, and simmer, Steps 1–3 (page 88).

    13. Veal Shanks with Wild Mushrooms: Brown the veal shanks, add the onions, garlic, celery, and carrots. Combine with the wine, tomato purée, and chicken stock. Season and simmer, Steps 1–3 (page 90).

    14. Chicken with Green Olives: Prepare the chicken with garlic, tomato, wine, and stock through Step 3 (page 91).

    15. Cool all dishes to room temperature; refrigerate or freeze, following the instructions in "To Store" of each recipe.

KETTLE OF GARLIC SAUSAGES
WITH WHITE BEANS AND VEGETABLES

Here is one of those meal-in-a-kettle arrangements that covers every course: soup, meat, and vegetable. This dish is virtually done with once you have prepared all the vegetables, but that should take a matter of minutes. Add a round, chewy, peasant kind of bread and offer several strengths of mustards for the sausages.

1 cup dried Great Northern white beans
4 tablespoons olive oil
3 onions, chopped
2 garlic cloves, finely chopped
4 carrots, diced
4 ribs celery heart, diced
1 turnip, diced
4 waxy boiling potatoes, peeled and cubed
1-pound head of cabbage, trimmed, cored, and thinly sliced

8 canned plum tomatoes, coarsely chopped
leaves from 2 sprigs of fresh thyme
6 parsley sprigs tied with 1 imported bay leaf
7 cups beef stock
freshly ground pepper

To Serve

1 pound sausages
salt

1. Put the beans in a large bowl and add enough cold water to cover them by at least 3 inches. Leave at room temperature to soak overnight.

2. Heat the olive oil in a soup pot and add the chopped onions. Sauté for 2 minutes. Stir in the chopped garlic and diced carrots; sauté for 2 minutes. Add the celery, turnip, potatoes, and cabbage, stirring them in in separate lots and sautéing for 2 minutes after each vegetable is added.

3. Stir in the plum tomatoes, add the thyme leaves and parsley bundle, and pour in the beef stock. Season to taste with pepper. Bring the contents of the kettle to a simmer, cover, and simmer slowly for 2½ hours.

To Store Cool the "kettle" to room temperature, remove the herb bundle, then transfer the contents to a storage container. Cover tightly and refrigerate for up to 6 days.

To Serve Drain the beans. Reheat the "kettle," add the beans, cover, and simmer for 20 minutes. Add the sausages and simmer for an additional 20 minutes, until the beans are tender and the sausages cooked through. Season with salt to taste and serve.

Menu Suggestion Finish with a lovely Rhubarb Compote (page 311).

SHOPPING LIST
Meat: sausages
Vegetables: onions, garlic, carrots, celery, turnip, boiling potatoes, cabbage

Staples: Great Northern white beans, olive oil, canned plum tomatoes, beef stock
Herbs: bay leaf, parsley, fresh thyme

PORK IN RED WINE WITH PEARL BARLEY

This is a garlic-lover's pork dish. In addition, the braise works astonishingly well in another form—by using 4 large onions and substituting 1½ cups of "light" beer (and a pinch of sugar) for the red wine.

4 tablespoons vegetable oil
2¾–3 pounds boneless pork shoulder, cut into 2-inch cubes
salt and freshly ground pepper
2 onions, chopped
3 large heads garlic, cloves separated but not peeled
1½ cups dry red wine

2 teaspoons fresh rosemary leaves, chopped
1¾ cups beef stock
1 imported bay leaf

To Serve

1½ cups pearl barley

1. Heat the vegetable oil in a heavy 6-quart casserole. Brown the pork cubes in several batches in the hot oil. Remove them to a plate as they are done and season with salt and pepper.

2. Stir in the chopped onions and sauté them in the remaining oil for 4 minutes. Stir in the garlic cloves and pour in the wine. Bring the wine to a boil, stirring the bottom of the casserole as the wine begins to bubble. Add the rosemary leaves and beef stock. Drop in the bay leaf.

3. Put the pork cubes back into the casserole. Bring the liquid to the simmer, and cover the casserole. Cook the pork in the lower third of a preheated 325° F oven for 2 hours or until the pork is tender. Alternately, simmer the pork on the stove top.

To Store   Remove the meat from the casserole with a slotted spoon and place in a storage bowl. Put the liquid and all solids through a food mill to purée, and pour over the pork. When completely cool, cover and refrigerate for up to 5 days or freeze up to 1 month.

To Serve   Cook the pearl barley in gently boiling salted water about 25–30 minutes until tender. Heat up the pork in a covered casserole. Drain the barley and transfer it to a large saucepan, season with salt and pepper, and pour on 1 cup of the hot liquid from the pork and heat. Correct the seasoning of both the barley and the pork. Transfer the barley to a serving platter and top with the pork, or put the pork in the center of the platter and surround with the barley.

Menu Suggestion Follow the pork with a mixed green salad in a wine, vinegar, mustard, and oil dressing; for dessert, Baked Spiced Apple Slices (page 269).

SHOPPING LIST
Meat: boneless pork shoulder
Vegetables: onions, garlic
Staples: vegetable oil, dry red wine, beef stock, pearl

barley
Herbs: rosemary, bay leaf

LAMB WITH GRAPEFRUIT

Fruit and meat play well against each other, sometimes in a mildly sweet way, other times pleasantly sharp, fresh, and sprightly like the manner of the lamb and grapefruit below.

3 tablespoons vegetable oil
3 tablespoons butter
3 pounds boneless lamb shoulder, cut into 2-inch cubes, with some of the shoulder bones, cracked, if possible
salt and freshly ground pepper
2 onions, chopped
2 ribs celery heart, chopped
2 garlic cloves, chopped
6 parsley stems tied with 1 small imported bay leaf

1 cup dry white wine
2 cups beef stock

To Serve

3 tablespoons butter
2 dozen pearl onions, peeled
6 carrots, cut into 2-inch segments
1 grapefruit, peeled and cut into segments, seeds removed
1 tablespoon finely chopped parsley

1. Heat the vegetable oil and 1 tablespoon butter in a heavy 6-quart casserole. Brown the lamb cubes in the hot oil-butter, a batch at a time. Remove them to a plate as soon as they are browned and season them with salt and pepper. Brown the cracked lamb bones, too, adding more oil, if necessary, to brown them properly.

2. Pour out the oil-butter from the casserole and add 2 tablespoons fresh butter. Stir

in the chopped onions and sauté for 3 minutes. Stir in the chopped celery and garlic and sauté for 3 minutes longer. Add the parsley stem bundle and pour in the wine. Bring the wine to a boil, stirring all the while.

3. Pour in the beef stock and add all the browned lamb cubes. Top with the browned bones. Bring the contents of the casserole to a simmer, cover, and cook in the lower third of a preheated 325° F oven for 1¾–2 hours, or until the lamb is tender. Alternately, simmer the lamb on the stove top.

To Store When the meat is tender, transfer the cubes to a storage bowl with a slotted spoon. Discard the parsley bundle and bones. Boil the liquid for 5 minutes, then put all the liquid plus the vegetables through a food mill. Pour this over the lamb cubes, cool to room temperature, then cover tightly and refrigerate for up to 5 days or freeze for up to 1 month.

To Serve Put the 3 tablespoons butter in a skillet and set over moderate heat. Add the pearl onions and sauté them until they begin to glaze over. Stir in the carrot segments and continue to sauté for an additional 4 minutes.

Reheat the lamb in a covered casserole. After several minutes, stir in the onions and carrots and simmer until the vegetables are tender. Adjust the seasoning with more salt and pepper as necessary. Add the grapefruit segments, cover, and simmer for a few minutes longer to heat up the fruit. Transfer the contents to a warm platter and serve.

Menu Suggestion Follow the lamb with Bibb Lettuce Salad (page 257).

Shopping List
Meat: boneless lamb shoulder
Vegetables and fruit: cooking onions, pearl onions, celery, garlic, carrots, grapefruit

Dairy: butter
Staples: vegetable oil, dry white wine, beef stock
Herbs: parsley, bay leaf

VEAL SHANKS WITH WILD MUSHROOMS

These veal shanks cook on a vegetable bed moistened with white wine and stock: a prelude to the addition of woody, aromatic wild mushrooms. So that the flavor of the mushrooms is clear and present, they are added to simmer with the veal on serving day.

2 veal shanks, to yield eight 1¼-inch-thick pieces
2 tablespoons butter
2 tablespoons vegetable oil
salt and freshly ground pepper
1 onion, chopped
2 garlic cloves, chopped
2 ribs celery heart, chopped
2 carrots, chopped

⅔ cup dry white wine
¾ cup tomato purée (homemade) or chopped canned plum tomatoes
1½ cups chicken stock

To Serve

1 ounce dried wild mushrooms
2 tablespoons butter
1 tablespoon finely chopped parsley

1. Dry the veal shanks with paper toweling. Heat 2 tablespoons butter and the vegetable oil in a 12-inch oval casserole. Brown the shanks in the butter-oil, several at a time, then transfer to a side dish. Season with salt and pepper.

2. When you have browned all the pieces of veal, stir in the chopped onions and sauté for 3 minutes. Stir in the chopped garlic and celery and sauté, stirring, for 3 minutes. Stir in the chopped carrots; cook and stir for 2 minutes.

3. Pour in the wine, raise the heat, and let it bubble up for 30 seconds. Give the casserole a few stirs as the wine bubbles away. Stir in the tomato purée or canned tomatoes and chicken stock. Put back the veal shanks and bring the contents of the casserole to a simmer, basting the shanks with some of the liquid. Cover the casserole and cook at a gentle simmer on the stove top for 2 hours or in the lower third of a preheated 325° F oven for 2 hours.

To Store   Transfer the cooked shanks to a storage container. Pour over the cooking liquid, and when cooled off completely, cover and refrigerate for up to 5 days or freeze for up to 1 month.

To Serve   Soak the mushrooms in 1 cup warm water for 20 minutes. Heat up the veal shanks in a covered casserole. Drain the mushrooms, rinse them off, and chop coarsely. Heat the 2 tablespoons butter in a small skillet and cook the mushrooms over moderate heat for 5 minutes. Season lightly with salt and pepper; stir in the chopped parsley. Swirl the chopped mushrooms, and all the savory cooking juices, into the veal shanks. Simmer the veal shanks until they are piping hot throughout. Correct the seasoning, and transfer the shanks with all of the vegetables to a warmed platter for serving.

Menu Suggestion   Start off with Cream of Onion Soup (page 217); for dessert, Fruit Layered in Caramel Syrup (page 285).

SHOPPING LIST
Meat: veal shanks
Vegetables: onion, garlic, celery, carrots
Dairy: butter
Staples: vegetable oil, dry white wine, tomato purée

or canned plum tomatoes, chicken stock, dried wild mushrooms
Herb: parsley

CHICKEN WITH GREEN OLIVES

Crisp-textured pimento-stuffed green olives have a bite more forward and assertive than some of the black varieties. Even a small handful, as used in this recipe, energizes.

4 tablespoons vegetable oil
2¾–3-pound whole chicken, cut into 8 serving pieces
salt and freshly ground pepper
2 tablespoons olive oil
2 garlic cloves, chopped
¾ cup dry white wine
½ cup tomato purée (homemade) or chopped canned plum tomatoes

2 cups chicken stock
6 parsley stems tied with 1 small imported bay leaf

To Serve

12 pimento-stuffed green olives, halved
¼ pound sliced lean cooked country ham, cut into narrow strips

1. Heat the vegetable oil in a 10-inch sauté pan and brown the chicken, a few pieces at a time. When the chicken pieces have browned, remove them to a dish and season with salt and pepper.

2. Pour out all of the vegetable oil, add the olive oil, and stir in the chopped garlic. Sauté for 1 minute. Pour in the wine, raise the heat to moderately high, and bring the wine to a boil, scraping the bottom of the pan with a spoon to loosen any clinging particles. Add the tomato purée or canned tomatoes and chicken stock. Stir. Add the parsley bundle.

3. Put the chicken back into the pan, baste with some of the pan juices, and bring to the simmer. Cover the pan and simmer the chicken for 30 minutes, or until tender.

To Store   Let the chicken cool in the cooking liquid, discard the parsley bundle, and transfer to a storage container. Refrigerate for up to 2 days or freeze up to 1 month.

(*continued*)

To Serve Reheat the chicken in a covered pan until hot. If the liquid seems very thin, remove the chicken pieces from the pan with a slotted spoon and keep them warm while you boil down the liquid until it has taken on some body. Add the olives and ham strips to the chicken, stir, and simmer everything for 5–6 minutes, uncovered. Correct the seasoning and serve the chicken from a warm platter.

Menu Suggestion Accompany the chicken with steamed potatoes and follow with a crisp green salad.

SHOPPING LIST
Meat and poultry: cooked country ham, chicken
Vegetable: garlic
Staples: vegetable oil, olive oil, dry white wine, to-
mato purée or canned plum tomatoes, chicken stock, pimento-stuffed green olives
Herbs: parsley, bay leaf

✷ OYSTERS WITH SPINACH AND PERNOD

A fast dish, as good as the quality of the raw materials: pure heavy cream; tender, deep emerald spinach; and freshly shucked oysters.

6 tablespoons butter
5 shallots, finely chopped
½ pound spinach, cooked and finely chopped
2 tablespoons Pernod
¼ cup fish stock

¾ cup heavy cream, heated
3 dozen oysters, shucked
salt and freshly ground pepper
several gratings of nutmeg
dash of cayenne pepper

1. Melt the butter in a skillet or sauté pan. Add the shallots, stir, and soften them in the butter until translucent. Stir in the spinach and sauté for 2 minutes. Stir in the Pernod.
2. Pour the fish stock and heavy cream into the pan, blend both in, and bring just to the simmer. Add the shucked oysters. Season with salt, pepper, and nutmeg. Cook, stirring, until the oysters are cooked (the edges will flute slightly). Sprinkle on a dash of cayenne pepper and turn out onto a warm serving platter.

Menu Suggestion For dessert, serve orange slices bathed in orange juice, orange brandy, and brown sugar to sweeten.

❋ SCALLOPS WITH LEEKS AND FENNEL

Diced fennel and the creamy white part of the leek are the two vegetables that make up the base for this scallop dish. To this, a little white wine, a few stirs, and onto a serving platter in a flash.

4 tablespoons butter
1 tablespoon olive oil
1 bunch leeks, white part only, thinly sliced
1 fennel bulb, trimmed and diced
2 garlic cloves, finely chopped

2 tablespoons finely chopped parsley
salt and freshly ground pepper
½ cup dry white wine
1½ pounds scallops, preferably bay scallops

1. Place the butter and olive oil in a skillet and set over moderate heat. When the butter has melted, stir in the sliced leeks and diced fennel. Stir and cook for 2 minutes. Reduce the heat slightly, partially cover the pan, and cook until the vegetables are tender.

2. Stir in the chopped garlic and parsley; stir and cook for 2 minutes. Season the vegetables with salt and pepper to taste. Pour in the white wine, raise the heat to moderately high, and let it bubble away until reduced by half.

3. Add the scallops, fold them through the fennel and leeks, and cook them gently until they just turn opaque, about 2 or 3 minutes. Correct the seasoning, if necessary, and turn the scallops and vegetables onto a warm serving platter.

Menu Suggestion   Follow the scallops with a Watercress Salad with Mustard and Herbs (page 262).

MAIN COURSES

* Shrimp in Garlic and Wine

Veal Cubes with Broccoli

Chicken with Button Mushrooms and Shallots

Pork with Glazed Fennel

Lamb with Cured Olives, or Lamb Shanks
on a Bed of Eggplant

* Fish and Shellfish Stew

Beef with Sweet Potatoes and Apricots

THE COOK'S PLAN

NOTE: The following plan can be used whichever one of the alternate recipes you select. If you choose Lamb with Cured Olives, eliminate those ingredients followed by a dagger. If you choose Lamb Shanks on a Bed of Eggplant, eliminate those followed by an asterisk.

1. Set out: 6-quart casserole with lid for the Veal Cubes with Broccoli, 6-quart casserole with lid for the Pork with Glazed Fennel, 6-quart casserole with lid for the Beef with Sweet Potatoes and Apricots, 12-inch casserole with lid for the Lamb Shanks on a Bed of Eggplant (if chosen), 10-inch sauté pan for the Chicken with Button Mushrooms and Shallots.

2. Thaw and measure out 6¼ cups beef stock* or 6 cups beef stock†, 4¼ cups chicken stock.

3. Wash and dry a small bunch of parsley, 5 ribs celery heart.

4. Peel 8 onions, 7 shallots, 8 carrots, 7 garlic cloves.

5. Finely chop 1 tablespoon parsley; chop 5 onions, 4 carrots, 4 ribs celery heart* or 2 ribs of celery heart†, 7 shallots, 1½ teaspoons rosemary leaves* or 3½ teaspoons rosemary leaves†; slice 1 onion, 2 carrots, 1 rib celery heart; cube ¼ pound bacon.*

6. Measure out 3¼ cups dry red wine* or 2¼ cups dry red wine†, 2 cups dry white wine* or 3 cups of dry white wine†, ¾ cup tomato purée* or canned plum tomatoes,* 1½ tablespoons tomato paste, 6 cloves, 3-inch cinnamon stick.

7. Set out vegetable oil, butter, salt, pepper, flour.

8. Tie 6 parsley stems with 1 bay leaf.*

9. Beef with Sweet Potatoes and Apricots: Brown the beef cubes; simmer with the sautéed vegetables, spices, and liquid, Steps 1–3 (page 96).

10. Pork with Glazed Fennel: Brown the pork; sauté the vegetables; add wine, stock, and herb bundle; simmer, Steps 1–2 (page 97).

11. Lamb with Cured Olives, or Lamb Shanks on a Bed of Eggplant: Brown the lamb; simmer with the sautéed vegetables, seasonings, and liquid, Steps 1–3 (page 98) for the Lamb with Cured Olives; Steps 1–2 (page 99) for the Lamb Shanks on a Bed of Eggplant.

12. Veal Cubes with Broccoli: Brown the veal; simmer with the sautéed onions, shallots, herbs, tomato paste, and liquid, Steps 1–3 (page 101).

13. Chicken with Button Mushrooms and Shallots: Brown the chicken in the oil and butter, add onions and shallots. Stir in rosemary, red wine and chicken stock, and bring to a simmer, Steps 1–3 (page 102). Prepare through Step 3 (page 102).

14. Cool all dishes to room temperature; refrigerate or freeze, following the instructions in "To Store" of each recipe.

BEEF WITH SWEET POTATOES AND APRICOTS

Here, cloves and cinnamon flatter the beef in a softly sweet way and enhance the whole apricots that soak up the spicy cooking liquid on serving day.

3 pounds rump pot roast, cut into 2-inch cubes
4 tablespoons vegetable oil
salt and freshly ground pepper
1 onion, sliced
2 carrots, sliced
1 rib celery heart, sliced
1 small imported bay leaf
6 whole cloves

3-inch piece of cinnamon stick
1 cup dry red wine
2 cups beef stock

To Serve

4 slender sweet potatoes
⅓ pound whole dried apricots
1 tablespoon finely chopped parsley

1. Dry the pieces of meat on paper toweling. Heat the vegetable oil in a 6-quart casserole. Brown the meat in batches in the hot oil. Transfer the browned cubes to a plate; season with salt and pepper.

2. Sauté the onion in the oil (it should film the bottom of the casserole), stirring, for 3 minutes. Stir in the sliced carrot and celery and sauté for 2 minutes. Stir in the bay leaf, cloves, and cinnamon stick. Sauté for 3 minutes.

3. Pour the wine into the casserole, raise the heat to moderately high, and bring the wine to a boil, stirring the casserole to dislodge any bits clinging to the bottom. Add the beef stock and meat cubes. Bring to the simmer. Cover tightly and cook the meat in the lower third of a preheated 325° F oven for 3 hours or until the beef cubes are tender.

To Store   Remove the meat from the cooking liquid with a slotted spoon and transfer to a storage container. Degrease the cooking liquid and boil it over high heat, if necessary, to condense. Strain the liquid through a food mill and pour it over the meat. Cool completely, and refrigerate for up to 5 days or freeze for up to 1 month.

To Serve   Simmer the sweet potatoes in a pot of water until tender (about 20 minutes), peel, and cube. While the potatoes are cooking, begin to reheat the meat in a covered casserole. Add the apricots, stir, and simmer covered for 15 minutes. By this time the potatoes should be tender; add them to the casserole and simmer everything together for 5 minutes. Turn the beef onto a serving platter and scatter the chopped parsley on top.

Menu Suggestion   Follow the beef with a Watercress Salad with Lemon Vinaigrette (page 261); for dessert, Bread Pudding with Dates and Walnuts (page 276).

Meat: rump pot roast
Vegetables and fruit: onion, carrots, celery, sweet
potatoes, dried apricots

Staples: vegetable oil, dry red wine, beef stock
Herbs and spices: bay leaf, parsley, cloves, cinnamon
stick

PORK WITH GLAZED FENNEL

Despite the earthy character of pork, this is a gentle, mild dish, enhanced with the slightly sweet flavor of fennel which has been cooked until tender in olive oil.

4 tablespoons vegetable oil
2¾–3 pounds boneless pork shoulder,
    cut into 2-inch cubes
salt and freshly ground pepper
1 onion, chopped
3 garlic cloves, chopped
2 carrots, chopped
2 ribs celery heart, chopped
1 cup dry white wine
2¼ cups beef stock

6 parsley sprigs tied with 1 bay leaf

To Serve

¼ cup olive oil
2 garlic cloves, chopped
3 firm fennel bulbs, trimmed and cut
    into 2-inch chunks
1 tablespoon lemon juice
1 tablespoon finely chopped parsley

1. Heat the vegetable oil in a heavy 6-quart casserole. Brown the pork cubes, a batch at a time, in the hot oil. Transfer the cubes to a plate as they are browned and season with salt and pepper.

2. Put the chopped onion in the casserole and sauté for 3 minutes. Stir in the 3 chopped garlic cloves, carrots, and celery. Sauté for 2 minutes. Pour in the wine, raise the heat to moderately high, and scrape the bottom of the casserole of any clinging bits as the wine bubbles up. Pour in the beef stock and add the parsley bundle. Add the browned pork cubes and bring the liquid to a rapid simmer. Cover and cook at a simmer on the stove top or in the lower third of a preheated 325° F oven for 2 hours, or until the pork is fork tender.

To Store   Remove the pork to a storage container. Discard the parsley bundle and degrease the cooking liquid. Strain the liquid through a food mill directly over the pork. Cool to room temperature, cover, and refrigerate for up to 5 days or freeze for up to 1 month.

To Serve   Reheat the pork in a covered casserole. Put the olive oil and 2 chopped garlic cloves in a saucepan large enough to hold all the fennel pieces. Sauté the garlic for 2 minutes over moderate heat. Stir in the fennel and lemon juice. Cover tightly and cook until the fennel is tender, lightly golden, and glazed over, about 20–25 minutes. Stir the fennel into the pork and blend in the chopped parsley. Correct the seasoning and simmer uncovered for 5 minutes, then serve.

Menu Suggestion   Follow the pork with a Salad of Red Leaf Lettuce with Herbs (page 260); for dessert, Pears Under Shortcake (page 301).

SHOPPING LIST
Meat: boneless pork shoulder
Vegetables and fruit: onion, garlic, carrots, celery, fennel, lemon

Staples: dry white wine, beef stock, vegetable oil, olive oil
Herbs: parsley, bay leaf

LAMB WITH CURED OLIVES

The tiniest cured olives, glistening and slightly shriveled, give this lamb dish an edge of piquancy. The best olives for this recipe are available either jarred or by the barrelful at food emporiums. They are not very salty, and the flesh is moist and soft.

2¾ pounds boneless lamb shoulder, cut into 2-inch cubes
4 tablespoons vegetable oil
salt and freshly ground pepper
¼-pound piece of bacon, cut into cubes, simmered in water for 8 minutes, drained, and dried
2 onions, chopped
2 garlic cloves, chopped
2 carrots, chopped

2 ribs celery heart, chopped
¾ cup tomato purée (homemade) or chopped canned plum tomatoes
1 cup dry red wine
2 cups beef stock

To Serve

1 dozen cured black olives
1 tablespoon red wine vinegar
1 tablespoon finely chopped parsley

1. Dry the lamb cubes on paper toweling. Heat the vegetable oil in a heavy 6-quart casserole, and brown the cubes in several shifts. Remove them to a plate as they brown and season with salt and pepper. Remove all but 2 tablespoons oil from the casserole.

2. Add the bacon cubes to the casserole and sauté until lightly browned. Add the chopped onion; sauté 2 minutes. Add the chopped garlic, carrots, and celery; sauté 3 minutes. Stir in the tomato purée or canned tomatoes and pour in the wine. Raise the heat and bring the contents to a rapid simmer, stirring all the time.

3. Pour in the beef stock and add the parsley bundle. Replace the meat and bring the

contents of the casserole to a rapid simmer. Cover tightly and cook in the lower third of a preheated 325° F oven for 2 hours or on the stove top at a simmer, until the lamb is tender.

To Store Transfer the lamb to a storage bowl, discard the parsley bundle, and defat the liquid. Boil the liquid for 5 minutes and pour it over the meat. Cool thoroughly, then cover and store in the refrigerator for up to 5 days or freeze for up to 1 month.

To Serve Reheat the lamb until piping hot. Add the olives, vinegar, and chopped parsley. Correct the seasoning with more salt and pepper if necessary. Simmer, uncovered, for 6 minutes. Serve.

Menu Suggestion Accompany the lamb with Buttered Noodles (page 253); for dessert, Oranges and Grapes in Hot Orange Sauce (page 293).

SHOPPING LIST
Meat: boneless lamb shoulder, bacon
Vegetables: onions, garlic, carrots, celery
Staples: vegetable oil, tomato purée or canned plum
tomatoes, dry red wine, cured olives, red wine vinegar
Herbs: parsley, bay leaf

LAMB SHANKS ON A BED OF EGGPLANT

Lamb takes to eggplant: just think of that Greek bake which layers the two together with tomatoes and spices. It is a fine union, and while this recipe does not combine them initially, the two blend favorably at the end.

4 tablespoons vegetable oil
2 meaty lamb shanks, or enough shanks
    to yield eight 1¼-inch-thick pieces
salt and freshly ground pepper
2 onions, chopped
2 garlic cloves, chopped
2 carrots, chopped
2 teaspoons rosemary leaves, chopped
1 small imported bay leaf
1 cup dry white wine
1¾ cups beef stock

To Serve

2 eggplants, peeled and cubed
6 tablespoons olive oil
3 ribs celery heart, diced
1 cup tomato purée (homemade) or
    chopped canned plum tomatoes
1½ teaspoons red wine vinegar
1 teaspoon capers, rinsed in cool water
    and dried

1. Heat the vegetable oil in a 12-inch casserole, preferably oval. Brown the lamb shanks in the oil a few at a time. Remove them to a plate as they are browned and season with

salt and pepper. Stir the onions into the casserole and sauté them for 3 minutes. Stir in the chopped garlic, carrots, and rosemary leaves. Sauté for 3 minutes. Add the bay leaf, wine, and beef stock. Bring the contents of the casserole to a boil, stirring.

2. Add the lamb shanks to the casserole, baste with some of the liquid, and bring to a simmer. Cover and simmer for 2 hours, turning the shanks over a few times as they cook.

To Store   Transfer the shanks to a storage container. Discard the bay leaf and boil down the liquid for 6 minutes. Pour the cooking liquid over the meat and cool everything to room temperature. Cover tightly and refrigerate for up to 5 days or freeze for up to 1 month.

To Serve   Salt the eggplant cubes, dump them in a colander, and leave about 20 minutes to disgorge any bitter juices. Dry the cubes on paper toweling. Heat 2 tablespoons of the olive oil in a skillet and brown half the eggplant in it; repeat with the remaining eggplant and 2 tablespoons oil. Remove. Add the last 2 tablespoons oil to the skillet, add the celery, and sauté until soft. Pour in the tomato purée or canned tomatoes, vinegar, and capers. Stir in the eggplant and season with salt and pepper. Bring to a simmer, cover, and simmer until the eggplant is tender, about 15–20 minutes. Meanwhile, reheat the shanks in a covered casserole. Spoon the hot eggplant onto a warm platter, top with the lamb shanks and some of the cooking liquid (which should be reduced and lightly syrupy), and serve.

Menu Suggestion   Follow the lamb with a simple green salad; for dessert, Baked Kiwi Custard (page 286).

SHOPPING LIST
Meat: lamb shanks
Vegetables: onions, garlic, celery, carrots, eggplants
Staples: vegetable oil, olive oil, dry white wine, beef
stock, tomato purée or canned plum tomatoes, red wine vinegar, capers
Herbs: rosemary, bay leaf

VEAL CUBES WITH BROCCOLI

One of the nicest ways to please veal-lovers is with this recipe in which thyme, shallots, and white wine underpin the taste of the veal. At the end, in brilliant green, the broccoli finishes off the exchange and the whole tastes simple and clean.

2¾–3 pounds boneless veal shoulder, cut
   into 2-inch cubes
4 tablespoons vegetable oil
salt and freshly ground pepper
1 onion, chopped
3 shallots, chopped
2 garlic cloves, chopped
2 teaspoons fresh thyme leaves, chopped

1 tablespoon finely chopped parsley
1½ tablespoons tomato paste
1 cup dry white wine
2¼ cups chicken stock

To Serve

1 bunch broccoli, trimmed and cut into
   flowerets

1. Dry the veal cubes on paper toweling. Heat the oil in a heavy 6-quart casserole and brown the veal cubes in batches. As as the veal browns, remove the cubes to a plate. Season with salt and pepper.

2. Remove all but 2 tablespoons oil from the casserole. Stir in the onions and sauté for 2 minutes. Stir in the shallots and sauté for 2 minutes. Stir in the garlic, thyme, parsley, and tomato paste. Cook and stir for 2 minutes. Pour in the wine and chicken stock.

3. Put the veal back in the casserole and bring the contents to a rapid simmer. Cover and cook the veal in the lower third of a preheated 325° F oven for 1¾–2 hours, or until tender, or simmer until tender on the stove top.

To Store   Remove the veal to a storage bowl. Boil the liquid for 3 minutes, then pour it over the veal. Refrigerate for up to 5 days or freeze for up to 1 month.

To Serve   Simmer the broccoli until just tender (about 10 minutes) as you reheat the meat in a covered casserole. Drain the broccoli and add it to the casserole. Adjust the seasoning, adding more salt and pepper if necessary. Simmer for 5 minutes longer to blend the flavors. Turn the veal, broccoli, and sauce onto a warm serving platter.

Menu Suggestion   Follow the veal with Hot Lemon Sponge Pudding (page 290) or Chocolate and Orange Velvet (page 278).

Shopping List
Meat: boneless veal shoulder
Vegetables: onion, shallots, garlic, broccoli
Staples: vegetable oil, tomato paste, dry white wine,

chicken stock
Herbs: fresh thyme, parsley

CHICKEN WITH BUTTON MUSHROOMS AND SHALLOTS

Chicken and mushrooms is a combination likely found fashioned in cream sauce with wine and rich in egg yolks. Here is a change from the cream and egg yolk route, a recipe in which the chicken is bolstered by shallots and red wine.

2¾–3-pound whole chicken, cut into 8 serving pieces
3 tablespoons vegetable oil
1 tablespoon butter
½ cup all-purpose flour, in a shallow bowl
salt and freshly ground pepper
1 onion, chopped
4 shallots, chopped

1½ teaspoons rosemary leaves, chopped
1¼ cups dry red wine
2 cups chicken stock

To Serve

3 tablespoons butter
1 pound button mushrooms, caps only
1 teaspoon lemon juice
1 tablespoon finely chopped parsley

1. Dry the chicken pieces on paper toweling. Heat the vegetable oil and 1 tablespoon butter in a 10-inch sauté pan. Flour the chicken pieces, a few at a time, and brown them on both sides in the hot oil-butter. Transfer to a plate and season with salt and pepper.

2. When all the chicken pieces have browned, stir in the chopped onions and shallots. Stir and cook for 4 minutes. Stir in the rosemary. Pour in the wine and chicken stock.

3. Bring the contents of the pan to a rapid boil, scraping up any bits clinging to the bottom of the pan. Add the chicken pieces and baste them with the cooking liquid. Cover the pan and simmer the chicken for 30 minutes or until tender.

To Store   Remove the chicken to a storage container. Boil the liquid in the pan for 5 minutes so that it condenses slightly and pour that over the chicken. Cool the chicken to room temperature, cover, and refrigerate for up to 2 days or freeze for up to 2 weeks.

To Serve   Reheat the chicken in a covered casserole. Melt the 3 tablespoons butter in a skillet, add the mushroom caps, and sauté until lightly golden. Remove from the heat, add the lemon juice, and season with salt and pepper. If the chicken cooking liquid seems thin, keep the chicken warm while you boil down the liquid. Add the mushrooms and simmer uncovered for 5–6 minutes. Correct the seasoning and fold in the chopped parsley.

Menu Suggestion   Begin with Lentil and Potato Soup (page 221) and finish with Rhubarb Baked with Brown Sugar and Cinnamon (page 310).

SHOPPING LIST
Poultry: chicken
Vegetables and fruit: onion, shallots, mushrooms, lemon
Dairy: butter

Staples: vegetable oil, flour, dry red wine, chicken stock
Herbs: fresh rosemary, parsley

❊ SHRIMP IN GARLIC AND WINE

As the shrimp is turned in the chopped garlic, shallots, wine, and butter, you will see how these ingredients, quickly and simply put together, produce a delicious dish handy for a cook's stock file. It's glamorous and quite definite in flavor, and the buttery, garlicky sauce means that a crusty loaf of bread is in order.

8 tablespoons butter
6 shallots, chopped
1¼ pounds shrimp, peeled, with the tails left intact, and deveined
3 garlic cloves, peeled and chopped

⅓ cup dry white wine
juice of 1 small lemon
salt and freshly ground pepper
1½ tablespoons finely chopped parsley
lemon wedges

1. Heat 3 tablespoons of the butter in a skillet, stir in the shallots and soften over moderate heat. Add the remaining 5 tablespoons butter.

2. When the butter is hot, stir in the shrimp and sauté over a fast flame until they *start* to turn opaque. Stir in the chopped garlic; stir and cook 30 seconds. Pour in the wine and lemon juice, season with salt and pepper, and cook-stir until the shrimp are just cooked and the butter and wine glaze over them.

3. Stir in the parsley and serve with lemon wedges on the side.

Menu Suggestion Begin with Leeks, Glazed and Baked (page 240) as a first course.

SHOPPING LIST
Shellfish: shrimp
Vegetables and fruit: garlic, shallots, lemons
Dairy: butter

Staple: dry white wine
Herb: parsley

✳ FISH AND SHELLFISH STEW

You can always cook up a sophisticated stew of this sort as long as a little time has been invested to furnish the freezer with a fine, potent fish stock. Fish stock is indeed one pure gold of the cooking trade and preferable, by far, to bottled clam juice.

3 tablespoons olive oil
1 onion, diced
2 leeks, white part only, thinly sliced
1 small hot pepper, cored, seeded, and chopped
¾ cup dry white wine
1 cup tomato purée (homemade) or chopped canned plum tomatoes
2 cups fish stock
salt and freshly ground pepper

To Serve

1 pound fish fillets, such as bass, haddock, or halibut, cut into 2-inch chunks
1 dozen mussels, well scrubbed
1 dozen clams, well scrubbed
⅓ pound scallops
½ pound shrimp, peeled, with tails left intact, and deveined
2 tablespoons finely chopped parsley
1 recipe Crisp Bread Slices (page 154)

If you are preparing the fish base in advance, put the olive oil in a 1½-quart saucepan to heat up; otherwise, to prepare the stew in one session, use a casserole large enough to contain all the ingredients above. Sauté the onions and leeks in the hot oil until soft. Stir in the hot pepper and sauté for 30 seconds, then pour in the wine. Raise the heat to moderately high and bring the wine to a boil. Stir in the tomato purée or canned tomatoes and fish stock. Season with salt and pepper. Simmer, partially covered, for 20 minutes.

To Store   Cool the fish base and store in a covered container in the refrigerator for 1 day or in the freezer for up to 1 week.

To Serve   Bring the stew base to a low boil. Add the fish fillet chunks and simmer gently for 3 minutes. Add the mussels and clams, baste with some of the tomato liquid, cover, and cook until they just begin to open. Stir in the scallops and shrimp. Cover and cook until the clams and mussels open fully, and the shrimp and scallops just turn opaque. Turn the stew onto a deep platter, dust over with the chopped parsley, and tuck the crisp bread slices amid the fish and shellfish.

Menu Suggestion   Follow the stew with Bibb Lettuce Salad (page 257).

SHOPPING LIST
Fish and shellfish: fish fillets (such as bass, haddock, or halibut), mussels, clams, scallops, shrimp
Vegetables: onion, leeks, hot pepper

Staples: olive oil, dry white wine, tomato purée or canned plum tomatoes, fish stock
Herb: parsley
For serving: Crisp Bread Slices (see recipe)

4
THE SPRING WEEKS

MAIN COURSES

∗ Swordfish Cubes with Vegetables and Wine

Veal Shanks with Early Green Peas

Chicken with Asparagus and White Wine

Lamb with Artichokes

Tripe with Zucchini

Oxtail in Red Wine with Oil-Cured Olives

∗ Mussels Broiled with Mustard and Garlic Butter
(first course) and

Haddock in Saffron Cream (second course)

THE COOK'S PLAN

1. Set out: 6-quart casserole with lid for the Tripe with Zucchini, 6-quart casserole with lid for the Lamb with Artichokes, 6-quart casserole with lid for the Oxtail in Red Wine with Oil-Cured Olives, 12-inch oval casserole with lid for the Veal Shanks with Early Green Peas, 10-inch sauté pan for the Chicken with Asparagus and White Wine.

2. Thaw and measure out 2½ cups beef stock, 7¼ cups chicken stock.

3. Wash and dry 5 ribs celery heart.

4. Peel 15 garlic cloves, 3 shallots, 6 onions, 4 carrots.

5. Chop 2 garlic cloves, 3 garlic cloves with 1 tablespoon fresh rosemary and 8 plum tomatoes, 1 onion, 3 shallots, 2 teaspoons fresh thyme, 2 teaspoons fresh rosemary, 2 teaspoons fresh savory, ½ cup celery leaves; slice 1 onion, 1 carrot; dice 3 onions, 2 carrots, 5 ribs celery heart, ⅓ pound salt pork.

6. Measure out 1½ cups dry red wine, 3¼ cups dry white wine, 2¼ cups tomato purée or canned plum tomatoes.

7. Set out olive oil, vegetable oil, butter, salt, pepper, flour.

8. Tie 6 parsley stems with 1 bay leaf.

9. Oxtail in Red Wine with Oil-Cured Olives: Flour and brown the oxtail pieces; simmer with the pork, sautéed vegetables, and seasonings, Steps 1–3 (page 108).

10. Tripe with Zucchini: Boil the tripe and drain; sauté the vegetables and garlic; add tripe, tomato purée, liquids, seasonings; simmer, Steps 1–4 (page 109).

11. Veal Shanks with Early Green Peas: Brown the veal shanks; simmer with the sautéed vegetables, wine, stock, and seasonings, Steps 1–3 (page 111).

12. Lamb with Artichokes: Brown the lamb cubes; sauté the onion; add rosemary and tomato purée, liquid; season and simmer, Steps 1–2 (page 113).

13. Chicken with Asparagus and White Wine: Brown the floured chicken in the oil and butter; combine with the sautéed onions and shallots, herbs, wine, and stock; simmer, Steps 1–3 (page 114).

14. Cool all dishes to room temperature; refrigerate or freeze, following the instructions in "To Store" of each recipe.

OXTAIL IN RED WINE WITH OIL-CURED OLIVES

For reasons of practicality and good taste, oxtail makes good main-course material for advance preparation. It is after the dish has cooled down and is refrigerated that the layer of fat, which surrounds the meaty joints and melts down into the cooking liquid, rises to the surface. After the fat solidifies, it should be removed. Oxtail achieves finesse by long simmering and careful seasoning, and I like to do this with a tablespoon of fresh rosemary leaves, pinched right from the branch.

3½ pounds oxtail, cut into 3-inch pieces
½ cup flour, in a shallow bowl
2 tablespoons olive oil
2 tablespoons butter
salt and freshly ground pepper
⅓ pound salt pork, as lean as possible, diced
2 onions, diced
2 carrots, diced
2 ribs celery heart, diced

3 garlic cloves, chopped with 1 tablespoon chopped fresh rosemary and 8 plum tomatoes
1 small imported bay leaf
1½ cups dry red wine
2½ cups beef stock

To Serve

1½ dozen oil-cured black olives

1. Dredge the oxtail pieces in flour, a few at a time, and brown them in olive oil and butter heated in a heavy skillet. As the pieces brown, remove them to a plate and season with salt and pepper.

2. Pour the remaining fat into a heavy 6-quart casserole, adding a little extra butter, as needed, if there is less than 3 tablespoons. Stir in the diced salt pork and cook until lightly browned. Add the diced onions, carrots, and celery and sauté for 2 minutes. Stir in the chopped garlic, rosemary, and tomato mixture. Add the bay leaf, red wine, and beef stock. Bring to the boil. Season with salt and pepper. Put in the browned oxtail and bring to the boil, skimming the foam that surfaces.

3. Cover the casserole and cook the oxtail in the lower third of a preheated 325° F oven for 3–3½ hours, until the oxtail pieces are tender.

To Store   Defat the cooking liquid as well as you can. Discard the bay leaf. Place the oxtail in a storage container; boil down the sauce until lightly condensed, if it is not already that way. Pour the sauce over the meat; cool to room temperature. Store, covered, in the refrigerator. The next day, remove the layer of fat that rose and solidified on the surface. Refrigerate for up to 5 days or freeze for up to 2 weeks.

To Serve   Reheat the oxtail in a covered container until piping hot. Adjust the seasoning and stir in the olives. Simmer for 4–5 minutes longer or until the olives are hot, then serve.

Menu Suggestion   Begin with Asparagus with Creamy Herb Dressing (page 234); accompany the oxtail with Buttered Noodles (page 253).

SHOPPING LIST
Meat: oxtail, salt pork
Vegetables and fruit: onions, carrots, celery, garlic, plum tomatoes, oil-cured olives

Dairy: butter
Staples: flour, olive oil, dry red wine, beef stock
Herbs: fresh rosemary, bay leaf

TRIPE WITH ZUCCHINI

If you have ever cooked tripe (the stomach muscle of ruminants), you know that once you get past reducing the rubbery honeycombed folds into strips and combine the narrow pieces with other ingredients, it begins to turn into a splendidly earthy dish. This stew is redolent of garlic and wine and contains a modest amount of vegetables that simmer in with the pale white lengths of tripe. It is a dish for those who are not inhibited by its preparation and for those who enjoy honest and robust flavors.

3 pounds ready-to-cook honeycomb tripe, thawed in the refrigerator (do not leave at room temperature to thaw)
1 imported bay leaf
3 tablespoons butter
3 tablespoons olive oil
1 onion, diced
2 garlic cloves, peeled and chopped
3 ribs celery heart, diced
1 carrot, diced
¾ cup dry white wine

1¼ cups tomato purée (homemade) or chopped canned plum tomatoes
1½ cups chicken stock
salt and freshly ground pepper
pinch of cayenne pepper

To Serve

2 firm, slender zucchini
1 tablespoon butter
1 tablespoon olive oil
1 tablespoon finely chopped parsley

1. Wash the tripe thoroughly under cold running water. Put the tripe and bay leaf in a large pot of boiling water and boil slowly for 10 minutes. Let the tripe stand in the water for 10 minutes, with the heat source cut off.

2. Drain the tripe in a colander and rinse it in cold water. Drain, dry, and cut the tripe into thin strips.

3. In a 6-quart casserole, heat the 3 tablespoons butter and 3 tablespoons olive oil. Sauté

the onion in the butter-oil for 3 minutes. Stir in the garlic and cook for 1 minute. Stir in diced celery and carrot and cook until the vegetables look glazed, about 3–4 minutes.

4. Pour in the wine, raise the heat, and bring the wine to a boil. Add the tripe, tomato purée or canned tomatoes, chicken stock, salt, pepper, and cayenne pepper. Bring the contents of the casserole to a simmer, cover, and simmer for 2 hours 15 minutes or until the tripe is tender; it will, characteristically, retain a slight edge of chewiness.

To Store   Cool the tripe to room temperature, then refrigerate in a covered container for up to 4 days or freeze for up to 2 weeks.

To Serve   Reheat the tripe in a covered casserole. Cut the zucchini into strips or cubes, salt lightly, and leave in a colander for 15 minutes. Dry the zucchini on paper toweling.

Heat the 1 tablespoon butter and 1 tablespoon olive oil in a skillet. Add the zucchini pieces and toss them around in the hot fat for 2 minutes, without letting them brown. Season the zucchini with salt and pepper, then add to the simmering tripe along with the chopped parsley. Simmer, uncovered, until the zucchini is tender, about 10 minutes. Check the seasoning and serve.

Menu Suggestion   Precede the tripe with White Bean Soup with Basil and Cheese (page 227); serve fresh fruit for dessert.

SHOPPING LIST
Meat: honeycomb tripe
Vegetables: onion, celery, carrot, garlic, zucchini
Dairy: butter

Staples: olive oil, dry white wine, tomato purée or canned plum tomatoes, chicken stock
Herbs and spice: bay leaf, parsley, cayenne pepper

VEAL SHANKS WITH EARLY GREEN PEAS

Here is a dish not designed for snobby eaters who dote on more expensive cuts of veal that are usually sautéed. As with oxtail, you have to relish the meat surrounding the bone that cooks up tender. You must simmer the pieces slowly in the liquid—wine and stock—and, for this recipe, add whole garlic cloves, which will be reduced (after the long simmering) into a nutty and sweet purée as part of the sauce. Although the taste of this is vibrant and full-flavored, it is not unrefined. Choose the tiniest, freshest peas in the pod for this preparation. At the market, break open a pod and sample the peas. If they seem to be large, mealy, and flat-tasting, choose another vegetable to go along with the veal, like a half pound of slender string beans, which you should simmer in salted water before adding to the sautéed pancetta (cured bacon in a tightly rolled log available at some specialty stores and sliced or cut into a large chunk on order).

4 tablespoons butter

2 tablespoons vegetable oil

2 veal shanks, or enough for eight 1½-inch-thick slices

salt and freshly ground pepper

1 onion, sliced

1 carrot, sliced

10 garlic cloves, peeled and left whole

2 teaspoons chopped fresh thyme

½ cup dry white wine

1½ cups chicken stock

6 parsley stems tied with 1 small imported bay leaf

To Serve

1 tablespoon olive oil

2 tablespoons butter

⅓ pound pancetta, cut into small cubes

1½ pounds fresh green peas, shelled

1 teaspoon lemon juice

1 tablespoon chopped fresh mint, if available, or chopped parsley

1. Heat the 2 tablespoons of the butter and the vegetable oil in a heavy 12-inch casserole. Dry the veal shanks on paper toweling and brown them in the hot fat. Remove the shanks to a dish as they are browned and season with salt and pepper.

2. Pour out the browning fat, add 2 more tablespoons of butter, and sauté the onion and carrot slices for 3 minutes. Add the garlic cloves and thyme. Pour in the wine and raise the heat so that the wine comes to the boil, stirring all the while. Pour in the chicken stock and add the parsley bundle.

3. Nestle the veal shanks amid the vegetables and liquid. Bring to the simmer. Cover the pot closely and simmer on the stove top for 2 hours, carefully turning the shanks a few times during cooking. The shanks may also be cooked in the lower third of a preheated 325° F oven.

To Store   Transfer the shanks to a storage container. Discard the parsley bundle and put the liquid and vegetables through a food mill. Pour this over the shanks. When the veal has cooled thoroughly, place, covered, in the refrigerator for up to 5 days or in the freezer for up to 1 month.

To Serve   Put the veal shanks in a covered casserole to reheat. Heat the olive oil and 2 tablespoons butter in a large saucepan. Stir in the pancetta and sauté for 4 minutes. Add the peas and lemon juice. Season with salt and pepper. Pour ½ cup of the sauce from the veal shanks over the peas, and add about 2 tablespoons water. Bring the contents to a simmer, cover closely, and cook until the peas are tender (about 4 minutes if the peas are quite fresh and small). Stir in the chopped mint or parsley. Simmer for 3–4 minutes longer, uncovered, so that everything blends perfectly. Serve from a warm platter.

(continued)

Menu Suggestion　Begin with Cream of Mushroom and Leek Soup (page 216) or Spinach and Leek Soup (page 225); for dessert, Strawberries Marinated in Red Wine and Honey (page 314).

Shopping List
Meat: veal shanks, pancetta
Vegetables and fruit: onion, carrot, garlic, green peas, lemon
Dairy: butter

Staples: vegetable oil, olive oil, dry white wine, chicken stock
Herbs: fresh thyme, parsley, bay leaf, fresh mint

LAMB WITH ARTICHOKES

This lovely presentation of lamb uses small tenderly cooked artichokes thrown into a sharp but happy blend of olive oil, butter, garlic, anchovies, and lemon juice before they are combined with the cooked lamb, which is reheating on serving day on a nearby burner.

If you have trouble locating small artichokes, exchange freshly cooked hearts from the larger variety. The baby artichokes, by the way, take so well to this sort of flavoring that you could stew them for another version of Artichoke Stew (see page 231). For that kind of stew, you would not need to boil them in advance, but trim and cook them in an inch or two of stock (or water) once they are stuffed with this savory mixture: the anchovy fillets, blended with the lemon juice, garlic, salt, and pepper in the amounts below and a handful of fresh parsley, chopped—about ⅓ cup—and enough good olive oil to bind everything together, about 3–4 tablespoons. Spread open the leaves and fill with a small amount of this blend. In a heavy casserole, sauté an onion in a little olive oil. Add the artichokes and the liquid of your choice. Simmer until the artichokes are tender and serve them with the pan juices cooked down until concentrated, with lots of crusty bread on the side.

3 tablespoons vegetable oil
3 tablespoons butter
2¾–3 pounds boneless lamb shoulder, cut into 2-inch cubes
salt and freshly ground pepper
1 onion, chopped
2 teaspoons chopped rosemary leaves
¾ cup tomato purée (homemade) or chopped canned plum tomatoes
1¼ cups dry white wine

2½ cups chicken stock
1 small imported bay leaf

To Serve

8 baby artichokes, trimmed
2 tablespoons butter
3 garlic cloves, chopped
4 anchovy fillets, chopped
2–3 teaspoons lemon juice
1 tablespoon finely chopped parsley

1. Heat the vegetable oil and 1 tablespoon of the butter in a heavy 6-quart casserole. Dry the lamb cubes on paper toweling to absorb any moisture, then brown the cubes, in batches, in the hot fat. As the cubes are browned, put them in a large side dish and season with salt and pepper.

2. Pour out the browning fat and add 2 tablespoons butter to the casserole. Sauté the onion in the butter for 3 minutes. Stir in the chopped rosemary and tomato purée or canned tomatoes. Pour in the wine and bring to the boil. Pour in the chicken stock and add the bay leaf and the browned lamb cubes. Bring the contents of the casserole to a boil, cover, and simmer on the stove top or in the lower third of a preheated 325° F oven for 1¾–2 hours or until the lamb is tender.

To Store   When the lamb is tender, remove the cubes to a storage container. Degrease the cooking liquid and boil it down for a few minutes if it seems rather thin. Pour the liquid over the lamb. Cool thoroughly, then refrigerate, covered, for up to 2 days or freeze for up to 1 month.

To Serve   Simmer the trimmed artichokes in an ample amount of salted water until tender, about 25 minutes if they are nice and small. Drain. While the artichokes are simmering, reheat the lamb in a covered container until very hot. Do this slowly. Heat the 2 tablespoons butter in a skillet and toss the small artichokes in the butter. Stir in the chopped garlic cloves and anchovy fillets and season with lemon juice, salt, and pepper to taste. Cook slowly, stirring, for 4 minutes.

Put the artichokes in the lamb container and simmer everything together to combine the flavors, then serve sprinkled with chopped parsley.

Menu Suggestion   Serve Buttered Noodles (page 253) or rice with the lamb; for dessert, Kiwi Fruit with Grapes and Mango Slices (page 287).

Shopping List
Meat: boneless lamb shoulder
Vegetables and fruit: onion, garlic, artichokes, lemon
Dairy: butter

Staples: vegetable oil, tomato purée or canned plum tomatoes, dry white wine, chicken stock, anchovies
Herbs: rosemary, bay leaf, parsley

CHICKEN WITH ASPARAGUS AND WHITE WINE

The holding properties of this chicken dish are the white wine and chicken stock, which make it as splendid on serving day as the day the chicken was transferred into the storage container. And it is a formula which you should know well if you have cooked from other do-ahead compositions in this book. The fresh herbs help, too, to add a clear fresh quality to the dish, but the finishing stroke is the complement of fresh asparagus, turned in butter and a sizzle of vinegar before it is added to the chicken.

2½ tablespoons vegetable oil
1 tablespoon butter
2¾–3-pound whole chicken, cut into 8
   serving pieces
½ cup all-purpose flour, in a shallow
   bowl
salt and freshly ground pepper
1 onion, chopped
3 shallots, chopped
2 teaspoons chopped fresh rosemary
2 teaspoons chopped fresh savory leaves
   (optional)

½ cup chopped celery leaves
¾ cup dry white wine
1¾ cups chicken stock

To Serve

½ pound fresh asparagus
2 tablespoons butter
2 tablespoons good vinegar, not plain
   white distilled, but a kind such as
   sherry wine or white wine vinegar
1 tablespoon finely chopped parsley

1. Heat the vegetable oil and 1 tablespoon butter in a 10-inch sauté pan. Take up a few chicken pieces, flour them, and brown in the hot fat. Transfer the browned pieces to a dish and season with salt and pepper. Flour and brown the rest of the chicken.

2. In the remaining fat (add a knob of butter if a skimpy amount of fat is left), sauté the onions and shallots until soft. Stir in the rosemary, savory, and celery leaves; cook 1 minute.

3. Pour in the wine; bring to the boil. Pour in the chicken stock and add the chicken pieces. Baste over with some of the liquid. Bring the liquid to a boil, then reduce the heat so that it simmers. Cover and simmer for 30 minutes, turning the chicken once or twice as it cooks.

To Store　Remove the chicken to a storage container and boil down the liquid for 3 minutes or until it is glossy and lightly thickened, then pour it over the chicken. When completely cooled, refrigerate covered for up to 2 days or freeze for up to 2 weeks.

To Serve　Reheat the chicken in a covered pan. Trim the asparagus spears, peeling off a very thin outer layer beginning just under the tips to the base. Put the spears in a deep skillet of cold water, salt, and bring to the boil. Simmer until crisply tender, about 8 minutes. Drain, pour cold water over to cool, and dry. Cut the spears into 2-inch lengths.

In a skillet, heat the 2 tablespoons butter and, when hot, add the asparagus. Season with salt and pepper. When the asparagus is hot, sprinkle on the vinegar and let it bubble and glaze the spears. Add the asparagus to the chicken and simmer everything together, uncovered, for 2 minutes longer. Correct the seasoning, fold in the chopped parsley, and serve from a warm platter.

Menu Suggestion   Begin with White Bean Soup with Basil and Cheese (page 227); for dessert, any of the strawberry compotes.

SHOPPING LIST
Poultry: chicken
Vegetables: onion, shallots, celery leaves, asparagus
Dairy: butter

Staples: vegetable oil, flour, dry white wine, chicken stock, sherry wine or white wine vinegar
Herbs: fresh rosemary, fresh savory (optional), parsley

*MUSSELS BROILED WITH MUSTARD AND GARLIC BUTTER

Mussels can be cooked in a number of agreeable ways. The preparations are mostly a haven for lots of garlic, butter, parsley, and bread crumbs.

You can steam mussels open in a white wine and chopped shallot mixture. Add them to the mixture and cook steadily until their bright shells open; then combine them with buttered and garlicked bread crumbs and serve them up. A nice first course.

Another way to do mussels, which you will be purchasing through the good part of spring, is to put together the garlic-butter-bread-crumb version offered here. In this recipe, you top the mussel halves with a flavored butter once they have been steamed just long enough to ease open the hinge. Absent here is the liberal amount of bread crumbs that frequently can be found kneaded into the butter. Instead, I like to sprinkle enough bread crumbs over the butter so that the top turns golden when broiled. You will, however, like to have some crusty bread for mopping up the garlic butter pools that settle in the mussel shells.

6 tablespoons butter, softened	3 tablespoons finely chopped parsley
1 tablespoon good-quality prepared mustard	1 tablespoon lemon juice
	salt and freshly ground pepper
3 garlic cloves, finely chopped	2 dozen mussels, well scrubbed
2 anchovy fillets, chopped	2–3 tablespoons dry bread crumbs

1. Put the softened butter into a mixing bowl and beat in the mustard, garlic, anchovy fillets, chopped parsley, and lemon juice by sprinkles. (To do this successfully, the butter must be softened; the seasonings and other ingredients cannot be introduced into cold, waxy-hard butter.) Season the butter with salt and pepper to taste. Reserve.

2. Put the mussels in a heavy casserole with a tight-fitting lid. There is no need to add water. Cover the pan and place over high heat to steam the mussels until they just open; this will take only a few minutes.

3. Remove the mussels from the shells and put them back into half of the shells. Spread a small spoonful of the prepared butter evenly on top of each mussel. Sprinkle a pinch of bread crumbs over the top of each.

4. Set the mussel shells in a baking pan, preferably filled with a layer of kosher salt (any coarse salt works well) to steady the shells. Run the mussels under a preheated hot broiler for about 3 minutes, or until the mussels and butter are bubbly hot. Serve right away, 6 to a person.

SHOPPING LIST
Shellfish: mussels
Vegetable and fruit: garlic, lemon
Dairy: butter

Staples: prepared mustard, anchovies, bread crumbs
Herb: parsley

✳ SWORDFISH CUBES WITH VEGETABLES AND WINE

An uncomplicated dish is this one of swordfish cubes simmered in a vegetable mixture which needs to be cooked on its own before the fish is added. This dish hints at the trappings for a grander fish stew and is nice when presented with some crisp slices of bread rubbed down with a split garlic clove. These bread slices can be broiled, but an equally good variation would be to fry the slices in hot oil until golden.

4 tablespoons olive oil	½ cup dry white wine
1 onion, diced	1½ cups fish stock
2 garlic cloves, finely chopped	salt and freshly ground pepper
4 ribs celery heart, diced	2 tablespoons finely chopped parsley
2 carrots, diced	2-pound piece of swordfish, cut into
1 green pepper, cored, seeded, and cut into small cubes	chunks
1 cup chopped plum tomatoes	1 recipe Crisp Bread Slices (page 154)

1. Put the olive oil in a skillet, add the diced onion, and sauté for 3 minutes. Stir in the chopped garlic and diced celery; sauté for 2 minutes. Stir in the diced carrots and cubed pepper; stir and cook for 3 minutes longer.

2. Pour in the tomatoes and wine. Bring to the boil and boil for 1 minute. Pour in the fish stock. Season with salt and pepper. Stir in the chopped parsley and simmer the mixture, partially covered, for 20 minutes.

3. Put the swordfish pieces into the vegetable mixture, spooning it over to moisten the fish chunks.

4. Simmer the swordfish, covered, for 10 minutes or until it is cooked through. Adjust the seasoning and serve the fish and vegetable sauce on a serving platter. Dot with the bread slices.

Menu Suggestion   Follow with Mango Cream (page 291) or Strawberries with Warm Lemon-Rum Sauce (page 317).

Shopping List
Fish: swordfish
Vegetables: onion, garlic, celery, carrots, green pepper
Staples: olive oil, plum tomatoes, dry white wine, fish stock
Herb: parsley
For serving: Crisp Bread Slices (see recipe)

✳ HADDOCK IN SAFFRON CREAM

The mixture of saffron and cream, carrots, tarragon, and wine is a nice base for lozenges of haddock. The essence of this kind of fish dish is a base of impeccably seasoned materials in which the fish cooks and is flavored through and through. The cream should be thick and fresh and, by choice, not ultrasterilized. The kind of heavy cream which comes in charming old-fashioned glass bottles (or sometimes small plastic containers) at health-food stores far and away produces the silkiest sauce. And I also must tell you that Devonshire cream, a thick double cream now available in the United States, makes the sauce dense and rich.

2 tablespoons butter	2 pinches saffron threads, lightly crushed
3 leeks, white part only, thinly sliced	with the back of a spoon
1 garlic clove, finely chopped	1¼ cups fish stock
2 carrots, diced	salt and freshly ground pepper
2 tablespoons finely chopped parsley	2 pounds haddock fillets, cut into chunks
1 tablespoon roughly chopped tarragon	¾ cup heavy cream
leaves	2 egg yolks
½ cup dry white wine	

1. Melt the butter in a wide sauté pan that has a cover. Stir in the leeks and soften them in the butter over a low flame. Stir in the chopped garlic and diced carrots; sauté for 3 minutes.

2. Stir in 1 tablespoon of the chopped parsley and tarragon. Pour in the wine and bring to the simmer. After the wine has simmered for a few seconds, flick in the saffron threads and stir them in the liquid. Pour in the fish stock and season with salt and pepper.

3. Simmer the fish base for 15 minutes, covered. Uncover, add the haddock pieces, and cover and simmer for 10 minutes, spooning over some of the liquid halfway during the cooking time. The haddock should be flake tender.

4. When the fish is tender, carefully transfer the pieces to a dish and keep warm. Boil down the cooking liquid until it has reduced by a third. While the liquid is boiling, combine the heavy cream and egg yolks in a mixing bowl. Blend several spoonfuls of the hot cooking liquid into the cream, then take the sauté pan off the heat and blend in the cream. Bring to the simmer, stirring. Return the pieces of fish to the pan, check the seasoning; let the fish absorb some of the creamy mixture for a second or two. Serve the fish, the top flecked over with the remaining tablespoon of finely chopped parsley, from a warm platter.

Menu Suggestion Begin with Mussels Broiled with Mustard and Garlic Butter (page 115).

Fish: haddock fillets

Vegetables: leeks, garlic, carrots

Dairy: butter, heavy cream, eggs

Staples: dry white wine, fish stock

Herbs and spice: parsley, tarragon, saffron

MAIN COURSES

* Soft-Shelled Crabs in Spinach-Scallion Sauce

Chicken with Zucchini Strips and Basil

Lamb with Spring Carrots and Onions

* Veal with Asparagus and Cucumber Wedges

Pork with Glazed Celery

Beef Short Ribs with Spices and Walnuts

* Shad Stew with Rice and Vegetables

THE COOK'S PLAN

1. Set Out: 6-quart casserole with lid for the Beef Short Ribs with Spices and Walnuts, 6-quart casserole with lid for the Pork with Glazed Celery, 6-quart casserole with lid for the Lamb with Spring Carrots and Onions, 10-inch sauté pan for the Chicken with Zucchini Strips and Basil.

2. Thaw and measure out 8 cups beef broth, 2¼ cups chicken broth.

3. Wash and dry 12 parsley sprigs, 2 ribs celery heart.

4. Peel 16 garlic cloves, 8 onions, 4 carrots.

5. Chop 8 garlic cloves, 5 onions, 2 teaspoons fresh rosemary leaves, 2 tablespoons parsley; slice 1 onion, 1 carrot; dice 2 onions, 3 carrots, 2 ribs celery heart; quarter 8 garlic cloves.

6. Measure out 1½ cups dry red wine, 3¼ cups dry white wine, 2 teaspoons sharp prepared mustard, ¾ cup tomato purée or canned plum tomatoes, 3-inch cinnamon stick, 6 allspice berries, 6 cloves.

7. Set out olive oil, vegetable oil, butter, salt, pepper, flour.

8. Tie 2 herb bundles, each containing 6 parsley stems and 1 bay leaf.

9. Beef Short Ribs with Spices and Walnuts: Brown the floured short ribs in oil; simmer with the diced vegetables, spices, and liquid, Steps 1–3 (page 122).

10. Pork with Glazed Celery: Brown the pork cubes; combine with sautéed onions, carrots, and garlic; stir in mustard and liquid; bring to the boil, then simmer, Steps 1–3 (page 124).

11. Lamb with Spring Carrots and Onions: Brown the lamb cubes; simmer with the onions, garlic, rosemary, tomato purée, and liquid, Steps 1–3 (page 125).

12. Chicken with Zucchini Strips and Basil: Brown the chicken; simmer with the sautéed vegetables, parsley, wine, stock, and bay leaf, Steps 1–3 (page 127).

13. Cool all dishes to room temperature; refrigerate or freeze, following the instructions in "To Store" of each recipe.

BEEF SHORT RIBS WITH SPICES AND WALNUTS

It's tasty to submerge beef short ribs in an onion- and spice-laden liquid where the spices intensify the flavor of the simmering red wine and stock. Most people do a catch-as-catch-can version of short ribs, likely cooking the meaty ribs with water and vegetables, thickening everything with fat, flour, and extra stock, all of which has a certain public, I guess. This version has a different set of flavorings and adds walnuts sautéed in a little butter, and spices for sprinkling over the tender ribs on serving day.

4 tablespoons vegetable oil
3 pounds meaty beef short ribs
½ cup all-purpose flour, in a shallow
    bowl
salt and freshly ground pepper
2½ tablespoons butter
1 tablespoon olive oil
2 onions, diced
1 carrot, diced
2 ribs celery heart, diced
2 garlic cloves, chopped
6 whole cloves

6 whole allspice berries
3-inch piece of cinnamon stick
1 small imported bay leaf
1½ cups dry red wine
3 cups beef stock

To Serve

1½ tablespoons butter
½ cup walnut halves, coarsely chopped
pinch each of ground cinnamon, cloves,
    and allspice
1½ tablespoons finely chopped parsley

1. Heat the vegetable oil in a heavy 6-quart casserole. Dust a few of the short ribs in the flour and brown them in the hot oil. Remove to a plate. Flour and brown the rest of the short ribs. Afterward, season them with salt and pepper.

2. Pour out all of the browning oil and add the 2½ tablespoons butter and the olive oil to the casserole. Stir in the diced onions, carrot, and celery. Sauté for 3 minutes. Stir in the chopped garlic and sauté for 1 minute. Stir in the cloves, allspice berries, and cinnamon stick. Stir and cook over moderate heat until the spices darken somewhat. Add the bay leaf.

3. Pour in the red wine and bring the contents of the casserole to a boil. Pour in the beef stock and add the browned short ribs. Bring to a boil, cover, and simmer on the stove top or cook in the lower third of a preheated 325° F oven for about 3 hours or until very tender.

To Store   Remove the cooked short ribs to a storage container, making sure that you push away any clinging spices or vegetables. Boil down the cooking liquid so that it takes on the consistency of a light sauce. Put the liquid and vegetables through a food mill, discarding the spices. Pour the purée mixture over the beef. When the beef has cooled, store covered in the refrigerator for up to 5 days or freeze for up to 1 month.

To Serve   Reheat the beef in a covered casserole. Heat the 1½ tablespoons butter in a small skillet. Sauté the chopped walnuts in the butter until lightly browned and, as the nuts cook, sprinkle them with the ground spices. Stir the chopped parsley into the short ribs, adjust the seasoning, and turn onto a warm platter. Sprinkle the hot, spiced nuts on top.

Menu Suggestion   Start off the meal with Artichoke Stew (page 231); accompany the beef with steamed potatoes, rice, or Buttered Noodles (page 253); for dessert, Strawberries and Pineapple with Strawberry Purée Sauce (page 315).

SHOPPING LIST
Meat: beef short ribs
Vegetables: onions, garlic, carrot, celery
Dairy: butter
Staples: vegetable oil, olive oil, flour, dry red wine, beef stock, walnuts
Herbs and spices: whole cloves, whole allspice berries, cinnamon stick, bay leaf, ground cinnamon, ground cloves, ground allspice, parsley

PORK WITH GLAZED CELERY

If one dish or another could mirror a thought or capture a scene, or imitate a feeling, this one would call to mind the forthright simplicity of country cooking. Celery heart, the choicest and most tender part of the vegetable, is given a sheer glassy coating by simmering chunks of it with butter and beef stock. The flavor becomes subdued and balances perfectly with the pork, which has its own measure of seasoning.

You could also follow the same formula for Pork with Glazed Turnips (page 79), turning this dish into one which could be done on serving day, instead of preparing part of it in advance. Using this method, you would be crafting an equally delicious, informal kind of dish. And somehow, it seems, it is assuring to know that you can carry out the plan of this recipe in more than one mode.

3½ tablespoons vegetable oil
2¾ pounds boneless pork shoulder, cut into 2-inch cubes
salt and freshly ground pepper
3 tablespoons butter
1 tablespoon olive oil
2 onions, chopped
2 carrots, diced
3 garlic cloves, chopped
2 teaspoons sharp prepared mustard
1½ cups dry white wine
2½ cups beef stock

6 parsley stems tied with 1 small imported bay leaf

To Serve

3 bunches firm, unblemished celery hearts
3 tablespoons butter
2 garlic cloves, peeled and halved
2 teaspoons lemon juice
1 tablespoon finely chopped parsley
1 cup beef stock

1. Heat the vegetable oil in a heavy 6-quart casserole. Brown the pork cubes in the hot oil, doing this in several batches, in order not to crowd the pan. Transfer the browned cubes to a plate and season them with salt and pepper.

2. When all the pork cubes have been browned, pour out all of the remaining vegetable oil. Put in the butter and olive oil. Sauté the onions and carrots in the fat for 2 minutes. Stir in the garlic, and sauté for 1 minute. Stir in the mustard and wine. Bring to the boil. Pour in the 2½ cups beef stock and drop in the parsley bundle. Add the pork.

3. Bring the contents of the casserole to a simmer, cover, and cook at a simmer on the stove top or in the lower third of a preheated 325° F oven for 2 hours or until the pork is tender.

To Store   Transfer the pork cubes with a slotted spoon to a storage container. Discard the parsley bundle and boil down the liquid until it is lightly condensed, about 4–5 minutes. Pour the vegetable and liquid "sauce" over the pork. Cool the pork to room temperature, then refrigerate tightly covered for up to 5 days or freeze for up to 1 month.

To Serve   Remove any fat solidified on top of the pork. Put the pork in a casserole, cover, and reheat very slowly. Prepare the celery ribs: detach the ribs from the stalk, trim, and cut into 3-inch lengths. Plunge them into a large quantity of boiling salted water and simmer for 10 minutes. Drain in a colander and freshen with several cupfuls of cold water. Dry well.

Melt the 3 tablespoons butter in a large saucepan. Fold the celery segments through. Stir in the garlic, lemon juice, and parsley. Season with salt and pepper and pour on the 1 cup beef stock. Bring to the simmer, then cover and simmer until the celery is almost tender. Cook, uncovered, to simmer away part of the liquid, about 3 minutes. Fold the glazed celery into the hot pork and simmer, uncovered, for a few seconds to combine the flavors. Serve from a warm platter.

Menu Suggestion   Follow the pork with Watercress Salad with Mustard and Herbs (page 262).

SHOPPING LIST
Meat: boneless pork shoulder
Vegetables and fruit: onions, garlic, carrots, celery, lemon
Dairy: butter

Staples: vegetable oil, olive oil, prepared mustard, dry white wine, beef stock
Herbs: parsley, bay leaf

LAMB WITH SPRING CARROTS AND ONIONS

The oniony pan sauce in this dish is a good escort for the lamb, along with rosemary, white wine, and garlic. If you can get bunches of those tender, young, reedy carrots, altogether about 3 inches long, snap them up for this dish. Otherwise, use slender bunch carrots cut into manageable pieces. As for the onions, the small and lustrous pearl ones complete this gathering of vegetables.

4 tablespoons vegetable oil
2¾ pounds boneless lamb shoulder, cut into 2-inch cubes
salt and freshly ground pepper
3 tablespoons butter
3 onions, chopped
3 garlic cloves, chopped
2 teaspoons rosemary leaves, chopped
¾ cup tomato purée (homemade) or chopped canned plum tomatoes
1 cup dry white wine
6 parsley stems tied with 1 imported bay leaf

2½ cups beef stock

To Serve

2½ tablespoons butter
18 pearl onions, peeled and trimmed
8 small tender carrots, cut into 2-inch lengths
sprinkling of granulated sugar
1 cup beef stock
1 tablespoon finely chopped parsley

1. Heat the vegetable oil in a heavy 6-quart casserole. Brown the lamb cubes, in batches, in the vegetable oil. As the cubes are browned, remove them to a side plate and season with salt and pepper.

2. Pour out any oil that is left in the casserole and add 3 tablespoons butter. Sauté the

onions in the butter 3 minutes. Stir in the chopped garlic and rosemary. Stir in the tomato purée or canned tomatoes and bring to the simmer. Stir in the wine and bring to the boil. Add the parsley bundle and pour in the 2½ cups beef stock. Put the lamb cubes in the liquid and bring to the boil.

3. Cover the casserole and simmer the lamb cubes on the stove top or cook in the lower third of a preheated 325° F oven for 2 hours or until the lamb is tender.

To Store   Remove the lamb with a slotted spoon to a storage container. Discard the parsley bundle and defat the cooking liquid. Boil the vegetable-stock liquid for 4 minutes to condense it. Pour that over the lamb cubes. Cool the lamb completely, then store, covered, in the refrigerator for up to 5 days or freeze for up to 1 month.

To Serve   Heat the 2½ tablespoons butter in a skillet, stir in the onions, and brown them lightly. Stir in the carrots and sprinkle a little sugar over all; stir-cook for 2 minutes. Season the carrots and onions with salt and pepper. Pour on the 1 cup beef stock, bring to the boil, and simmer until the vegetables are tender, about 15 minutes.

In the meantime, reheat the lamb in a covered casserole until very hot. When the lamb is ready, add the cooked vegetables and simmer uncovered for a few minutes longer. Check the seasoning and fold in the chopped parsley. Serve from a heated platter.

Menu Suggestion   Serve Buttered Noodles (page 253) along with the lamb; for dessert, Strawberries Steeped in Orange Brandy (page 316).

SHOPPING LIST
Meat: boneless lamb shoulder
Vegetables: cooking onions, garlic, pearl onions, carrots
Dairy: butter

Staples: vegetable oil, tomato purée or canned plum tomatoes, dry white wine, beef stock, sugar
Herbs: rosemary, parsley, bay leaf

CHICKEN WITH ZUCCHINI STRIPS AND BASIL

This is a recipe that is typical of the way you can combine aspects of do-ahead cooking with the lively taste of fresh vegetables and come up with a dish that is ideal for full schedules and demanding palates. The zucchini strips are added on serving day so that they do not taste tired from overcooking. And when the shredded basil is added, the dish takes on added flavor, just as when you whisk an herb-imbued cream into pan juices to pour on top of veal chops or when you swirl an emerald green spoonful of basil, cheese, and oil into soup.

3 tablespoons vegetable oil
4 tablespoons butter
2¾–3-pound whole chicken, cut into 8
   serving pieces
salt and freshly ground pepper
1 onion, sliced
8 garlic cloves, peeled and quartered
1 carrot, sliced
2 tablespoons chopped parsley
¾ cup dry white wine

2¼ cups chicken stock
1 small imported bay leaf

To Serve

2 zucchini, cut into narrow strips
3 tablespoons butter
½ pound pearl onions, carefully peeled
   and trimmed
5 fresh basil leaves, shredded
6 canned plum tomatoes, chopped

1. Heat the vegetable oil and 1 tablespoon of the butter in a 10-inch sauté pan. Brown the chicken pieces, a few at a time, in the hot fat and transfer them to a plate as they brown. Season the chicken with salt and pepper.

2. When all of the chicken pieces have browned, pour out any of the existing fat and add a fresh 3 tablespoons of butter. Stir in the sliced onion and sauté for 3 minutes. Stir in the garlic and sliced carrot; cook, stirring, for 2 minutes. Add the chopped parsley, stir, and pour in the wine. Bring the wine to the boil, then pour in the chicken stock. Add the bay leaf and put in the chicken pieces.

3. Bring the contents of the pan to a simmer, and baste the chicken with some of the pan liquid. Cover the pan and simmer the chicken for 30 minutes or until it is tender.

To Store   Put the chicken pieces into a storage container. Discard the bay leaf; boil the pan juices for 3 minutes or until lightly condensed. Put the condensed liquid and vegetables through a food mill and pour that over the chicken. Refrigerate the chicken, tightly covered, when cooled completely, for up to 2 days or freeze for up to 2 weeks.

To Serve   Salt the zucchini lightly and leave in a colander for 15 minutes. In the meantime, put the chicken in a casserole, cover, and reheat slowly. Drain the zucchini and pat dry the strips on paper toweling.

Melt the 3 tablespoons butter in a skillet, add the pearl onions, and sauté them for

5 minutes. Stir in the zucchini strips and sauté for 3 minutes. Stir in the basil and plum tomatoes, bring to the simmer, and simmer uncovered for 4 minutes. Cover and simmer for 5 minutes. Season the vegetables lightly with salt and pepper; combine them with the chicken and simmer everything together for several minutes to blend the flavors. Serve from a warm platter.

Menu Suggestion Begin with Garlic Soup (page 220) and end with any of the strawberry desserts.

SHOPPING LIST
Poultry: chicken
Vegetables: cooking onion, garlic, carrot, pearl onions, zucchini
Dairy: butter

Staples: vegetable oil, dry white wine, chicken stock, canned plum tomatoes
Herbs: parsley, bay leaf, fresh basil

* VEAL WITH ASPARAGUS AND CUCUMBER WEDGES

This dish is modeled after one cooked for me by one of my itinerant friends, whose passion is collecting great food ideas from all kinds of dining havens. This recipe uses stalks of ample asparagus and a "European" cucumber, the kind that you don't have to peel, so you can keep the beautiful green case on. It is seasoned by fresh savory, the soft-leafed summer type. The asparagus and cucumber preparation in Steps 4–5 can also be added to the syrupy pan juices of a veal roast which has been casserole cooked, and poured over the carved slices (this makes a delicious Sunday supper).

3½ tablespoons vegetable oil
4 rib veal chops, cut 1-inch thick
salt and freshly ground pepper
5 shallots, finely chopped
5 tablespoons butter
2 carrots, chopped
½ cup dry white wine
1 cup chicken stock
½ pound fat asparagus, trimmed, simmered in salted water until barely tender, and cut into 2-inch pieces
½ small "European" cucumber, cut in half, then cut into wedges, or 1 small regular cucumber, peeled and cut into wedges
2 teaspoons prepared mustard (choose a piquant one)
1 tablespoon chopped fresh savory
⅓ cup *crème fraîche*

1. Heat the vegetable oil in a heavy skillet and brown the veal chops on both sides in the hot oil. Remove them to a plate and season with salt and pepper.

2. In a 10-inch casserole soften the chopped shallots in 2 tablespoons of the butter over a low flame. Stir in the chopped carrots and sauté for 2 minutes. Raise the heat to moderately high and pour in the wine, letting it bubble up vigorously for about 30 seconds. Pour in the chicken stock and add the browned veal chops.

3. Baste the veal chops with the liquid several times, bring the liquid to a boil, then cover and cook the chops in the lower third of a preheated 325° F oven for 55 minutes to 1 hour or until tender.

4. Have the cooked asparagus at hand. Sprinkle the cucumber wedges with a little salt and leave to drain in a colander for 15 minutes; dry the pieces on paper toweling.

5. In a skillet, heat the remaining 3 tablespoons butter and add the cucumber wedges; sauté them quickly for 3 minutes. Stir in the asparagus, mustard, and chopped savory. Stir and cook for 1 minute. Keep the chops warm while you stir the *crème fraîche* into the cooking liquid. Add the vegetables, season with salt and pepper, and heat everything through.

6. Put the chops on a serving platter and pour the vegetable mixture over them.

Menu Suggestion   For dessert, Stuffed Prunes and Whole Apricots in White Wine and Spices (page 307).

SHOPPING LIST
Meat: veal chops
Vegetables: shallots, carrots, asparagus, cucumber
Dairy: butter, *crème fraîche*

Staples: vegetable oil, dry white wine, chicken stock, prepared mustard
Herb: fresh savory

✳ SOFT-SHELLED CRABS IN SPINACH-SCALLION SAUCE

One part of spring cookery, before the time we are whisked into early summer, is the gradual leavening of dishes from the intense enveloping warmth of durable soups and the like. If winter is a nurturing kettle of lentil soup and wild mushrooms meandering through some soul-satisfying braises, spring is eating the first soft-shelled crabs of the season. They are very good in some fish stews, although not all that common, and special when combined with vegetables (see Soft-Shelled Crabs with Vegetables on page 153) and here, in a symmetry of chopped spinach, thin scallion rounds, tomatoes, white wine, and a few currants.

3 tablespoons olive oil	salt and freshly ground pepper
2 bunches scallions, trimmed, leaving 1 inch of the green, and thinly sliced	2 tablespoons butter
	2 tablespoons vegetable oil
2 garlic cloves, chopped	8 soft-shelled crabs
¾ pound fresh spinach, cooked and finely chopped	½ cup all-purpose flour, in a shallow bowl
⅓ cup dry white wine	juice of ½ lemon
1 cup chopped canned plum tomatoes	2 tablespoons moist, dried currants

1. Heat the olive oil in a sauté pan large enough to accommodate all of the crabs. Stir in the scallions and sauté until soft. Add the chopped garlic and sauté for 1 minute. Stir in the chopped spinach. Pour on the wine and raise the heat to make the wine bubble up.

2. As soon as the wine bubbles, stir in the plum tomatoes and season with salt and pepper to taste. Simmer, partially covered, for 15 minutes.

3. While the spinach-scallion mixture is simmering, heat the butter and vegetable oil in a large heavy skillet. Dredge half of the crabs in the flour and brown them on both sides in the hot fat. Put the browned crabs on a plate and season them lightly with salt and pepper. Add extra butter and oil, if necessary, to brown the remaining crabs.

4. Put all of the browned crabs in the spinach-scallion sauce, sprinkle with the lemon juice, scatter in the currants, and moisten the crabs with the sauce.

5. Simmer the crabs, covered, for 12–15 minutes until they are cooked through, basting with the sauce once or twice during the cooking time. Check the seasoning and serve the crabs from a warm dish with the sauce spooned over and around them.

Menu Suggestion   For dessert, Gratin of Kiwi and Papaya (page 288).

Shopping List
Fish: soft-shelled crabs .
Vegetables and fruit: scallions, garlic, spinach, lemon
Dairy: butter

Staples: olive oil, vegetable oil, dry white wine, canned plum tomatoes, flour, currants

✳ SHAD STEW WITH RICE AND VEGETABLES

The painstaking ritual of boning shad: it contains what seems like an infinite number of bones, many so small and thin that you could be tweezing out bones forever. You might just depend on your fish dealer to do the boning, one extravagance (and rite) of spring, and follow through on this stew. While it is very simple, it is one of the shad preparations I do every time the season comes round. It reminds me, in part, of my grandmother's glorious way for shad, and I regret that her recipe was never passed down to me.

3 tablespoons olive oil
2 onions, chopped
1 garlic clove, chopped
1 carrot, diced
2 ribs celery heart, diced
1 tablespoon minced parsley
2 teaspoons chopped fresh savory (optional)
1 cup tomato purée (homemade) or chopped canned plum tomatoes
½ cup dry white wine

1½ cups fish stock
salt and freshly ground pepper
1 small imported bay leaf
2 pounds fillet of shad, cut into large pieces
3 tablespoons long-grain rice, cooked in boiling salted water for 12 minutes and drained
1 teaspoon capers
1 dozen oil-cured black olives

1. Heat the olive oil in a wide casserole or a heavy-bottomed sauté pan. Sauté the onions in the oil until translucent; add the garlic and cook for 1 minute. Stir in the diced celery and carrots; cook for 2 minutes.

2. Stir in the parsley and savory, if you are using it, along with the tomato purée or canned tomatoes. Simmer, uncovered, for 5 minutes. Pour in the wine and bring to the boil. Pour in the fish stock. Season the mixture with salt and pepper. Drop in the bay leaf.

3. Bring the contents of the pan to the boil, cover, and simmer for 10 minutes. Sprinkle the pieces of shad lightly with salt and pepper. Add them to the vegetable-wine mixture. Cover and simmer for 5 minutes. Stir in the rice, capers, and olives, cover, and simmer for 5 minutes longer until the fish flakes tender.

4. Carefully transfer the fish and all the good pan sauce to a warm serving dish.

Menu Suggestion   Follow the stew with a Salad of Watercress and Red Leaf Lettuce (page 262).

SHOPPING LIST
Fish: fillet of shad
Vegetables: onions, garlic, carrot, celery
Staples: olive oil, tomato purée or canned plum

tomatoes, dry white wine, fish stock, rice, capers, oil-cured black olives
Herbs: parsley, savory (optional), bay leaf

MAIN COURSES

* Shrimp with Thyme and *Crème Fraîche*

Breast of Lamb Stuffed with Ground Lamb and Olives

Chicken with Green Beans and Tarragon

Beef with Capers

* Veal Chops with Glazed Carrots and Cream

Pork Braised with Onions, Paprika, and Caraway

* Shad Roe with Asparagus and Celery, or

* Red Snapper with Asparagus and Chives

THE COOK'S PLAN

1. Set out: 6-quart casserole with lid for the Pork Braised with Onions, Paprika, and Caraway, 6-quart casserole with lid for the Beef with Capers, 12-inch oval casserole with lid for the Breast of Lamb Stuffed with Ground Lamb and Olives, 10-inch sauté pan with lid for the Chicken with Green Beans and Tarragon.

2. Thaw and measure out about 7½ cups beef stock, 1¾ cups chicken stock.

3. Wash and dry a bunch of parsley.

4. Peel 9 garlic cloves, 8 onions, 1 carrot.

5. Finely chop 3 onions, 1 tablespoon parsley, 2 garlic cloves; chop 2 tablespoons parsley, 7 garlic cloves, 1 onion, 1 carrot, 2 fresh rosemary leaves, 8 canned plum tomatoes; slice 4 onions; cube ⅓ pound salt pork.

6. Measure out 2¼ cups dry red wine, 1⅔ cups dry white wine, 2 tablespoons red wine vinegar, ½ cup bread crumbs, 2 tablespoons paprika.

7. Set out vegetable oil, olive oil, butter, salt, pepper, flour.

8. Tie herb bundles: 6 parsley stems with 1 bay leaf; 1 branch tarragon with 6 parsley stems and 1 bay leaf; in a cheesecloth bag, 4 allspice berries, 1 teaspoon caraway seeds, 1 bay leaf, and 6 parsley stems.

9. Beef with Capers: Brown the floured beef cubes; sauté salt pork cubes and onions; add vinegar, parsley, garlic, bay leaf, wine, and stock; simmer, Steps 1–3 (pages 134).

10. Breast of Lamb Stuffed with Ground Lamb and Olives: Prepare the lamb stuffing; fill the pocket of the lamb breast with the stuffing and sew it up; simmer the breast on the bed of sautéed vegetables to which the seasonings, wine and stock have been added, Steps 1–3 (page 135).

11. Pork Braised with Onions, Paprika, and Caraway: Brown the pork cubes; simmer with the sautéed onions, garlic, paprika, liquid, and seasonings, Steps 1–3 (page 137).

12. Chicken with Green Beans and Tarragon: Brown the floured chicken; simmer with the onion, garlic, chopped tomatoes, liquid, and herb bundle, Steps 1–3 (page 138).

13. Cool all dishes to room temperature; refrigerate or freeze, following the instructions in "To Store" of each recipe.

BEEF WITH CAPERS

A fairly robust and, thanks to the capers, zesty beef dish which works equally well with some three pounds of meaty short ribs. For the bulk of short ribs, increase the quantity of red wine by ½ cup and the beef stock by ½ cup. Another flourish, for either, would include 5 anchovy fillets, chopped and added along with the garlic.

4 tablespoons vegetable oil
2¾ pounds grainy chuck or rump pot
   roast, cut into 2-inch cubes
½ cup all-purpose flour, in a shallow
   bowl
salt and freshly ground pepper
2 tablespoons olive oil
⅓ pound lean salt pork, cut into cubes
2 onions, finely chopped
2 tablespoons red wine vinegar

2 tablespoons chopped parsley
4 garlic cloves, chopped
1 imported bay leaf
1½ cups dry red wine
1¾ cups beef stock

To Serve

2 tablespoons imported nonpareil capers,
   rinsed quickly in cool water, drained,
   and dried

1. Heat the vegetable oil in a heavy 6-quart casserole. A batch at a time, dredge the meat cubes in the flour and brown them in the hot oil. Remove the cubes to a dish and season them with salt and pepper.

2. When you have browned all of the cubes, pour out the vegetable oil and add the olive oil. Sauté the salt pork cubes in the oil until lightly golden. Stir in the onions and sauté for 2 minutes. Stir in the vinegar, chopped parsley, and chopped garlic. Stir and cook for 30 seconds. Add the bay leaf and pour in the wine. Bring the wine to a boil, then pour in the beef stock. Add the browned beef cubes.

3. Bring the contents of the casserole to a boil, cover, and simmer on the stove top or in the lower third of a preheated 325° F oven for 2½–3 hours or until the meat is very tender, but not falling apart.

To Store   Remove the beef cubes with a slotted spoon to a storage container. Boil down the liquid until it has lightly condensed, then pour it over the beef. Pick out and discard the bay leaf. Cool completely, then refrigerate in a covered container for up to 5 days or in the freezer for up to 1 month.

To Serve   Reheat the meat in a covered casserole, stirring in the capers. Check the seasoning and turn the beef onto a warm serving platter.

Menu Suggestion   Begin with a vegetable first course, Gratin of Zucchini with Onions and Herbs (page 245); for dessert, Cantaloupe with Cassis, White Wine, and Honey (page 277).

BREAST OF LAMB STUFFED WITH GROUND LAMB AND OLIVES

This particular stuffing for breast of lamb contains bits of olive and carrot along with the ground lamb in addition to chopped fresh rosemary. In a straitened circumstance, ½ teaspoon dried rosemary leaves chopped along with the parsley could be used to replace the fresh herb in the stuffing.

For the Stuffing

2 tablespoons vegetable oil

1 onion, chopped

2 garlic cloves, chopped

1 carrot, chopped

2 teaspoons chopped fresh rosemary leaves

1 tablespoon finely chopped parsley

½ cup bread crumbs soaked in ⅓ cup beef stock

1 egg

¼ cup whole green olives, pitted and coarsely chopped

10 ounces ground lamb

salt and freshly ground pepper

For the Lamb Breast

3–3½-pound boneless lamb breast, with a pocket cut for stuffing

2 tablespoons vegetable oil

2 tablespoons butter

1 tablespoon olive oil

1 onion, sliced

1 carrot, sliced

1 rib celery heart, sliced

6 parsley stems tied with 1 small imported bay leaf

¾ cup dry red wine

2 cups beef stock

1. First prepare the stuffing. Heat 2 tablespoons vegetable oil in a small skillet. Cook the chopped onion, garlic, and carrot in the oil until soft. Cool slightly. In a large mixing bowl, place the rosemary leaves, chopped parsley, bread crumb mixture, egg, olives, and ground lamb. Blend the ingredients well. Season with salt and pepper. Beat in the cooled vegetable mixture.

2. Fill the pocket of the lamb breast with the stuffing. Sew up the open seam with a piece of heavy-duty kitchen string.

3. Heat 2 tablespoons vegetable oil in a 12-inch oval casserole (or one which can hold

the lamb in one layer). Brown the lamb breast on both sides in the hot oil. Remove to a plate and season with salt and pepper. Pour out the vegetable oil.

4. Put the butter and olive oil into the casserole and place over moderate heat. Stir in the onion, carrot, and celery slices and cook for 3 minutes. Add the parsley bundle and pour in the wine. Bring the wine to a boil, stirring. Pour in the beef stock and add the lamb breast. Bring the contents of the casserole to a boil. Cover tightly and cook in the lower third of a preheated 325° F oven for 2½ hours or until tender.

To Store   Let the lamb breast cool in the cooking liquid for about 15 minutes. Carefully remove it to a storage bowl. Boil down the cooking liquid for several minutes to thicken it a bit. Discard the parsley bundle. Pass the liquid and vegetables through a food mill to purée and pour that over the lamb. When cool, store, covered, in the refrigerator for up to 4 days.

To Serve   Reheat the lamb in a covered casserole until hot. Correct the seasoning. Take out the lamb breast, remove the binding string, and carve it into long slices to include a large strip of filling in each slice. Arrange the slices on a platter, and pour over them some of the vegetable-enriched pan juices.

Menu Suggestion   Begin with Spring Vegetable Soup (page 226).

Shopping List

Meat: boneless lamb breast, ground lamb
Vegetables: onions, garlic, carrots, celery
Dairy: butter, egg

Staples: vegetable oil, olive oil, dry red wine, beef stock, green olives, bread crumbs
Herbs: rosemary, parsley, bay leaf

PORK BRAISED WITH ONIONS, PAPRIKA, AND CARAWAY

The caraway seeds appear in two ways here with the pork, once in a cheesecloth pouch and again, crushed, on the day that the dish is reheated, for adding right along with the pork. And if, for some reason, you are not able to work with the pork shoulder for a day or two, you could marinate the piece with slivers of garlic, a few peppercorns and 2 allspice berries, cracked, a bay leaf crumbled up, 2 tablespoons olive oil, a few pinches of salt, and a branch of thyme if you have it. Massage all of this over the pork and store it in a porcelain bowl, covered. Flick away all the clinging spices and dry the pork on paper toweling before using.

4 tablespoons vegetable oil

2¾ pounds boneless pork shoulder, cut into chunks

½ cup all-purpose flour, in a shallow bowl

salt and freshly ground pepper

3½ tablespoons olive oil

4 onions, sliced

3 garlic cloves, chopped

2 tablespoons paprika

1 cup dry white wine

2½ cups beef stock

4 whole allspice berries, ¼ teaspoon caraway seeds, 1 bay leaf, and 6 parsley stems, enclosed in clean square of cheesecloth

To Serve

¼ teaspoon caraway seeds, crushed with the back of a spoon or mallet

½ cup sour cream

1½ tablespoons finely chopped parsley

1. Heat the vegetable oil in a heavy 6-quart casserole. Dredge the pork cubes in the flour, a batch at a time, and brown them in the hot oil. Remove to a bowl and season with salt and pepper.

2. When all of the cubes have been browned, pour out the vegetable oil and add the olive oil. Sauté the sliced onions in the oil for 3 minutes. Stir in the chopped garlic and paprika; stir and cook for 1 minute. Pour the wine into the pan; bring the wine to the boil, stirring. Pour in the beef stock and add the browned pork and cheesecloth package.

3. Bring the contents of the casserole to the boil, cover, and simmer on the stove top or cook in the lower third of a preheated 325° F oven for 2 hours, or until the pork is tender. Remove the pork cubes with a slotted spoon to a casserole, leaving behind the solids. Discard the cheesecloth package.

To Store   Boil the cooking liquid for 4 minutes, defat, then purée through a food mill. Pour the puréed mixture over the pork and cool completely. Refrigerate, covered, for up to 5 days or freeze for up to 1 month.

To Serve   Reheat the pork in a covered casserole. Stir in the caraway seeds when the pork is hot. Put the sour cream in a mixing bowl. Blend ½ cup of the cooking liquid from the pork into the sour cream and stir the sour cream back into the pork along with the chopped parsley. Heat everything through and serve.

Menu Suggestion   Begin with Artichoke Stew (page 231); serve steamed potatoes, rice, or Buttered Noodles (page 253) with the pork; for dessert, Strawberry, Melon, and Kiwi Bowl with Ginger and Port (page 318).

SHOPPING LIST

Meat: boneless pork shoulder

Vegetables: onions, garlic

Dairy: sour cream

Staples: vegetable oil, olive oil, flour, dry white wine,

beef stock

Herbs and spices: paprika, whole allspice berries, caraway seeds, bay leaf, parsley

CHICKEN WITH GREEN BEANS AND TARRAGON

I always look for the firmest, thinnest green beans for any sort of preparation—in a vegetable course or for combining them with fresh herbs and butter in a dish that has been looked after in advance such as this one, which keeps its own distinction by having the vegetable added to it on serving day.

3½ tablespoons vegetable oil
2¾–3-pound whole chicken, cut into 8 serving pieces
½ cup all-purpose flour, in a shallow bowl
salt and freshly ground pepper
2 tablespoons butter
1 tablespoon olive oil
1 onion, finely chopped
2 garlic cloves, finely chopped
8 canned plum tomatoes, chopped
⅔ cup dry white wine

1¾ cups chicken stock
1 branch tarragon tied with 6 parsley stems and 1 small imported bay leaf

To Serve

½ pound green beans
2 tablespoons butter blended with 1 small garlic clove, chopped
1 tablespoon chopped fresh tarragon leaves
1 teaspoon lemon juice
1 tablespoon finely chopped parsley

1. Heat the vegetable oil in a 10-inch sauté pan. A few pieces at a time, dust the chicken pieces with flour and brown them in the hot oil. As the chicken pieces are browned, remove them to a plate and season with salt and pepper. Brown the rest of the chicken.

2. Pour out any oil that remains in the pan and add the 2 tablespoons butter and the olive oil. Sauté the onion in the butter-oil until it is light golden. Stir in the chopped garlic and plum tomatoes; cook for 2 minutes, stirring occasionally. Pour in the wine and let it bubble up for 1 minute. Pour in the chicken stock and add the herb bundle.

3. Return the chicken pieces to the pan and baste over with the cooking liquid several times. Bring the contents of the pan to the boil, then simmer, covered, for 30 minutes, turning the chicken once during that time.

To Store   Transfer the chicken to a storage container. Discard the herb bundle. Boil down the liquid for 3 minutes, pour it over the chicken, and cool completely. Store, in a covered container, in the refrigerator for up to 2 days or in the freezer for up to 2 weeks.

To Serve   Reheat the chicken in a covered casserole. As the chicken heats up, plunge the green beans into boiling salted water and boil steadily for 5 minutes or until the beans are barely tender. Drain the beans in a colander and refresh them with a blast of cold water. Drain again; pat them dry on paper toweling. Trim the beans and cut them into 2-inch pieces.

Put the garlic butter into a heavy skillet and set over moderately high heat. As soon as the butter ceases to foam, toss in the beans, tarragon, and lemon juice. Cook, stirring, for 1 minute. Season lightly with salt and pepper. Fold in the chopped parsley. Fold the beans into the chicken and simmer for a minute to blend the flavors. Turn out onto a heated dish for serving.

Menu Suggestion   For dessert, Mango Cream (page 291).

SHOPPING LIST
Poultry: chicken
Vegetables and fruit: onion, garlic, green beans, lemon
Dairy: butter

Staples: vegetable oil, olive oil, flour, canned plum tomatoes, dry white wine, chicken stock
Herbs: fresh tarragon, parsley, bay leaf

✻ SHRIMP WITH THYME AND *CRÈME FRAÎCHE*

This is a recipe for one of those days when all you want is a nice main course, approachable in about 20 minutes, because you have spent either part of the day cooking or all of the day working and need some good-natured sustenance. I am meticulous about the use of fresh thyme here, but if you do not have fresh thyme you could eliminate it (and change the name of the dish) and, in its place, add a spoonful of Dijon mustard with the *crème fraîche* and add another tablespoon of finely chopped parsley.

4 tablespoons butter
1 onion, finely chopped
2 garlic cloves, chopped
2 teaspoons fresh thyme leaves, chopped
1¼ pounds fresh shrimp, peeled, with

the tail left on, and deveined
⅓ cup dry white wine
salt and freshly ground pepper
1½ tablespoons finely chopped parsley
½ cup *crème fraîche*

1. Heat the butter in a skillet and stir in the chopped onion. Cook slowly until the onion turns soft. Stir in the chopped garlic and thyme. Stir and cook for 1 minute.

2. Add the shrimp to the pan and sauté for 2 minutes over a lively flame. Pour in the wine and let it bubble up and glaze over the shrimp.

3. Season the shrimp with salt and pepper. Stir in the chopped parsley and *crème*

fraîche, stirring until the contents of the skillet are well heated through. Correct the seasoning and serve.

Menu Suggestion   Follow with Bibb Lettuce Salad (page 257).

SHOPPING LIST
Shellfish: shrimp
Vegetables: onion, garlic
Dairy: butter, *crème fraîche*

Staples: dry white wine
Herbs: fresh thyme, parsley

✳ VEAL CHOPS WITH GLAZED CARROTS AND CREAM

It's the carrots simmered until they are shiny and tender that provide much of the filigree work for this dish, with a healthy dose of heavy cream. Fresh carrots in the bunch, with the greenery still attached, would be my first choice for this preparation. They are sweet and very flavorful. But if you are faced with a plastic bag of carrots as your only option, after the usual peeling, cut the carrots into long quarters and remove the inner core, which is apt to be unpleasantly tough. Then cut the sticks into chunks before simmering.

3 tablespoons vegetable oil	1 cup chicken stock
4 rib veal chops, cut 1-inch thick	1 fresh bunch of carrots (4–5), peeled
salt and freshly ground pepper	and sliced into thin rounds
5 tablespoons butter	¼ teaspoon granulated sugar
1 onion, chopped	¾ cup chicken stock
4 shallots, chopped	1 tablespoon finely chopped parsley
2 celery heart ribs, chopped	2 teaspoons snipped chives
1 small imported bay leaf	½ cup heavy cream, warmed
½ cup dry white wine	

1. Heat the vegetable oil in a heavy skillet. Brown the veal chops in the hot oil. Season them with salt and pepper and set aside.

2. Melt 3 tablespoons of the butter in a 10-inch casserole, stir in the chopped onions and shallots, and soften them in the butter. Add the chopped celery and continue to cook for 2 minutes. Add the bay leaf and wine; bring the wine to a boil. Pour in the chicken stock and add the veal chops, overlapping them slightly to fit. Bring the liquid to a boil.

3. Cover the casserole and cook the veal in the lower third of a preheated 325° F oven for 50 minutes to 1 hour or until tender, basting several times as the chops cook.

4. While the veal cooks, prepare the carrots. Melt the remaining 2 tablespoons butter in a saucepan. Stir in the carrot rounds, sugar, chicken stock, and parsley. Season with salt and pepper. Bring the liquid to a boil, then cover and simmer the carrots until tender and absorbed with stock, about 15 minutes. Uncover the saucepan and carefully boil down the liquid until it is almost completely absorbed. Stir in the chives.

5. Stir the warmed cream into the carrots, then combine the carrots with the cooked veal chops and the pan liquid. Correct the seasoning and serve.

Menu Suggestion   Serve Buttered Noodles (page 253) with the veal chops, and finish with any of the strawberry desserts.

Shopping List
Meat: veal chops
Vegetables: onion, shallots, celery, carrots
Dairy: butter, heavy cream

Staples: vegetable oil, dry white wine, chicken stock, sugar
Herbs: parsley, chives, bay leaf

⋇ SHAD ROE WITH ASPARAGUS AND CELERY

The candor of anchovy fillets, bound in softened butter, is added to the asparagus after the shad roe has cooked with onion, garlic, celery, and white wine.

¾ pound firm fresh asparagus
2 tablespoons butter
2 tablespoons olive oil
1 onion, finely chopped
2 garlic cloves, finely chopped
3 ribs celery heart, diced
½ cup dry white wine

salt and freshly ground pepper
4 pairs of shad roe
3 tablespoons butter, softened
5 anchovy fillets, finely chopped
1½ tablespoons chopped parsley
juice of ½ lemon
lemon wedges

1. Remove the tough ends from the asparagus and, with a swivel-bladed peeler, peel off a thin top layer from the asparagus from just underneath the closed tips straight down to the base. Put the asparagus into a skillet of salted water, bring to the boil, and simmer uncovered until barely tender, about 8 minutes. Drain, refresh in cold water, drain again, and dry. Cut the spears into 2-inch lengths. Set aside.

2. Melt the 2 tablespoons butter with the olive oil in a sauté pan large enough to accommodate all of the roe. Stew the onion, garlic, and celery in the butter-oil until soft. Pour in the wine and bring to the boil. Season with pepper and very lightly with salt. Place the shad roe on top of the vegetable mixture. Cover and cook at a simmer for 6 minutes.

3. After 6 minutes, turn the shad roe over, cover, and cook for 2 minutes. Add the asparagus and cook for 4 more minutes, covered.

4. While the shad roe and asparagus are cooking, blend the 3 tablespoons softened butter with the chopped anchovies. Beat in the parsley and the lemon juice.

5. Cut each cooked roe in half along the natural membrane and keep warm while you finish the sauce. Whisk in the anchovy butter, off the heat, in two portions. Put the shad roe on a serving platter and turn the asparagus-anchovy sauce over and around the roe. Serve with lemon wedges.

Menu Suggestion   First course: Clams, Served Soup Style, with White Wine, Leeks, and Coriander (page 213).

SHOPPING LIST
Fish: shad roe
Vegetables and fruit: asparagus, onion, garlic, celery, lemons

Dairy: butter
Staples: olive oil, dry white wine, anchovies
Herb: parsley

✳ RED SNAPPER WITH ASPARAGUS AND CHIVES

Every spring, when an outpour of radiant asparagus fills produce bins at the market in strong sculpturelike vertical bundles, I carry home several pounds and begin to work them into old favorites and new configurations.

On a warm spring day, I might serve a pâté made from a few kinds of fish and settle snugly within it some choice asparagus spears. When you cut down into the pâté, a beautiful marbled green design shows up, and I enhance it all with a spirited herb sauce. Or I might mist cooked spears in an assertive vinaigrette or spoon over a graceful creamy sauce heightened with garlic or mustard.

But when I travel from greengrocer to fish market, and it's one of those work-filled days, I rely on this dish of red snapper and asparagus, in a "pan sauce," fortified with heavy cream and chives. For this dish, I am inclined to use asparagus of ample thickness.

¾ pound fresh green asparagus
3 leeks, white part only, thinly sliced
1 carrot, diced
2½ tablespoons butter
½ cup dry white wine
1 cup tomato purée (homemade) or chopped canned plum tomatoes
4 basil leaves, shredded
salt

cayenne pepper
2 pounds fillet of red snapper, cut into large chunks
½ cup heavy cream, simmered 10 minutes
1 tablespoon butter, softened
1½ tablespoons finely snipped chives
½ tablespoon finely chopped parsley

1. Trim the base of each asparagus and take off a thin outer layer with a swivel-bladed vegetable peeler, starting just under the tip, to the base. Put the asparagus in a skillet of salted water, bring to the boil, and simmer about 8 minutes until barely tender. Drain well, pour on a few cups of cold water, drain again, and dry. Cut the spears into 2-inch pieces.

2. In a skillet, sauté the carrots and leeks in the 2½ tablespoons butter until lightly softened. Pour on the wine, bring to the boil, and boil for 45 seconds. Pour in the tomato purée or canned tomatoes, add the shredded basil, and season with salt. Sprinkle in a dusting of cayenne pepper. Simmer, uncovered, for 10 minutes.

3. Add the red snapper chunks to the tomato-leek mixture, baste over with some of it, and simmer gently, covered, for 5 minutes. Add the asparagus, cover, and simmer for another 5 minutes or until the fish flakes tender.

4. Pour in the heavy cream and heat through. Off the heat, blend in the softened butter, chives, and parsley. Check the seasoning and serve from a warm platter.

Menu Suggestion   Follow the suggestion for Shad Roe with Asparagus and Celery (page 141).

SHOPPING LIST
Fish: red snapper
Vegetables: asparagus, leeks, carrot
Dairy: butter, heavy cream
Staples: dry white wine, tomato purée or canned

plum tomatoes
Herbs and spice: fresh basil, chives, parsley, cayenne pepper

MAIN COURSES

✳ Soft-Shelled Crabs with Vegetables

Lamb with Flageolets

Chicken with Green Peas and Lettuce

✳ Calves' Liver with Watercress, Mustard,
and Walnut Sauce

Tongue in Mustard-Raisin Sauce

Braised Veal Cubes with Mushrooms and Tarragon

✳ Fish Stew with Garlic Sauce

THE COOK'S PLAN

1. Set out: large kettle, with lid, for simmering the tongue in Tongue in Mustard-Raisin Sauce, 6-quart casserole with lid for the Braised Veal Cubes with Mushrooms and Tarragon, 6-quart casserole with lid for the Lamb with Flageolets, 10-inch sauté pan with lid for the Chicken with Green Peas and Lettuce.

2. Thaw and measure out 2¼ cups beef stock, 4 cups chicken stock.

3. Wash and dry 4 ribs celery heart.

4. Peel 7 garlic cloves, 5 onions, 2 carrots, 7 shallots.

5. Chop 4 onions, 7 garlic cloves, 7 shallots; cube 2 carrots, 2 ribs celery heart, ⅓ pound bacon.

6. Measure out 1¾ cups dry white wine, 1 cup red wine, ¾ cup tomato purée or canned plum tomatoes, 6 peppercorns.

7. Set out vegetable oil, olive oil, butter, salt, pepper, flour.

8. Tie herb bundles: 6 parsley stems with 3 strips dried orange peel and 1 bay leaf; 1 sprig tarragon with 6 parsley stems and 1 bay leaf; 6 parsley stems with 2 sprigs thyme and 1 bay leaf.

9. Tongue in Mustard-Raisin Sauce: Simmer the tongue in water; drain and simmer again in fresh water with the flavorings, Steps 1–2 (page 146).

10. Lamb with Flageolets: Brown the lamb cubes, season, and simmer with the sautéed vegetables, herb bundle, and liquid, Steps 1–3 (page 147).

11. Braised Veal Cubes with Mushrooms and Tarragon: Brown the veal cubes; add the sautéed onions, garlic, wine, tomato purée, herb bundle, and chicken stock; simmer, Steps 1–3 (page 149).

12. Chicken with Green Peas and Lettuce: Brown the chicken pieces; simmer with the sautéed bacon, shallots, herb bundle, and liquid, Steps 1–3 (page 150).

13. Cool all dishes to room temperature; refrigerate or freeze, following the instructions in "To Store" of each recipe.

TONGUE IN MUSTARD-RAISIN SAUCE

This is a potent dish I remember being served as a child. I have worked with a few versions, upgraded some ingredients, and included the results here.

1 pickled tongue, approximately 2½–3 pounds
1 garlic clove, peeled
1 onion, peeled and halved
1 imported bay leaf
2 ribs celery heart, sliced in half
6 peppercorns

To Serve

2 tablespoons butter
½ onion, finely chopped

1 carrot, finely chopped
1 rib celery heart, finely chopped
1 tablespoon all-purpose flour
3 tablespoons dark-brown sugar
2 tablespoons lemon juice
grated rind of 1 small lemon
2 teaspoons prepared mustard
⅛ teaspoon ground ginger
1½ cups beef stock
salt and freshly ground pepper
⅓ cup dark raisins

1. Put the tongue in a large kettle and pour in enough cold water to cover completely. Bring to the boil slowly, and simmer for 45 minutes.

2. Drain the tongue. Rinse out the kettle, add the tongue, and cover with fresh water. Add the garlic, onion, bay leaf, celery, and peppercorns. Bring to the boil and simmer slowly, covered, for 2½ hours or until tender.

To Store Let the tongue cool in the water, then remove it, peel off the skin, and trim away any gristle, cartilage, and fat. Cool completely, wrap in plastic wrap, and refrigerate in a covered container for up to 4 days.

To Serve Melt the 2 tablespoons butter in a heavy saucepan. Stir in the chopped onion, carrot, and celery. Cook slowly until the vegetables are soft. Blend in the flour and cook for 2 minutes over moderate heat, whisking. Stir in the brown sugar, lemon juice, lemon rind, mustard, and ginger. Pour in the beef stock and bring to the boil over moderate heat. Season with salt and pepper and simmer for 5 minutes.

Slice the tongue into ½-inch-thick slices. Spoon a little of the mustard sauce on the bottom of a heavy 4-quart casserole, layer in the tongue, and dot with raisins. Create layers of sauce, raisins, and tongue, finishing with a thin layer of sauce. Cover tightly and simmer until the tongue is piping hot. Correct the seasoning, transfer the slices with the sauce to a warm platter, and serve.

Menu Suggestion Accompany the tongue with Buttered Noodles (page 253); follow with Watercress and Bibb Lettuce Salad (page 260).

Meat: pickled tongue
Vegetables and fruit: garlic, onions, celery, carrot, lemon
Dairy: butter

Staples: flour, dark-brown sugar, prepared mustard, beef stock, dark raisins
Herb and spices: bay leaf, peppercorns, ground ginger

LAMB WITH FLAGEOLETS

Flageolets, an oval, green legume, are easiest to buy in the dried state, boxed. The cooked beans are ideal with lamb and are also good in soups based on onions, cream, and other kinds of dried beans.

3½ tablespoons vegetable oil
1½ pounds boneless lamb shoulder and 1½ pounds boneless lamb breast or 3 pounds boned lamb shoulder, cut into 2-inch cubes
salt and freshly ground pepper
3½ tablespoons olive oil
2 onions, chopped
2 garlic cloves, chopped
2 carrots, cubed
2 ribs celery heart, cubed

2 teaspoons chopped fresh rosemary
6 parsley stems tied with 3 strips dried orange peel and 1 small imported bay leaf
1 cup dry white wine
2¼ cups beef stock

To Serve

1½ cups dried flageolets
1½ tablespoons finely chopped parsley

1. Heat the vegetable oil in a heavy 6-quart casserole. Brown the lamb cubes in the hot oil, and as they are browned, remove to a plate. Season with salt and pepper.

2. When you have browned all of the lamb, pour out the vegetable oil and add the olive oil. Sauté the chopped onions in the oil for 2 minutes, stirring once or twice. Stir in the garlic, carrots, and celery. Sauté for 2 minutes longer. Add the rosemary and the herb and orange peel bundle. Pour the wine. Bring the wine to a boil, stirring. Pour in the beef stock and add the lamb cubes.

3. Bring the contents of the casserole to a boil, then cover and simmer on the stove top or in the lower third of a preheated 325° F oven for 1¾–2 hours or until the lamb is tender.

To Store   Discard the herb bundle, remove the lamb chunks to a storage container, and degrease the cooking liquid. Boil down the cooking liquid for a minute or two, if necessary, to condense it lightly. Pour it over the lamb and cool to room temperature. Refrigerate, covered, for up to 5 days or freeze for up to 1 month.

To Serve   The night before the lamb is to be served, put the flageolets in a large bowl and cover with 3 inches of cold water. Leave the beans to soak overnight.

The next day, drain the beans and put them in a large pot. Cover them with cold water, bring to the boil, and simmer gently about 40 minutes until they are tender. While the beans are cooking, heat the lamb in a covered casserole until piping hot throughout. When the beans are tender, drain them in a colander and carefully stir them into the lamb. Season with salt and pepper. Simmer, uncovered, for a moment longer to blend. Fold in the chopped parsley and serve from a warm platter.

Menu Suggestion   Follow the lamb with a plain green salad; for dessert, Frozen Maple Cream with Pecans (page 292).

SHOPPING LIST
Meat: boneless lamb shoulder, boneless lamb breast
Vegetables: onions, garlic, carrots, celery
Staples: vegetable oil, olive oil, dry white wine, beef stock, dried flageolets
Herbs and spices: fresh rosemary, parsley, dried orange peel, bay leaf

BRAISED VEAL CUBES WITH MUSHROOMS AND TARRAGON

What you should remember, primed to make this, is that the tarragon does not have an anonymous taste. Tarragon appears twice, once bound with parsley stems and a bay leaf and once again, chopped, along with the mushrooms on serving day.

3 tablespoons vegetable oil
2¾ pounds boneless veal shoulder, cut into 2-inch cubes
½ cup all-purpose flour, in a shallow bowl
salt and freshly ground pepper
3 tablespoons butter
2 onions, chopped
2 garlic cloves, chopped
1 cup dry red wine
¾ cup tomato purée (homemade) or chopped canned plum tomatoes
1 large sprig of tarragon tied with 6 parsley stems and 1 small imported bay leaf
2 cups chicken stock

To Serve

1½ tablespoons butter
¾ pound small fresh mushrooms, caps only
1½ tablespoons tarragon leaves, roughly chopped
½ tablespoon chopped parsley

1. Heat the vegetable oil in a 6-quart casserole. Dust the veal cubes, a batch at a time, in the flour and brown them in the hot oil. Remove them to a plate and season with salt and pepper. Flour and brown the rest of the veal.

2. When all of the veal cubes have been browned, pour out the vegetable oil from the casserole, add the 3 tablespoons butter, and sauté the chopped onions for 3 minutes. Stir in the chopped garlic and cook for 1 minute, stirring. Pour in the wine and bring to the boil. Stir in the tomato purée or canned tomatoes, and add the herb bundle and chicken stock. Return the veal cubes. Bring the contents of the casserole to a boil.

3. Cover the casserole and cook at a simmer on the stove top or in the lower third of a preheated 325° F oven for 1¾ hours.

To Store With a slotted spoon, remove the veal cubes to a storage container. Boil the liquid down for 3–4 minutes or until lightly condensed. Discard the herb bundle and pour the reduced cooking liquid over the veal. Cool and refrigerate, covered, for up to 5 days or freeze for up to 1 month.

To Serve Reheat the veal in a covered casserole. Melt the 1½ tablespoons butter in a heavy skillet and sauté the mushroom caps until lightly browned. Season with salt and pepper, and sprinkle on the chopped tarragon. Add the mushrooms to the veal and simmer for a minute or so longer to finish cooking the mushrooms. Correct the seasoning, fold in the parsley, and serve.

Menu Suggestion Begin the meal with Cream of Carrot Soup (page 214).

SHOPPING LIST

Meat: boneless veal shoulder
Vegetables: onions, garlic, mushrooms
Dairy: butter

Staples: vegetable oil, flour, dry red wine, tomato purée or canned plum tomatoes, chicken stock
Herbs: fresh tarragon, parsley, bay leaf

CHICKEN WITH GREEN PEAS AND LETTUCE

This dish looks rather homespun, probably because when the lettuce is added to the cooked chicken on serving day, it melts down, softens, and intermingles with the peas, making everything look like a rough-hewn stew. That's the allure of this dish.

3 tablespoons vegetable oil

2¾–3-pound whole chicken, cut into 8 serving pieces

½ cup all-purpose flour, in a shallow bowl

salt and freshly ground pepper

3 tablespoons butter

⅓-pound piece of bacon, rind removed, cubed, simmered in water for 5 minutes, and drained

7 shallots, chopped

3 garlic cloves, chopped

¾ cup dry white wine

2 cups chicken stock

6 parsley stems tied with 2 sprigs of thyme and 1 small imported bay leaf

To Serve

4 tablespoons butter

1 onion, finely chopped

2 tablespoons chopped parsley

1 tablespoon snipped chives

2 heads Boston lettuce, trimmed and shredded

1½ pounds fresh young peas in the pods, shelled

1. Heat the vegetable oil in a 10-inch sauté pan. Lightly dredge a few pieces of chicken in the flour and brown in the hot oil. When browned, remove the pieces to a plate and season with salt and pepper. Dredge, brown, and season the rest of the chicken.

2. Pour out any vegetable oil that is left in the pan. Add the 3 tablespoons butter and, when it melts, stir in the bacon cubes. Sauté the cubes for a few minutes until a light golden color. Add the shallots and sauté for 3 minutes. Pour in the wine and bring to the boil, stirring. Pour in the chicken stock and add the browned chicken pieces. Drop in the herb bundle.

3. Bring the contents of the pan to a boil, cover, and simmer for 30 minutes, or until the chicken is tender. Turn the chicken over in the liquid at least one time while it cooks.

To Store   Discard the herb bundle and transfer the chicken to a storage container. Boil down the pan juices until they are lightly reduced and syrupy, skimming off the fat as well. Pour the liquid over the chicken, and cool all to room temperature. Store, covered, in the refrigerator for up to 2 days or freeze for up to 1 month.

To Serve   Reheat the chicken slowly in a covered casserole. Heat the 4 tablespoons butter in a nonmetallic saucepan. Stir in the chopped onions and cook until tender and translucent. Stir in the parsley, chives, lettuce, and peas. Season with salt and pepper. Pour on ⅓–½ cup of the chicken liquid, enough to moisten the contents of the saucepan. Bring the contents to a rapid simmer, cover, and simmer slowly until the peas are just tender—if they are very young and very fresh, this should take only a few minutes. Do not overcook.

Add the lettuce-pea stew to the chicken, baste all with a little of the pan liquid, and transfer to a warm platter for serving.

Menu Suggestion   For dessert, Gratin of Kiwi and Papaya (page 288).

✳ SOFT-SHELLED CRABS WITH VEGETABLES

This recipe contrasts diced vegetables with a very few anchovy fillets, shredded basil, and tomato. First you concentrate on doing the part of the recipe that uses these ingredients and then you brown the crabs before they mingle with the sauce for a final simmer.

Sometime, if you are feeling prodigal, make up a double quantity of the vegetable and white wine mixture in a deep casserole. Then cut up 4 live lobsters, about 1¼ pounds each, and sauté the pieces in a little oil and butter until the shells turn a bright red. Add the lobster pieces to the vegetables and simmer, covered, for about 13 minutes. Add the shredded romaine lettuce, simmer another 2 minutes, and serve in wide bowls with good bread.

For the Vegetable-Wine Mixture
2 tablespoons butter
1 tablespoon olive oil
1 onion, diced
2 garlic cloves, finely chopped
1 carrot, diced
2 ribs celery heart, diced
4 anchovy fillets, chopped
1 cup chopped canned plum tomatoes
1 teaspoon tomato paste
4 fresh basil leaves, shredded
½ cup dry white wine

1½ cups fish stock
salt and freshly ground pepper

For the Soft-Shelled Crabs

8 soft-shelled crabs
3 tablespoons butter
3 tablespoons vegetable oil
½ cup all-purpose flour, in a shallow bowl
6 tender romaine lettuce leaves, shredded
1 tablespoon finely chopped parsley

1. First prepare the vegetable base. Heat the 2 tablespoons butter and olive oil in a heavy pan large enough to hold all the crabs. Stir in the onion and garlic; stir and cook for

3 minutes. Stir in the carrot and celery. Sauté for 2 minutes. Stir in the anchovies, tomatoes, tomato paste, and basil. Simmer the tomato mixture for 5 minutes. Pour in the wine and bring to the boil. Pour in the fish stock and season with salt and pepper. Simmer, partially covered, for 15 minutes.

  2. Blot dry the soft-shelled crabs on paper toweling. Heat the 3 tablespoons butter and the vegetable oil in a skillet. Dredge the crabs, half at a time, in the flour and brown in the hot butter-oil. Dredge and brown the remaining crabs. Season the crabs with salt and pepper.

  3. Transfer the browned crabs to the vegetable mixture and baste over with some of the mixture. Simmer, covered, for 12 minutes, adding the lettuce after 6 minutes. Correct the seasoning.

  4. Put the crabs on a warm platter and spoon the sauce over and around them. Dust the top with chopped parsley.

Menu Suggestion   Follow the crabs with any of the strawberry desserts (refer to index).

SHOPPING LIST
Fish: soft-shelled crabs
Vegetables: onion, garlic, celery, carrot, romaine lettuce
Dairy: butter

Staples: olive oil, vegetable oil, anchovies, canned plum tomatoes, tomato paste, dry white wine, fish stock, flour
Herbs: fresh basil, parsley

❊FISH STEW WITH GARLIC SAUCE

The very rich palette of fish preparations should provoke adventure beyond simply broiling the fillets. It is appealing to take freshly caught fish, season them with fresh herbs, and grill them over a fire vivified with a few sprigs of fennel stalk and several branches of rosemary. You might even make a basting brush by joining together a few kinds of fresh herbs for glossing over the fish with oil as it cooks. This is an example of how carefully chosen attendants make the preparation shine. In this recipe, there's a little garlic in the fish base, which is thickened with potato, a natural binder. But the real energy of the dish comes from the last phase of cooking, when a generous amount of thick garlic mayonnaise is swirled into the cooking liquid. The mayonnaise is silky from fresh egg yolks and a good grade of olive oil.

For the Fish Base

3 tablespoons olive oil
1 onion, sliced
1 carrot, sliced
2 small ribs celery heart, sliced
2 garlic cloves, finely chopped
¾ cup dry white wine
¼ teaspoon saffron threads
2 small boiling potatoes, peeled and roughly sliced
2 cups fish stock
6 parsley stems tied with 2 sprigs of thyme and 1 imported bay leaf
salt and freshly ground pepper

For the Garlic Mayonnaise

7 garlic cloves, very finely chopped
3 egg yolks, at room temperature
1½ cups olive oil
juice of ½ lemon
1½ teaspoons prepared mustard of good quality
1–2 teaspoons boiling water

The Fish

2½ pounds fish fillets, skinned and boned, one or a combination of halibut, haddock, scrod, striped bass, cod, and the like, cut into large chunks
1 recipe Crisp Bread Slices (page 154)

1. First prepare the fish base by putting the 3 tablespoons olive oil in a heavy enameled saucepan. Stir in the onion, carrot, and celery slices; sauté for 3 minutes. Stir in the garlic and sauté for 1 minute. Pour in the wine and bring to the boil. Stir in the saffron, potatoes, fish stock, and herb bundle. Season with salt and pepper. Bring to the boil, then simmer, covered, for 20 minutes. After 20 minutes, discard the herb bundle and purée the base through a food mill. (If you would like to make this a day in advance, pour the base into a storage container and refrigerate covered.)

2. Prepare the garlic mayonnaise. Beat the chopped garlic with the egg yolks in a mixing bowl, using a hand-held electric beater. Beat in the olive oil by droplets until the mixture begins to emulsify; you will be adding about ½ cup in this way. Add the remaining oil in a very thin, steady stream, beating all the time. Beat in the lemon juice. Season with salt and pepper, and stir in the mustard. Add enough of the boiling water to thin the mayonnaise very slightly. Place a piece of plastic wrap directly over the surface of the mayonnaise. Use at room temperature.

3. In a wide casserole, simmer the fish base until hot. Add the fish pieces, cover, and cook at a very gentle simmer for 10 minutes or until the fish flakes tender and done. Do not overcook. To finish the sauce, remove the fillets and keep warm briefly. Put one-third of the garlic mayonnaise into a mixing bowl and stir in a few spoonfuls of the fish base. Off the heat, stir that back into the main saucepan. Correct the seasoning, add the fish, and transfer all to a deep platter. Serve each helping with a few crisp bread slices tucked in and extra garlic mayonnaise to be added in dollops by each individual.

(continued)

Menu Suggestion   As a salad or vegetable course, serve Vinaigrette of Zucchini (page 264).

SHOPPING LIST
Fish: fish fillets (choose among halibut, haddock, scrod, striped bass, cod)
Vegetables and fruit: onion, garlic, carrot, celery, boiling potatoes, lemon
Dairy: eggs

Staples: olive oil, dry white wine, fish stock, prepared mustard
Herbs and spices: parsley, thyme, bay leaf, saffron
For serving: Crisp Bread Slices (following recipe)

CRISP BREAD SLICES

⅓ loaf French bread or a similar plain, unsweetened crusty loaf, sliced
1 garlic clove, peeled and halved

4–5 tablespoons olive oil
cayenne pepper

1. Arrange the bread slices on a cookie sheet lined with aluminum foil. Rub both sides of the bread with the split garlic clove and brush each side with a light film of olive oil.

2. Sprinkle one side with a few grains of cayenne pepper.

3. Bake the slices on the middle level of a preheated 350° F oven until golden brown on both sides, turning the slices once. Alternately, brown both sides under a broiler.

SHOPPING LIST
Vegetable: garlic
Staples: French bread, olive oil

Spice: cayenne pepper

*CALVES' LIVER WITH WATERCRESS, MUSTARD, AND WALNUT SAUCE

In this preparation, you could use ½-inch slices of calves' liver in place of the thin slices, although my first choice is to do the liver in thin slices as opposed to the thicker steaks. As for the mustard, I like to use an aromatic mustard of some texture that contains the crushed seeds and earmarks the sauce in a tasty way.

6 tablespoons butter	3 tablespoons vegetable oil
1 bunch watercress, leaves only, finely chopped	½ cup all-purpose flour, in a shallow bowl
1½ tablespoons prepared mustard	salt and freshly ground pepper
¼ cup dry white wine	1 cup heavy cream
8 thin slices calves' liver	3 tablespoons chopped walnuts

1. Melt 2 tablespoons of the butter in a saucepan. Stir in the chopped watercress and cook for 2 minutes. Stir in the mustard; cook for 1 minute. Pour in the wine, raise the heat to high, and boil it down until it has reduced to a light glaze. Season the watercress with salt and pepper and set aside. Place the liver on paper toweling.

2. In a large heavy skillet, melt the remaining 4 tablespoons butter with the vegetable oil until the butter turns a light nut brown. Make sure that the liver slices are dry, then dredge them, 4 at a time, in the flour and cook them quickly, about a minute on each side, until brown on both sides in the hot butter-oil—they should be a juicy pink within. Season the slices with salt and pepper and keep them warm while you are cooking the rest of the liver.

3. Pour the cream into the watercress and simmer until thickened lightly, then stir in the chopped walnuts. Correct the seasoning.

4. Place the calves' liver on a warm platter and pour the sauce over and around the liver.

Menu Suggestion For dessert, Cantaloupe with Cassis, White Wine, and Honey (page 277).

SHOPPING LIST
Meat: calves' liver
Vegetable: watercress
Dairy: butter, heavy cream

Staples: prepared mustard, dry white wine, vegetable oil, flour, walnuts

5

THE SUMMER WEEKS

MAIN COURSES

Pot Roast Braised with Vegetables and Red Wine

Chicken with Roasted Peppers

* Shrimp with Mustard and Dill

* Summer Beef Salad with Vegetables

Veal Breast Stuffed with Zucchini and Ricotta Cheese

Lamb with Ripe Apricots and Cinnamon

* Crab, Clam, Halibut, and Bass Stew with Garlic
and Tomatoes

THE COOK'S PLAN

1. Set out: 6-quart casserole with lid for the Pot Roast Braised with Vegetables and Red Wine, 6-quart casserole with lid for the Lamb with Ripe Apricots and Cinnamon, 12-inch casserole with lid for the Veal Breast Stuffed with Zucchini and Ricotta Cheese, 10-inch sauté pan for the Chicken with Roasted Peppers.

2. Thaw and measure out 5¼ cups beef stock, 3¾ cups chicken stock.

3. Wash and dry a small bunch parsley, 3 ribs celery heart.

4. Peel 6 garlic cloves, 5 onions, 5 carrots.

5. Finely chop 1 garlic clove, 2 onions, 2 tablespoons parsley; chop 2 onions, 2 teaspoons fresh basil; slice 2 onions, 3 carrots, 3 ribs celery heart; shred 2 small zucchini; cube 2 carrots; mince 2 garlic cloves.

6. Measure out 2 cups dry red wine, 2¾ cups dry white wine, 1 tablespoon tomato paste, 4 allspice berries, 2 cloves, 1 cup ricotta cheese, ½ cup finely grated Gruyère cheese.

7. Set out oils, butter, salt, pepper, flour.

8. Tie 2 herb bundles, each containing 6 parsley stems and 1 bay leaf.

9. Pot Roast Braised with Vegetables and Red Wine: Brown the rump pot roast; simmer it with the vegetables and liquid, Steps 1–3 (page 160).

10. Veal Breast Stuffed with Zucchini and Ricotta Cheese: Prepare the zucchini and ricotta cheese stuffing; stuff and sew up the veal breast; simmer in the aromatic vegetables, liquid, and seasonings, Steps 1–4 (page 161).

11. Lamb with Ripe Apricots and Cinnamon: Brown the floured lamb cubes in the oil; season; simmer with the onions, carrots, spices, wine, and beef stock, Steps 1–4 (page 163).

12. Chicken with Roasted Peppers: Simmer the browned chicken pieces with the onion, garlic, parsley, tomato paste, and liquid, Steps 1–3 (page 165).

13. Cool all dishes to room temperature; refrigerate or freeze, following the instructions in "To Store" of each recipe.

POT ROAST BRAISED WITH VEGETABLES
AND RED WINE

This pot roast is cooked slowly with the usual aromatic vegetables in red wine and stock. One virtue of the dish is that the meat is just as delicious freshly braised as it is cubed in one of those perfectly orchestrated summer salads. You will use the extra braised meat in Summer Beef Salad with Vegetables (p. 167).

A rump pot roast, securely tied, would be my first choice for this dish. You could even marinate the meat in 2 cups of red wine, a bay leaf, several parsley stems (also a sprig of fresh thyme is nice here if you have it), a crushed garlic clove, and a few peppercorns. Strain this marinade and use it for the amount of red wine, adding a little extra wine if needed.

3 tablespoons vegetable oil	2 ribs celery heart, sliced
4-pound piece of rump pot roast, tied to hold its shape	2 garlic cloves, peeled and halved
salt and freshly ground pepper	6 parsley stems tied with 1 small imported bay leaf
1 onion, sliced	2 cups dry red wine
2 carrots, sliced	2½ cups beef stock

1. Heat the vegetable oil in a heavy 6-quart casserole. Pat the piece of meat dry with paper toweling. Brown the meat in the hot oil, then remove it to a large plate and season with salt and pepper.

2. In the remaining oil (heat a tablespoon or two more if a good part of the oil has been used up), sauté the sliced onion for 2 minutes. Stir in the carrot and celery slices; sauté for 2 minutes.

3. Add the garlic cloves and herb bundle. Pour in the red wine and bring to the boil, stirring. Pour in the beef stock and add the browned piece of meat. Bring to a boil, then cover and cook in the lower third of a preheated 325° F oven for 3 hours or until very tender.

To Serve   If the meat is prepared on the main cooking day, time this preparation to coincide with the dinner hour, adjusting your working schedule around the amount of time it takes to cook the meat as well as taking into account the other dishes you are preparing. Keep the meat warm while you reduce the cooking liquid over high heat until glazed-looking and full of body.

Put the sauce through a food mill to purée it, discarding the herb bundle. Adjust the seasoning. Cut part of the meat into slices, and moisten with some of the condensed pan sauce. Reserve the remaining unsliced meat to use in Summer Beef Salad with Vegetables (p. 167), later on in the week.

To Store Wrap the remaining unsliced piece of meat in plastic wrap and aluminum foil; place in an airtight container and refrigerate for up to 4 days.

Menu Suggestion Accompany the pot roast with Warm Potato Salad with Oregano and Red Onion (page 249); for dessert, Prune Plums Stewed in White Wine (page 306).

SHOPPING LIST

Meat: rump pot roast
Vegetables and fruit: onion, carrots, celery, garlic

Staples: vegetable oil, dry red wine, beef stock
Herbs: parsley, bay leaf

VEAL BREAST STUFFED WITH ZUCCHINI AND RICOTTA CHEESE

This is one of the two stuffed veal breast recipes that appear in the summer section. By my own design for summer fare, I think that this kind of dish—slices of veal containing ground veal, vegetables, and cheese—is a very appealing, even elegant, way to dine during the hot and hazy days of summer. The veal breast is very easy to slice once it has been refrigerated because then the filling and the surrounding meat have had a chance to set. Small cubes of eggplant, lightly sautéed until just tender, could replace the shredded zucchini. Then I would add 4 tablespoons of chopped tomatoes and 2 small basil leaves torn into tiny pieces.

The Stuffing

3 tablespoons butter
1 onion, chopped
1 garlic clove, finely chopped
2 small zucchini, scrubbed and shredded
½ pound ground veal
2 teaspoons chopped fresh basil
several grindings of nutmeg
1 cup ricotta cheese
½ cup finely grated Gruyère cheese
1 egg, beaten lightly
salt and freshly ground pepper

The Veal Breast

2 tablespoons vegetable oil
1 3-pound boneless veal breast, with a pocket cut for stuffing
2½ tablespoons olive oil
1 onion, sliced
1 carrot, sliced
1 rib celery heart, sliced
6 parsley stems tied with 1 small imported bay leaf
1 cup dry white wine
2 cups chicken stock

1. To prepare the stuffing, melt the butter in a skillet and cook the chopped onion and garlic until soft and translucent. Add the zucchini shreds; stir and cook for 3 minutes. Remove from the heat and cool slightly.

2. In a large mixing bowl, combine the ground veal, basil, nutmeg, ricotta, Gruyère, egg, and salt and pepper to taste. Blend in the onion-zucchini mixture. Fill the pocket of the veal breast evenly with the stuffing and sew up the opening with a sturdy needle threaded with heavy-duty kitchen string.

3. Heat the vegetable oil in a 12-inch casserole. Brown the veal breast on both sides in the hot oil. Remove the breast to a side plate and season with salt and pepper. Pour out the vegetable oil, add the olive oil, and sauté the onion for 2 minutes. Stir in the sliced celery and carrot; sauté for 2 minutes.

4. Add the parsley bundle and wine. Bring the wine to a boil, pour in the chicken stock, and add the prepared veal breast. Bring the contents of the casserole to a boil, cover, and simmer for 2 hours on the stove top or in the lower third of a preheated 325° F oven. Baste the veal breast a few times during cooking, or carefully turn it over two or three times.

To Store   When the veal is tender, let it cool in the cooking liquid, then wrap it in plastic wrap and heavy-duty aluminum foil. Refrigerate in a covered container for up to 5 days. Discard the cooking liquid.

To Serve   Remove the trussing strings and cut the breast into long thin slices. Serve an herb mayonnaise or the following vegetable sauce on the side.

TOMATO-CUCUMBER-BASIL SAUCE

4 large ripe tomatoes, peeled, quartered, seeded, and cut into cubes

½ small "European" cucumber, cut into small cubes

1 small hot pepper, halved, cored, seeded, and finely chopped

1 small garlic clove, chopped

4 basil leaves, shredded

red wine vinegar

olive oil

salt

1. In a nonmetallic mixing bowl, combine the cubed tomatoes, cucumbers, hot pepper, garlic, and basil leaves.

2. Add the vinegar and olive oil in parts of about 1½ tablespoons vinegar to 5 tablespoons olive oil, to moisten the vegetables well. Season with salt.

3. Before serving, taste the sauce for salt and adjust the balance of oil and vinegar, if needed. Make this sauce the very evening that the veal is to be served.

Menu Suggestion   Begin with Crookneck Squash Soup with Chervil (page 219) and finish with Nectarines Steeped in Sweet Wine with Honey (page 293).

Shopping List

MAIN COURSE

Meat: ground veal, boneless veal breast
Vegetables: onions, zucchini, carrot, celery, garlic
Dairy: butter, ricotta cheese, Gruyère cheese, egg
Staples: vegetable oil, olive oil, dry white wine, chicken stock
Herbs and spice: fresh basil, parsley, bay leaf, ground nutmeg

SAUCE

Vegetables: tomatoes, cucumber, garlic
Staples: red wine vinegar, olive oil
Herb and spice: fresh basil, hot pepper

LAMB WITH RIPE APRICOTS AND CINNAMON

Part of the glory of summer fruit takes place in the simple patterns of all the luscious, satisfying baked desserts, covered with shortcake or nuts, sugar and butter. If the shape of your menu and market presents an opportune time for gathering some soft and yielding sweet and ripe apricots, I encourage you to use them in this recipe with lamb. The apricots are added on serving day when they are cooked until just tender before being added for a final communal simmering with the lamb and a few raisins.

3½ tablespoons vegetable oil
2¾ pounds boneless lamb shoulder, cut into 2-inch pieces
½ cup all-purpose flour, in a shallow bowl
salt and freshly ground pepper
1 cup dry white wine
3 tablespoons butter
2 small onions, finely chopped
2 carrots, cut into small cubes
1 cinnamon stick
4 whole allspice berries

2 whole cloves
⅛ teaspoon freshly ground nutmeg
1 small imported bay leaf
2¾ cups beef stock

To Serve

2 tablespoons dark raisins
2 tablespoons butter
8 small apricots, halved and pitted
½ cup water
1 tablespoon finely chopped parsley
1 tablespoon sesame seeds

1. Heat the vegetable oil in a heavy 6-quart casserole. As they are to be browned, lightly dust the lamb cubes in the flour and brown them in the hot oil. Remove the browned cubes to a bowl and season with salt and pepper.

2. When all of the lamb has been browned, pour out all of the oil and pour in the

wine, stirring, and allow it to boil up in the pan for a few seconds. Pour the wine into the bowl containing the lamb. Wipe out the casserole.

3. Melt the 3 tablespoons butter in the casserole and sauté the chopped onion for 2 minutes. Stir in the carrots and sauté for 2 minutes. Stir in the cinnamon stick, allspice berries, cloves, and ground nutmeg. Sauté the spices until they darken somewhat, about 3 minutes. Add the bay leaf, the meat with wine, and the beef stock.

4. Bring the contents of the casserole to a boil, then cover and simmer on the stove top or cook in the lower third of a preheated 325° F oven for 2 hours or until the lamb is tender, but not falling apart.

To Store Remove the meat with a slotted spoon to a storage container. Pick out and discard the allspice berries, cloves, and bay leaf. Defat the liquid and boil it down until it has reduced to the lightly thickened stage. Pour this over the meat, and when everything is completely cool, cover the container and refrigerate for up to 5 days or freeze for up to 1 month.

To Serve Slowly reheat the lamb in a covered casserole. After 10 minutes, add the raisins. Melt the butter in a skillet and add the apricots. Turn the apricots in the butter, but keep them flat side down. Pour in the water and bring to a simmer. Cover and simmer the fruit slowly until tender but not mushy, about 15 minutes. When the lamb is hot, remove and discard the cinnamon stick and carefully fold in the apricots. Simmer for a few minutes, uncovered, then fold in the chopped parsley. Turn the lamb onto a warm serving dish and sprinkle it with the sesame seeds.

Menu Suggestion Follow the lamb with Watercress Salad with Lemon Vinaigrette (page 261).

Shopping List

Meat: boneless lamb shoulder

Vegetables and fruit: onions, carrots, apricots

Dairy: butter

Staples: vegetable oil, dry white wine, flour, beef stock, dark raisins, sesame seeds

Herbs and spices: parsley, bay leaf, cinnamon stick, allspice berries, whole cloves, ground nutmeg

CHICKEN WITH ROASTED PEPPERS

The roasted peppers give the chicken a taste which is more full-bodied than if the peppers were, for instance, cut into strips, sautéed separately, then added to the chicken. Sometimes I roast the peppers over charcoal, which produces the tastiest of all results. It is very easy to do if I have the grill going for another one of my favorite summertime dinners, fish grilled with branches of fennel.

3 tablespoons vegetable oil
1 tablespoon butter
2¾–3-pound whole chicken, cut into 8
  serving pieces
salt and freshly ground pepper
3 tablespoons olive oil
1 onion, chopped
3 garlic cloves, minced
2 tablespoons finely chopped parsley

1 tablespoon tomato paste
1 small imported bay leaf
¾ cup dry white wine
1¾ cups chicken stock

To Serve

3 sweet red peppers
2 teaspoons red wine vinegar

1. Heat the vegetable oil and butter in a 10-inch sauté pan and brown the chicken pieces, a few at a time. Remove the pieces as they are browned to a plate and season with salt and pepper.

2. Pour away the vegetable oil and butter and pour in the olive oil. Sauté the onion in the oil for 3 minutes. Stir in the minced garlic, parsley, and tomato paste. Add the bay leaf and wine. Raise the heat and bring the wine to a boil, stirring as you do so. Pour in the chicken stock and put in the browned chicken,

3. Bring the contents of the sauté pan to a simmer, cover, and cook the chicken at a simmer for 30 minutes. Turn the chicken pieces once as they cook.

To Store   Transfer the chicken to a storage container. Boil down the cooking liquid for 3–4 minutes, until it has reduced by a third. Pour the liquid over the chicken. Cool to room temperature, then refrigerate covered for up to 2 days or freeze for up to 2 weeks.

To Serve   Roast the red peppers under a preheated hot broiler until charred on all sides. Wrap up the peppers in a large sheet of aluminum foil or put them into a clean heavy brown bag so that the steam they emit can loosen the skin from the flesh. When they have cooled down, skin, core, seed, and cut them into large squares or strips.

As the peppers cool, reheat the chicken in a covered casserole. When the peppers are ready, add them to the casserole along with the vinegar and heat everything together to blend the different tastes. Adjust the seasoning, adding more salt and pepper to taste, and serve the chicken from a warm platter.

Menu Suggestion As a first course or vegetable course, Baked Zucchini and Tomatoes (page 244); for dessert, any of the fruit compotes.

<small>Shopping List</small>
Poultry: chicken
Vegetables: onion, garlic, sweet red peppers
Dairy: butter

Staples: vegetable oil, olive oil, tomato paste, dry white wine, chicken stock, red wine vinegar
Herbs: parsley, bay leaf

❋ SHRIMP WITH MUSTARD AND DILL

When you combine the mustard, dill, and lemon juice part of this dish, taste it carefully for that perfect balance of sweet and sharp. Depending on the strength of your mustard and lemon juice, more or less sugar will be needed. Once the shrimp are peeled and deveined (leave the tails on—they lend an attractive touch to the presentation), all else goes quite fast. Sturdy, whole-grain black bread and mulled cucumbers are good partners for the shrimp.

3 tablespoons prepared mustard
3 tablespoons lemon juice
1 teaspoon white wine vinegar
2 teaspoons superfine sugar
4 tablespoons minced fresh dill
2 teaspoons finely chopped parsley

4 tablespoons olive oil
1¼ pounds shrimp, shelled, with the tails left on, and deveined
⅓ cup dry white wine
salt and freshly ground pepper
lemon wedges

1. In a small bowl, stir together the mustard, lemon juice, vinegar, sugar, dill, and parsley. Stir to dissolve the sugar. Taste for extra seasoning.

2. Heat the olive oil in a skillet large enough to accommodate all of the shrimp. Stir in the shrimp and sauté for 1 minute. Pour on the wine and let it bubble up around the shrimp, reducing the wine down to half the original amount.

3. Stir in the mustard and dill mixture, stir and cook the shrimp until they turn opaque; do not overcook. Check the seasoning and serve the shrimp very hot from a warm platter. Extra lemon wedges can be offered here.

Menu Suggestion   For dessert, Fresh Apricot Compote with Vanilla and Cinnamon (page 272).

✳ SUMMER BEEF SALAD WITH VEGETABLES

With a piece of braised pot roast, cut into thin strips or ample chunks, you can make a thoroughly satisfying main-course salad. The amounts for this kind of salad are relative to what's available and looks good. If you have less meat, add more vegetables. I am suggesting a mixture of cooked and raw vegetables, dressed with oil and vinegar, boosted with basil and parsley, tarragon if you have it. I have also had such a salad bound with a very light mayonnaise, which is a handy option, but then you should be careful to choose vegetables that blend well with the mayonnaise.

1 pound, more or less, cold cooked beef (if you like, from the Pot Roast Braised with Vegetables and Red Wine, page 160), cut into cubes or narrow strips
3 tablespoons red wine vinegar
1 teaspoon prepared mustard
9 tablespoons olive oil
freshly ground pepper
6 basil leaves, shredded
2 tablespoons finely chopped parsley
2 teaspoons chopped fresh tarragon (optional)
salt

Vegetable Ideas—Choose Among Them:

½ recipe Warm Potato Salad with Oregano and Red Onion (page 249)
5 cooked beets, cubed
½ pound green beans, cooked until tender
3 ripe tomatoes, peeled, cut into wedges, and seeded
½ recipe Pepper Strips with Garlic (page 242)
1 cup freshly cooked cranberry beans
1 bunch watercress, trimmed

1. Make sure the beef cubes or strips are well trimmed of all the fat, and set them aside.

2. Whisk the vinegar with the mustard. Blend in the olive oil, a tablespoon at a time. Season with pepper. Stir in the herbs and season to taste with salt.

(continued)

3. Of the vegetables you are using, which should be finished and ready at hand, combine them with a little of the vinaigrette dressing. Do this for all of them except the potato salad and the pepper strips—they have their own seasoning. Season the vegetables with salt and pepper as needed. Moisten the beef with some of the dressing, and season lightly with salt and pepper.

4. Ring a platter or line a bowl with the watercress. Combine the vegetables and meat and heap them on the watercress. The potato salad and pepper strips should be arranged separately. Pour any remaining dressing over the meat, to moisten as necessary.

Menu Suggestion Salad of Lentils with Basil (page 259) can replace one of the choices above or be added to it; finish with fresh raspberries and heavy cream.

SHOPPING LIST
Meat: cold cooked beef (see recipe)
Vegetables: your choice from the ingredients list

Staples: red wine vinegar, prepared mustard, olive oil
Herbs: fresh basil, parsley, tarragon (optional)

⁎ CRAB, CLAM, HALIBUT, AND BASS STEW WITH GARLIC AND TOMATOES

I am intrigued by the idea of using crabmeat in a stewlike arrangement of fish and shellfish. Luckily, I can buy masses of hard-shelled crabs in the summertime, found close at hand to Washington, D.C., at adjacent Maryland bays and shores. The extra-large and jumbo sizes are always succulent and full of big, fat pieces of crabmeat. And if I am not cracking crab claws and dividing the rest of the crab into chunks for some kind of wonderful crab soup, or if I am not steaming them whole with spices, I would be sinking the meat of the crab into this garlicky tomato base.

I have also used this cooking base, which boasts lots of very ripe chopped tomatoes, with shellfish alone: a couple of lobsters, the crabs, clams, and mussels. It's a very pretty sight, the gray-white clam shells and jet-black mussels and the red of the lobsters. For this you will need a big platter and a good, friendly, free-form group of eaters who like to dig into the goods, shells and all.

4 tablespoons olive oil	1½ cups fish stock
1 onion, chopped	salt and freshly ground pepper
8 garlic cloves, chopped	3 dozen clams, well scrubbed
4 tablespoons finely chopped parsley	1 pound halibut steak, skinned, boned,
8 large ripe tomatoes, peeled, seeded,	and cut into large chunks
and roughly chopped	1 pound bass (boned weight), skinned
1 small hot pepper, cored, seeded, and	and cut into large chunks
chopped	¾ pound lump crabmeat
½ cup dry white wine	8 green olives, pitted and chopped

Heat the olive oil in a large, heavy casserole (an 8-quart one is ideal if you are preparing the base of this recipe in advance; otherwise, a large, heavy nonmetallic saucepan will do). Stir in the chopped onion and cook until soft and translucent. Stir in the chopped garlic and sauté for 2 minutes. Add 3 tablespoons chopped parsley, the chopped tomatoes, juices and all, hot pepper, and wine. Bring to the boil; boil for 1 minute. Pour in the fish stock and season the mixture lightly with pepper, then add salt to taste. Bring to the boil and simmer, partially covered, for 25 minutes.

To Store   You may prepare this base a day in advance. Cool completely, and refrigerate in a covered container for 1 day.

To Serve   To complete the stew, heat up the fish base in the large casserole. Add the clams and cook them until they have opened partially. Add the halibut and bass chunks along with the crabmeat and olives. Simmer until the chunks are cooked through and the clams are fully opened, about 5 minutes. Correct the seasoning. Serve the stew from a deep platter. Dust the remaining tablespoon of chopped parsley on top and serve.

Menu Suggestion   Follow the stew with Bibb Lettuce Salad (page 257); for dessert, Blackberries in Nut-Lace Crisp (page 274), or exchange pitted cherries for the blackberries and bake just as you would the blackberry dessert.

SHOPPING LIST
Fish and shellfish: clams, crabmeat, halibut steak, bass
Vegetables: tomatoes, onion, garlic, hot pepper

Staples: olive oil, dry white wine, fish stock, green olives
Herb: parsley

MAIN COURSES

* Scallop Salad with Feta Cheese and Garden Vegetables

Sweetbreads with Summer Herbs

Chicken with Chickpeas

* Red Snapper Fillets with Fresh Tomato Sauce

Terrine of Chicken Livers, Veal, and Tongue

Pork with Summer Tomatoes

* Lump Crabmeat with Nova Scotia Salmon

THE COOK'S PLAN

1. Set out: 6-cup ovenproof terrine, with a lid, for the Terrine of Chicken Livers, Veal, and Tongue, 4-quart casserole with lid for the Sweetbreads with Summer Herbs, 6-quart casserole with lid for the Pork with Summer Tomatoes, 10-inch sauté pan for the Chicken with Chickpeas.

2. Thaw and measure out 5¼ cups chicken stock.

3. Peel 6 garlic cloves, 4 onions, 2 carrots, 7 tomatoes.

4. Chop 3 onions, 6 garlic cloves, 1 tablespoon thyme leaves, 2 teaspoons fresh rosemary, 1 tablespoon fresh oregano, 3 tomatoes; slice 1 onion, 2 carrots; dice ¼ pound salt pork; cube 4 tomatoes.

5. Measure out 2¾ cups dry white wine, ½ teaspoon ground allspice.

6. Set out olive oil, vegetable oil, butter, salt, pepper, flour.

7. Trim sweetbreads; soak, Step 1 (page 172).

8. Terrine of Chicken Livers, Veal, and Tongue: Put together the terrine; bake, Steps 1–5 (page 173).

9. Pork with Summer Tomatoes: Brown the pork cubes; season; simmer with the onions, garlic, herbs, tomatoes, and liquid, Steps 1–3 (page 175).

10. Sweetbreads with Summer Herbs: Simmer the sweetbreads with onion, carrot, white wine, and seasonings, Step 2 (page 172).

11. Chicken with Chickpeas: Brown the floured chicken; season; simmer with the onion, garlic, tomato, herbs, wine, and stock, Steps 1–2 (page 176).

12. Cool all dishes to room temperature; refrigerate or freeze, following the instructions in "To Store" of each recipe.

SWEETBREADS WITH SUMMER HERBS

Sweetbreads are lovely when completed with a collection of chopped fresh herbs (that grow very well in the summer) and a little *crème fraîche*. The sweetbreads are handled exactly as they are done in the autumn section of this book: washed, trimmed, soaked, and braised. This is the prelude to storing until the herbs and cream are added to the reduced cooking liquid. For some occasions the sweetbreads make a beautiful first course, in smaller amounts, appropriate for a multicourse dinner.

2½ pounds sweetbreads
2 tablespoons butter
1 onion, sliced
2 small carrots, sliced
½ cup dry white wine
1¾ cups chicken stock
1 small imported bay leaf
salt and freshly ground pepper

To Serve

4 tablespoons Madeira
½ cup *crème fraîche*
¼ cup light cream
2 teaspoons chopped fresh tarragon
2 teaspoons chopped fresh chervil
1 tablespoon finely chopped parsley

1. Prepare the sweetbreads according to the directions in Steps 1 and 2 of the recipe Sweetbreads with Spinach (page 16), washing, trimming, soaking, and so on as directed.

2. Melt the butter in a 4-quart casserole. Stew the sliced onion and carrots in the butter until soft. Pour in the wine and bring to the boil. Pour in the chicken stock and add the bay leaf. Season with salt and pepper. Put in the sweetbreads. Bring the contents of the casserole to a gentle simmer, cover, and simmer for 40 minutes.

To Store Let the sweetbreads cool in the cooking liquid, then put them in a storage container, picking off the vegetables. Boil the cooking liquid until it has reduced by half. Discard the bay leaf and purée the liquid and vegetables through a food mill. Pour the puréed mixture into a storage container, cool completely, cover, and refrigerate for 1 day. Refrigerate the sweetbreads, also well covered, for 1 day.

To Serve Cut the sweetbreads into large chunks. Put the Madeira into a skillet and cook it down rapidly until reduced by half. Add the puréed mixture and the sweetbreads and cook until the sweetbreads are hot.

In the meantime, place the *crème fraîche* and light cream into a mixing bowl and blend the two together. Stir a few spoonfuls of the sweetbread cooking liquid into the cream mixture, then stir the mixture back into the sweetbreads. Cook until the cream is hot. Blend in the fresh herbs. Correct the seasoning and serve very hot.

Menu Suggestion Accompany the sweetbreads with Spinach Gratin with Nutmeg (page 243), and finish with Fresh Apricot Compote with Vanilla and Cinnamon (page 272).

Meat: sweetbreads
Vegetables: onion, carrots
Dairy: butter, *crème fraîche,* light cream

Staples: dry white wine, chicken stock, Madeira
Herbs: bay leaf, fresh tarragon, fresh chervil, parsley

TERRINE OF CHICKEN LIVERS, VEAL, AND TONGUE

Here is one of the more layered terrines: there are lots of different goods, the veal, pork, dark chicken meat, chicken livers, salt pork, and some sliced tongue. The recipe certainly makes more than four servings, but you can pack up slices of this terrine to take for lunch. Or, cut the terrine into slices, then into squares or strips, and make a fancy salad arrangement with some freshly cooked vegetables—this is an absolutely fabulous way to use the last parts of the terrine.

½ pound sheets of pork fat, for lining the terrine
3 tablespoons vegetable oil
1 onion, chopped
2 garlic cloves, chopped
8 chicken livers, trimmed
½ cup Madeira
¾ pound ground veal
6 ounces ground pork
¾ pound dark meat of chicken, finely diced
¼ pound salt pork, diced

½ pound ground pork fat
2 eggs
2½ teaspoons coarse salt
freshly ground pepper, to taste, or ¼ teaspoon cracked peppercorns and only a few grinds of pepper
1 tablespoon fresh thyme leaves, chopped, or ½ teaspoon dried thyme
¼ teaspoon ground allspice
¼ pound sliced tongue, cut into strips
1 imported bay leaf

1. Line the bottom of a 6-cup ovenproof terrine with a few slices of the pork fat. Set aside.

2. Heat the oil in a skillet and sauté the chopped onion and garlic until the onion has softened. Raise the heat to medium-high and add the chicken livers. Sauté them quickly until they just lose their pink color, then remove the onions, garlic, and liver to a plate. Pour in the Madeira and bring to the boil. Boil for 1 minute and set aside.

3. In a large mixing bowl, put the ground veal, ground pork, diced chicken, diced salt

pork, and ground pork fat. Blend in the eggs, one at a time, then add salt, pepper (and peppercorns), and allspice. Stir in the onion-garlic (not the livers) and Madeira.

4. Pack one-third of the meat mixture on the bottom of the terrine. Lay on half the chicken livers and tongue strips. Pack on another third of the meat mixture, then layer in the remaining tongue and liver. Finish with a top layer of the last of the meat mixture. Press a bay leaf on top and cover the top with enough sheets of pork fat to envelop the meat. Trim off any scraps of fat that extend over the surface.

5. Cover the top of the terrine with a sheet of aluminum foil, then with the lid. Set the terrine in a baking pan filled with warm water (the warm water should reach halfway up the sides of the terrine) and set the whole unit in a preheated 350° F oven for 2 hours.

6. Remove the terrine from the oven, pour out the water from the pan, and return the terrine to the pan. Remove the lid and weigh down the top of the terrine with a brick (covered) or a board and a few canned goods.

To Store   After 2 hours, clean off the outside of the terrine and replace the foil with a double thickness of plastic wrap, followed by a fresh sheet of foil. Refrigerate the terrine, weighted, overnight. Remove the weights, make sure that the terrine is tightly covered, and refrigerate up to 1 week.

To Serve   Remove the top slices of pork fat from the terrine before serving in slices directly from the casserole.

Menu Suggestion   With the terrine, serve Warm Potato Salad with Savory (page 249) for an unusual contrast; for dessert, Double-Rich Peach Ice Cream (page 296).

SHOPPING LIST
Meat: pork fat sheets, ground pork fat, ground veal, ground pork, dark-meat chicken, salt pork, sliced tongue, chicken livers
Vegetables: onion, garlic

Dairy: eggs
Staple: vegetable oil
Herbs and spice: bay leaf, fresh thyme, ground all-spice

PORK WITH SUMMER TOMATOES

In this recipe, boneless pork shoulder is cooked slowly with chopped onions and garlic, with fresh basil and tomatoes, plus chicken stock. Tomatoes appear twice in this recipe, once while the pork braises and again folded into the pork along with the chopped parsley. This dish should be approached when tomatoes are at their home-grown ripest, for mealy gassed tomatoes would certainly lower the caliber of the dish.

3½ tablespoons vegetable oil
2¾ pounds boneless pork shoulder, cut
    into 1½–2-inch cubes
salt and freshly ground pepper
1¼ cups dry white wine
2 onions, chopped
2 garlic cloves, chopped
2 teaspoons chopped fresh rosemary or
    ½ teaspoon dried rosemary crumbled
    between the fingertips
4 leaves fresh basil, torn into small pieces

3 tomatoes, peeled, seeded, and roughly
    chopped
2 cups chicken stock
1 small imported bay leaf

To Serve

1½ tablespoons butter
2 tomatoes, peeled, seeded, and cut into
    narrow wedges
1 tablespoon finely chopped parsley

1. Heat the vegetable oil in a heavy 6-quart casserole and brown the pork cubes, a batch at a time. Remove them to a bowl as they are browned and season with salt and pepper.

2. When all the pork has been browned, pour out the oil into a small dish, reserving it for later use. Pour in the wine and bring to a boil, stirring the bottom of the casserole. Pour the wine over the pork cubes. Wipe out the casserole and add the oil plus a little extra to make 4 tablespoons.

3. Sauté the chopped onions in the oil for 2 minutes. Stir in the chopped garlic, rosemary, and basil. Stir and cook for 1 minute. Add the chopped tomatoes and cook over moderate heat for 1 minute. Pour in the chicken stock and add the bay leaf. Return the pork to the casserole, along with the wine. Bring the contents of the casserole to a simmer, then cook in the lower third of a preheated 325° F oven or simmer the pork on the stove top for 2 hours.

To Store   When the pork is tender, remove it to a storage container with a slotted spoon. Defat the cooking liquid, then boil it down until it is lightly condensed. Discard the bay leaf. Pour the cooking liquid over the pork, cool completely, cover, and refrigerate for up to 5 days or freeze for up to 1 month.

To Serve   Reheat the pork in a covered casserole. Melt the butter in a skillet and sauté the tomato wedges for 2 minutes. Stir in the parsley and season with salt and pepper. When the pork is hot, fold in the tomato-parsley mixture. Correct the seasoning. Allow the pork to simmer with the tomatoes for a minute or two longer. Serve very hot.

Menu Suggestion   Serve rice with this pork dish to catch all the savory juices; follow with Peach Slices Baked with Walnuts and Spices (page 297).

SHOPPING LIST
Meat: boneless pork shoulder
Vegetables: onions, garlic, tomatoes
Dairy: butter

Staples: vegetable oil, dry white wine, chicken stock
Herbs: rosemary, fresh basil, bay leaf, parsley

CHICKEN WITH CHICKPEAS

This is a chicken dish that combines some large juicy ripe tomatoes with chopped oregano and small pieces of fresh basil. On serving day, a teaspoonful of capers and some cooked chickpeas finish off the preparation. It is a very nice combination as the tomato cubes mingle with the herbs and garlic, and the chickpeas follow through with a firmness and texture that play well against the chicken. It is an excellent dish to do when ripe tomatoes inundate market stands.

3½ tablespoons vegetable oil
2¾–3-pound whole chicken, cut into 8 serving pieces
½ cup all-purpose flour, in a shallow bowl
salt and freshly ground pepper
2½ tablespoons olive oil
1 onion, chopped
2 garlic cloves, chopped
4 ripe tomatoes, peeled, seeded, and cubed
1 tablespoon fresh oregano leaves, chopped, or ½ teaspoon dried oregano crumbled between the fingertips
4 leaves fresh basil, torn into small pieces
1 cup dry white wine
1½ cups chicken stock
1 small imported bay leaf

To Serve

1 cup cooked chickpeas
1 teaspoon capers
1 tablespoon finely chopped parsley

1. Heat the vegetable oil in a 10-inch sauté pan. Dust the chicken pieces, a few at a time, in the flour and brown them in the hot oil. As they are browned, transfer them to a plate and season well with salt and pepper.

2. When all of the chicken has been browned, pour out the vegetable oil and add the olive oil. Sauté the onion in the oil for 3 minutes. Stir in the chopped garlic, tomatoes, and oregano. Stir and cook for 1 minute. Add the basil and pour in the wine. Bring to a boil. Pour in the chicken stock and add the bay leaf. Put back the browned chicken and baste once or twice with the liquid as you bring it to a boil. Cover the pan and simmer the chicken for 30 minutes or until it is tender.

To Store Put the cooked chicken into a storage container. Discard the bay leaf. Boil the vegetable liquid until it is reduced and syrupy, pour that over the chicken, and when all is cool, cover tightly and refrigerate for up to 2 days or freeze for up to 2 weeks.

To Serve Reheat the chicken in a covered casserole. After 10 minutes, add the chickpeas and capers, and continue simmering until all the components are hot. Fold in the chopped parsley and serve from a heated platter.

Menu Suggestion As a first course or vegetable course, serve Eggplant with Fennel and Onions (page 234); for dessert, any of the baked fruit desserts.

SHOPPING LIST
Poultry: chicken
Vegetables: onion, garlic, tomatoes
Staples: vegetable oil, olive oil, flour, dry white wine,

chicken stock, chickpeas, capers
Herbs: oregano, fresh basil, bay leaf, parsley

✳ SCALLOP SALAD WITH FETA CHEESE AND GARDEN VEGETABLES

This is a good salad for one of those sun-drenched days when a room-temperature main course is so much appreciated. Here you can have your scallops cool instead of steaming hot from the skillet. Adorning the salad are pieces of feta cheese, with its own measure of saltiness, and vegetables of good quality, which we can especially rely on in the warm months to lend a flavorsome crunch.

¼ cup dry white wine
2 cups water
1 slice of onion
1 small imported bay leaf
6 peppercorns
1 pound scallops, preferably bay scallops
2½ tablespoons lemon juice
1 teaspoon prepared mustard
6½ tablespoons olive oil
1 tablespoon chopped fresh oregano or ½ teaspoon crumbled dried oregano leaves
1 tablespoon finely chopped parsley
⅓-pound piece feta cheese, soaked in cold water for 10 minutes, drained well, and crumbled

salt and freshly ground pepper
3 juicy ripe tomatoes, peeled, cut into wedges, and seeded
½ "European" cucumber, cut into sticks or cubed
1 red onion, thinly sliced, soaked in ice water for 15 minutes, drained, dried, and broken into rings
1 green pepper, halved, cored, seeded, and cut into strips
10–12 tender, crisp romaine lettuce leaves, shredded or broken into small pieces
12 green or purple olives done in an oil and vinegar brine

1. In a nonmetallic saucepan, bring the wine, water, onion slice, bay leaf, and peppercorns to a boil. Boil slowly, covered, for 4 minutes. While the liquid is cooking, rinse the scallops quickly in cool water.

2. Add the scallops to the liquid and simmer at a very gentle bubble until the scallops turn opaque, a matter of a few minutes. Drain the scallops in a stainless-steel sieve. Discard the onion, bay leaf, and peppercorns.

3. In a mixing bowl, whisk together the lemon juice and mustard. Blend in the olive oil by tablespoons. Stir in the oregano and parsley and set aside. Just before you are ready

to assemble the salad, whisk the dressing thoroughly, then blend in the feta cheese, salt, and freshly ground pepper to taste.

4. Combine the scallops and all of the vegetables except the lettuce with the dressing. Correct the seasoning and pile on a bed of the romaine lettuce. Dot with the olives and serve.

Menu Suggestion   For dessert, serve Nectarines Steeped in Sweet Wine with Honey (page 293) or substitute juicy peaches for the nectarines for a lovely variation.

<small>SHOPPING LIST</small>
Shellfish: scallops
Vegetables and fruit: tomatoes, cucumbers, cooking onion, red onion, green pepper, romaine lettuce, lemon

Dairy: feta cheese
Staples: dry white wine, prepared mustard, olives
Herbs and spice: bay leaf, oregano, parsley, peppercorns

✳ RED SNAPPER FILLETS WITH FRESH TOMATO SAUCE

The "sauce" for the cooked red snapper, one of those magic source recipes that can be put together with haste, is useful for adventuring with other types of fish as well. The cool sauce can cover fillets that are warm or approaching room temperature. Each way is delicious.

2 large fillets of red snapper, 1¾–2 pounds
⅓ cup dry white wine
⅔ cup fish stock
salt
5 tablespoons olive oil
3 ripe tomatoes, peeled, seeded, and cubed
5 basil leaves, torn into very small pieces

1½ tablespoons white wine vinegar, or to taste
1 small hot pepper, cored, seeded, and finely chopped
2 tablespoons finely chopped parsley
freshly ground pepper
anchovy fillets (optional)
small black olives (optional)

1. Cut the red snapper fillets in half to make 4 pieces.

2. In a skillet large enough to hold all the fish in one layer, bring the wine and fish stock to a boil. Salt the fillets lightly, carefully lower them in the liquid, and adjust the heat so that the liquid simmers gently. Cover and cook the fish for 8–10 minutes, until cooked throughout. Cool in the liquid.

3. In a small nonmetallic bowl, put the olive oil, tomatoes, basil, vinegar, chopped hot pepper, and parsley. Season with salt to taste and add pepper if needed. Beat the ingredients together lightly to blend, then let them stand for 15 minutes.

4. Put the fish fillets, carefully taken from the cooking liquid and drained well, onto

a serving platter. Remix the tomato sauce to blend again and pour it over the fish. Garnish also, if you like, with a crisscross of anchovy fillets and small black olives.

Menu Suggestion   Follow the red snapper with Green Bean Salad with Shallots and Mixed Herbs (page 258); serve any of the fresh fruit desserts.

SHOPPING LIST
Fish: red snapper fillets
Vegetables: tomatoes, hot pepper
Staples: dry white wine, fish stock, olive oil, white

wine vinegar, anchovy fillets (optional), black olives (optional)
Herbs: fresh basil, parsley

✳ LUMP CRABMEAT WITH NOVA SCOTIA SALMON

This simple sauté depends on a very good grade of crabmeat, and I like to use "jumbo lump," which has big clusters of meat instead of tiny flakes. The minced dill goes well with the salmon strips and zucchini. One note about the cooking procedure: take care not to mash the big chunks of crabmeat into shreds—use a wooden spatula to turn the goods in the skillet.

1 pound crabmeat
4 tablespoons butter
1 onion, chopped
2 small, thin zucchini, cut into cubes
salt and freshly ground pepper

¼ cup dry white wine
⅓ pound sliced Nova Scotia salmon, cut
  into strips
3 tablespoons minced fresh dill

1. Pick over the crabmeat for any bones and cartilage, but try not to break up any of the large lumps.

2. Melt the butter in a skillet, stir in the chopped onion, and cook until it is soft. Stir in the zucchini cubes and season with salt and pepper. Sauté the zucchini until it is tender but still slightly crisp.

3. Stir in the crabmeat and cook steadily to heat it up. Stir in the wine and let it bubble up and glaze the crabmeat. Fold in the salmon strips and dill, correct the seasoning, and serve.

Menu Suggestion   For dessert, Raspberry Cream (page 308) or Blueberries in Maple–Brown Sugar Syrup (page 275).

SHOPPING LIST
Fish: crabmeat, Nova Scotia salmon
Vegetables: onion, zucchini
Dairy: butter

Staple: dry white wine
Herb: fresh dill

MAIN COURSES

* Swordfish in Basil Sauce

Spiced Stuffed Loin of Pork

Chicken with Corn and Lima Beans, or Chicken with
Zucchini and Red Peppers

Cod with Summer Vegetables

* Sausages with Cranberry Beans and Tomatoes

* Veal Chops with Red and Green Peppers

* Corned Beef with Herb Vinaigrette

THE COOK'S PLAN

NOTE: The following plan can be used whichever one of the alternate recipes you select. If you choose Chicken with Corn and Lima Beans, eliminate those ingredients followed by an asterisk. If you choose Chicken with Zucchini and Red Peppers, eliminate those followed by a dagger.

1. Set out: 6-quart casserole with lid for the vegetable part of the Cod with Summer Vegetables, 12-inch casserole with lid for the Spiced Stuffed Loin of Pork, 10-inch sauté pan for either of the chicken preparations, Chicken with Corn and Lima Beans or Chicken with Zucchini and Red Peppers.

2. Thaw and measure out 1 cup beef stock, 2 cups chicken stock.

3. Wash and dry several sprigs parsley, 3 sweet red peppers.

4. Peel 5 onions, 9 garlic cloves, 6 tomatoes, 3 boiling potatoes.

5. Finely chop 4 garlic cloves, 1 tablespoon parsley*; chop 3 onions, 2 garlic cloves, 2 teaspoons fresh thyme; slice 1 onion; cube 3 sweet red peppers, 3 boiling potatoes; dice 6 tomatoes.

6. Measure out ⅔ cup dry white wine* or ¾ cup dry white wine†, 10 whole dried apricots; 5 pieces ginger preserved in syrup, 3 cloves, ¼ teaspoon ground ginger, ¼ teaspoon ground allspice, ½ cup tomato purée* or canned plum tomatoes.*

7. Set out vegetable oil, olive oil, peanut oil, butter, salt, pepper, flour.

8. Spiced Stuffed Loin of Pork: Stuff the apricots; simmer in the Madeira; stuff the loin with apricots, push garlic slivers into the loin; brown in the oil; bake with the sautéed vegetables, beef stock, and reserved Madeira, Steps 1–4 (page 182).

9. Cod with Summer Vegetables: Prepare the vegetable stew, Step 1 (page 184).

10. Chicken with Corn and Lima Beans or Chicken with Zucchini and Red Peppers: Brown the chicken; simmer with the flavorings, stock, and wine (page 184 or page 186).

11. Cool all dishes to room temperature; refrigerate or freeze, following the instructions in "To Store" of each recipe.

SPICED STUFFED LOIN OF PORK

This loin of pork is stuffed with whole apricots. In the center of each apricot is placed a piece of preserved ginger, then the apricots are simmered briefly in Madeira. After the pork is browned and the sliced onion is sautéed, a healthy pinch of ground ginger and allspice goes in. The pork is very tasty done in this manner, since the remaining Madeira and beef stock are just enough liquid for cooking the pork and keeping it juicy. It is good hot or at room temperature.

10 whole dried apricots
5 pieces ginger preserved in syrup, halved
½ cup Madeira
1 clove garlic, peeled and cut in half
2¾-pound loin of pork, with a pocket cut for stuffing
3½ tablespoons peanut oil
salt and freshly ground pepper

1 onion, sliced
¼ teaspoon ground ginger
¼ teaspoon ground allspice
3 whole cloves
1 small imported bay leaf
1 cup beef stock
watercress (optional)

1. Lay out the apricots on a work surface. Put a piece of preserved ginger in the center of each apricot. Place the stuffed apricots in a nonmetallic saucepan and pour over the Madeira. Bring the Madeira to a simmer, cover the pan, and simmer the apricots for 10 minutes. Drain the apricots and reserve the Madeira.

2. Rub the cut garlic clove over the surface of the pork. Push the cooled, whole apricots at even intervals through the cut pocket of the pork loin.

3. Heat the peanut oil in a 12-inch casserole. Brown the loin in the hot oil, then remove it to a side dish and season well with salt and pepper. Add the onion slices to the casserole and sauté them for 2 minutes. Stir in the ginger, allspice, and cloves. Add the bay leaf and pour in the beef stock; pour in the reserved Madeira.

4. Bring the contents of the casserole to a boil. Add the pork loin and baste over with some of the liquid. Cover the casserole and bake the loin in a preheated 325° F oven for 2 hours, turning the piece over a few times while it cooks.

To Store Cool the pork in the liquid, then wrap it airtight and store in a covered container in the refrigerator for up to 4 days.

To Serve Cut the pork into slices and arrange on a serving platter. Garnish, if you like, with one bunch of crisp watercress.

Menu Suggestion For dessert, Sugar-Crust Custard with Raspberry Compote (page 280).

Meat: loin of pork
Vegetables and fruit: onion, garlic, watercress (optional), dried apricots

Staples: peanut oil, Madeira, beef stock
Herb and spices: bay leaf, preserved ginger, ground ginger, ground allspice, whole cloves

COD WITH SUMMER VEGETABLES

This cod dish depends upon finding the salted kind, mostly available frozen, in one-pound wooden crates with a sliding top, at the supermarket or from your fish dealer. The salt cod by R. E. Newell Fisheries Ltd., packed in Vogler's Cove, Nova Scotia, produces the most reliable cod, quality-wise. Since salt cod is free of all skin and bones, it is very easy to prepare. It stores well in the freezer, and it needn't be defrosted, just soaked overnight in a few changes of cold water. I like to combine the cod (once it has simmered for several minutes) with vegetables and herbs that are cooked together in the fashion of a vegetable stew. You could also try the cod with a slightly different vegetable combination, such as my Eggplant, Zucchini, and Fennel Stew (page 236).

¼ cup olive oil
4 garlic cloves, finely chopped
2 onions, chopped
3 sweet red peppers, cored, seeded, and cut into cubes
2 zucchini, cut into cubes
3 small boiling potatoes, peeled and cubed
6 tomatoes, peeled, seeded, and diced
6 leaves fresh basil, torn into small pieces

2 teaspoons chopped fresh thyme leaves
1 small imported bay leaf
salt and freshly ground pepper

To Serve

1½ pounds dried salt cod
¾ cup dry white wine
1 cup fish stock
1 tablespoon finely chopped parsley
cayenne pepper

Heat the olive oil in a 6-quart casserole. Stew the garlic and onions in the oil until the onions are translucent. Stir in the peppers and cook for 3 minutes. Stir in the zucchini and potatoes; cook and stir for 3 minutes. Add the tomatoes, basil, thyme, and bay leaf. Season with salt and pepper. Cover tightly and simmer until the vegetables are tender but still hold their shape—they should still have a crispy edge because they get cooked a little longer on serving day.

To Store Cool the vegetables and transfer them to a container, cover, and refrigerate up to 4 days in advance.

(*continued*)

To Serve   The night before serving the cod, soak it in a large bowl in 3 changes of cold water (twice in the evening and once in the morning). On serving day, put the cod in a large pot and cover with cool water. Bring to the boil, then simmer uncovered for 4 minutes. Drain and dry. Cut the cod into large chunks.

Put the vegetables in a casserole to reheat. Pour in the wine and bring to the boil. Pour in the fish stock and bring to the boil. Add the cod, cover, and simmer for 10 minutes, until the cod is tender. Fold in the chopped parsley and a little sprinkling of cayenne.

Menu Suggestion   For dessert, serve Blackberries in Nut-Lace Crisp (page 274).

Shopping List
Fish: salt cod
Vegetables: garlic, onions, red peppers, zucchini, tomatoes, boiling potatoes

Staples: olive oil, dry white wine, fish stock
Herbs: parsley, fresh basil, fresh thyme, bay leaf

CHICKEN WITH CORN AND LIMA BEANS

Here is another chicken dish that can be stored safely until you add the corn and lima beans, those radiant vegetables which are among the achievements of summertime crops.

3 tablespoons vegetable oil
2¾–3-pound whole chicken, cut into 8
   serving pieces
salt and freshly ground pepper
2 tablespoons butter
1 onion, chopped
2 garlic cloves, chopped
¾ cup dry white wine
2 cups chicken stock

To Serve

4 tablespoons butter
1 pound fresh lima beans, shelled
3 ears of corn, preferably white, kernels
   removed from the cob
3 leaves fresh basil, torn into small pieces
2 teaspoons snipped chives
1 tablespoon finely chopped parsley

1. Heat the vegetable oil in a heavy 10-inch sauté pan. Brown the chicken pieces in the hot oil, a few at a time; add more oil, if necessary, and let it heat up before any new

pieces are added. As the pieces are browned, remove them to a plate and season with salt and pepper.

2. Pour out any oil left in the pan. Add the 2 tablespoons butter, let it melt down, then stir in the chopped onion and sauté until lightly golden. Stir in the chopped garlic and sauté for a minute longer.

3. Pour in the wine and bring to the boil, stirring. Pour in the chicken stock and put back the browned chicken pieces. Bring the contents of the pan to a boil, then simmer, covered, for 30 minutes, or until the chicken is tender.

To Store Transfer the chicken to a container; boil down the liquid for 3 minutes, then pour it over the chicken. Cool the chicken completely, cover tightly, and refrigerate for up to 2 days or freeze for up to 2 weeks.

To Serve Reheat the chicken in a covered casserole. In a large saucepan, melt the 4 tablespoons butter and add the lima beans and ½ cup of the liquid that the chicken is reheating in. Cover and simmer until the lima beans are half cooked, about 7 minutes. Add the corn kernels, cover tightly, and cook until both the corn and the lima beans are tender, another 5 minutes. When the vegetables are cooked, season them with salt and pepper and fold in the basil and chives. Fold the vegetables into the chicken and simmer for a few moments longer. Fold in the chopped parsley and serve.

Menu Suggestion For dessert, Stewed Spiced Peaches (page 298).

Shopping List
Poultry: chicken
Vegetables: onion, garlic, lima beans, corn
Dairy: butter

Staples: vegetable oil, dry white wine, chicken stock
Herbs: fresh basil, chives, parsley

CHICKEN WITH ZUCCHINI AND RED PEPPERS

Here you cut the zucchini into rounds or matchsticks before sautéing in olive oil. The peppers should be cut into strips and cooked quickly until just crunchy before adding them to the chicken on reheating.

3 tablespoons vegetable oil

2¾–3-pound whole chicken, cut into 8 serving pieces

½ cup all-purpose flour, in a shallow bowl

salt and freshly ground pepper

⅔ cup dry white wine

2 tablespoons olive oil

1 tablespoon butter

1 onion, chopped

2 garlic cloves, chopped

1 tablespoon finely chopped parsley

2 cups chicken stock

½ cup tomato purée (homemade) or chopped canned plum tomatoes

1 small imported bay leaf

To Serve

2 small zucchini, cut into rounds or matchsticks

3 tablespoons olive oil

2 sweet red peppers, cored, seeded, and cut into narrow strips

2 teaspoons chopped fresh thyme (if available) or chopped parsley

1. Heat the vegetable oil in a 10-inch sauté pan. Dredge the chicken pieces in the flour, a few at a time, and brown them in the hot oil. As the pieces brown, transfer them to a bowl and season with salt and pepper.

2. When you have browned all of the chicken, pour out the vegetable oil and pour in the wine. Bring the wine to a boil, scraping the bottom of the pan to dislodge any clinging flavorful bits. Pour the wine over the chicken. Wipe out the pan.

3. Add the 2 tablespoons olive oil and 1 tablespoon butter to the pan. Stir in the chopped onion and sauté for 2 minutes. Stir in the chopped garlic and sauté for 1 minute longer. Add the chopped parsley. Blend together the chicken stock and tomato purée or canned tomatoes, and add the mixture. Drop in the bay leaf. Add the chicken pieces along with the wine. Bring the contents of the pan to a simmer, cover, and simmer for 30 minutes or until the chicken is tender.

To Store When the chicken has cooked, discard the bay leaf. Transfer the chicken to a container with tongs or a slotted spoon and boil down the cooking liquid until it has reduced by a third. Pour the liquid over the chicken, cool completely, and refrigerate, tightly covered, for up to 2 days or freeze for up to 2 weeks.

To Serve Salt the cut zucchini lightly and let the pieces stand in a colander for 15–20 minutes or until tiny beads of water appear on the surface of the pieces. Drain the zucchini well and dry thoroughly. Reheat the chicken in a covered casserole.

Heat 2 tablespoons of the olive oil in a skillet and cook the zucchini until crisply tender. Remove the zucchini and add the remaining 1 tablespoon of oil. Sauté the red pepper strips in the oil until tender, but still firm, about 5 minutes, adding the thyme or parsley during the last minute. Combine the vegetables and season them with salt and pepper; fold them into the chicken. Simmer everything together for a minute or two, then serve from a warm platter.

Menu Suggestion   For dessert, Stewed Spiced Peaches (page 298).

Shopping List
Poultry: chicken
Vegetables: onion, garlic, zucchini, sweet red peppers
Dairy: butter
Staples: vegetable oil, olive oil, dry white wine,
chicken stock, tomato purée or canned plum tomatoes
Herbs: parsley, bay leaf, fresh thyme

✴ SWORDFISH IN BASIL SAUCE

The mixture that the swordfish simmers in, along with a small amount of white wine, is redolent of fresh basil leaves, garlic, and anchovies. Be sure not to overcook the swordfish: if it measures one inch at its thickest part, a gentle simmering for 10 minutes should be correct. If the fish is cooked too long, the chunks will be tough and dry. What you want is the compact grain to stay succulent. This sauce is also delightful with lobster tails. Sauté the tails in a combination of hot oil and butter, then finish the recipe with the wine and basil mixture.

½ cup trimmed fresh basil leaves
3½ tablespoons olive oil
3 anchovy fillets, chopped
1 tablespoon finely chopped parsley
2 garlic cloves, minced
salt and freshly ground pepper
3 tablespoons butter

2-pound piece of swordfish steak, trimmed and cut into large cubes
⅓ cup dry white wine
½ tablespoon lemon juice, or more to taste
lemon wedges

1. Tear the basil leaves into small pieces. Pound them in a mortar with 2½ tablespoons of the olive oil until they turn into a pasty purée, or process in a food processor until well blended. Beat in the anchovies, parsley, and minced garlic. Season with salt and pepper.

2. In a skillet, heat the 3 tablespoons butter and remaining tablespoon of olive oil over moderate heat. Put the swordfish cubes into the pan and turn them in the hot oil and butter for 1 minute. Remove the fish from the pan to a dish.

3. Raise the heat to moderately high and pour in the wine. After the wine reaches the boil, boil it for 1 minute. Stir in the basil mixture. Place the fish back into the pan and baste the pieces with some of the sauce.

4. Cover the pan and cook over low heat for 5 minutes. After 5 minutes, uncover the pan and turn the pieces of swordfish over, cover, and cook for 4 minutes longer. Correct the seasoning. Sprinkle over the lemon juice and serve from a warm platter with lemon wedges for each eater to use at will.

Menu Suggestion For dessert, Spiced Compote of Cherries (page 278) or a flan made with fresh cherries.

Shopping List
Fish: swordfish steak
Vegetable and fruit: garlic, lemons
Dairy: butter

Staples: olive oil, dry white wine, anchovies
Herbs: parsley, fresh basil

＊SAUSAGES WITH CRANBERRY BEANS AND TOMATOES

Cranberry beans are held fast within a swirled pink and cream-colored shell, which should be smooth, free from wrinkles and any light brown spots. Once the beans are podded, you cook them in water until tender and drain, then you could dress them with some good olive oil and season with salt and pepper. They are a splendid addition to a composed salad, but the real treat is to do them with sausages and some ripe tomatoes that have been peeled and cubed.

2 pounds fresh cranberry beans
3 tablespoons vegetable oil
8 sausages
3 tablespoons olive oil
1 onion, chopped

½ cup dry white wine
5 fresh ripe tomatoes, seeded and cubed
2 tablespoons finely chopped parsley
salt and freshly ground pepper

1. Simmer the cranberry beans in a large pot of salted water about 20 minutes until they are tender. Drain them in a colander.

2. While the beans are simmering, heat the vegetable oil in a skillet. Prick the sausages, brown them in the hot oil, and remove them to a plate. Pour out the vegetable oil and pour in the olive oil. Stir in the onion and cook slowly until it has softened. Pour in the wine and let it boil away for 1 minute. Stir in the tomatoes and chopped parsley. Season with salt and pepper. Cover and simmer for 3 minutes.

3. Add the sausages, cover, and simmer for 20 minutes, basting the sausages once with the liquid. Add the cranberry beans, stir, cover, and continue to cook at a simmer for an additional 5–10 minutes until the sausages are cooked through and everything is hot. Check the seasoning.

4. Turn the sausages and beans out onto a platter and serve very hot.

Menu Suggestion For dessert, wonderful fresh figs, Figs in Black-Currant Syrup (page 283).

Shopping List
Meat: sausages
Vegetables: cranberry beans, onion, tomatoes

Staples: olive oil, vegetable oil, dry white wine
Herb: parsley

✳ VEAL CHOPS WITH RED AND GREEN PEPPERS

The lure of this dish is the two-tone color and flavor of the peppers and tomatoes against the veal chops. Definitely, this is a summer dish. Out-of-season tomatoes would be useless in this preparation; it is only during the time when the full repertory of garden vegetables abounds that this dish is most pleasing.

3 tablespoons vegetable oil
1 teaspoon butter
4 rib veal chops, cut 1 inch thick
salt and freshly ground pepper
½ cup dry white wine
1 cup chicken stock
1 small imported bay leaf
3 tablespoons olive oil
1 onion, thinly sliced

2 sweet red peppers, cored, seeded, and cut into strips
2 green peppers, cored, seeded, and cut into strips
2 ripe tomatoes, peeled, seeded, and cut into strips
2 teaspoons chopped fresh oregano
1 tablespoon finely chopped parsley

1. Heat the vegetable oil and butter in a skillet. Brown the veal chops on both sides in the hot butter-oil. Remove the chops to a plate and season with salt and pepper. Pour the wine into the skillet, raise the heat, and bring the liquid to a boil. Place the veal chops, wine, and chicken stock in a 10-inch casserole. Put in the bay leaf.

2. Bring the contents of the casserole to a boil, then cover and transfer it to the lower third of a preheated 325° F oven and cook until the chops are tender, about 50 minutes.

3. About 10 minutes before the veal is ready, heat the olive oil in a skillet. Stir in the onion and cook slowly until it is almost tender. Add the peppers and sauté until just tender, about 4 minutes. Stir in the tomato strips, oregano, and parsley. Season all with salt and pepper. Cook the tomatoes until they heat up but do not allow them to cook down too much.

4. When the chops are tender, stir in the cooked vegetables. Adjust the seasoning and serve the veal chops on a warm platter, spooning the vegetables over and around them.

Menu Suggestion   To begin, Chive-Corn Chowder (page 212); for dessert, any berry dessert, such as blackberries or blueberries.

Shopping List
Meat: veal chops
Vegetables: onion, green peppers, sweet red peppers, tomatoes
Dairy: butter

Staples: vegetable oil, olive oil, dry white wine, chicken stock
Herbs: bay leaf, fresh oregano, parsley

✳ CORNED BEEF WITH HERB VINAIGRETTE

Cubes or strips of corned beef are very attractive when served in a light herb vinaigrette dressing, combined with vegetables and strips of sour pickles. If you serve the corned beef with Eggplant Salad with Onions and Capers, as suggested, you may want to use only one of the vegetables called for below, such as the tomato strips.

1¼ pounds corned beef, cut into ⅓-inch-thick slices and trimmed of all fat
5 sour pickles (the tiny French cornichons), cut into strips
3 tablespoons red wine vinegar
2 shallots, minced
1 teaspoon prepared mustard
9 tablespoons olive oil
3 tablespoons chopped fresh herbs, such as a combination of parsley, tarragon, chives, chervil
Tabasco sauce

salt and freshly ground pepper
1 head lettuce, such as Boston or Bibb
a choice of some or all of the following:
   3 ribs celery heart, cut into strips
   1 bunch scallions, cut into thin lengths
   1 red onion, thinly sliced, soaked in ice water for 15 minutes, drained, dried, then divided into rings
   8 radishes, thinly sliced
   2 tomatoes, peeled, quartered, seeded, and cut into thin strips

1. Cut the corned beef into cubes or strips and place them in a mixing bowl with the strips of sour pickle.

2. In a small mixing bowl, whisk together the vinegar, shallots, and mustard. Beat in the olive oil a tablespoon at a time. Blend in the fresh herbs, and season with a few drops of Tabasco and salt and pepper to taste.

3. Line a platter or bowl with the lettuce leaves. Add the chosen vegetables to the corned beef and toss everything in the herb dressing. Check the seasoning and transfer the corned beef and vegetables to the lined bowl.

Menu Suggestion   To begin the meal, She-Crab Soup (page 224); along with the corned beef, Eggplant with Onions and Capers (page 235).

Shopping List
Meat: corned beef
Vegetables: shallots, Boston or Bibb lettuce, choice of: celery, scallions, red onion, radishes, tomatoes
Staples: sour pickles (cornichons), red wine vinegar, prepared mustard, olive oil, Tabasco sauce
Herbs: choose among a combination of parsley, tarragon, chives, chervil, as available

MAIN COURSES

✱ Scallops with Tomatoes and White Wine

Chicken in Mustard and Herb Sauce

✱ Composed Salad of New Potatoes, Ham, and Cheese

Breast of Veal Stuffed with Spinach and Pistachio Nuts

✱ Smoked Sablefish Steaks with Tuna, Caper, and Anchovy
Sauce

Country Terrine

✱ Shrimp Panned with Corn

THE COOK'S PLAN

1. Set out: 6-cup terrine, with lid, for the Country Terrine, 12-inch casserole for the Breast of Veal Stuffed with Spinach and Pistachio Nuts, 10-inch sauté pan for the Chicken in Mustard and Herb Sauce.

2. Thaw and measure out about 4 cups chicken stock.

3. Wash and dry ½ pound spinach, 1 rib celery heart, several parsley sprigs.

4. Peel 4 garlic cloves, 2 onions, 8 shallots, 1 carrot.

5. Finely chop 2 garlic cloves, 1 onion; chop 8 shallots, ½ pound spinach, 4 tablespoons parsley, 1 tablespoon fresh tarragon, 1 tablespoon chives, 4 branches thyme; slice 1 onion, 1 rib celery heart, 1 carrot; cut into strips ½ pound salt pork; mince 2 garlic cloves.

6. Measure out about 1½ cups dry white wine, 4 tablespoons brandy or port, ½ cup cognac or port, ¼ teaspoon ground nutmeg, ½ teaspoon ground allspice, ¼ teaspoon peppercorns, ¼ cup bread crumbs, ¼ cup heavy cream, ¼ cup skinned pistachio nuts, 2 tablespoons lemon juice, 2 teaspoons prepared mustard.

7. Set out olive oil, vegetable oil, peanut oil, butter, salt, pepper, flour.

8. Breast of Veal Stuffed with Spinach and Pistachio Nuts: Prepare the stuffing for the veal breast; stuff it and sew shut; brown the veal breast; simmer with the sautéed vegetables, seasonings, wine, and stock, Steps 1–4 (page 194).

9. Country Terrine: Put together the terrine and bake, Steps 1–4 (page 197).

10. Chicken in Mustard and Herb Sauce: Brown the chicken in oil; simmer with the shallots, white wine, and chicken stock, Steps 1–3 (page 198).

11. Cool all dishes to room temperature; refrigerate or freeze, following the instructions of each recipe.

BREAST OF VEAL STUFFED WITH
SPINACH AND PISTACHIO NUTS

Neat slices of veal breast, exposing a large band of light, savory filling, are a fine change from the more prestigious cuts and their standard sauces napped over. This pastel filling has a crunch of pistachios and repeats veal on the inside polished by mild spinach and heavy cream.

For the Stuffing
1 tablespoon olive oil
1 tablespoon butter
1 onion, finely chopped
2 garlic cloves, finely chopped
½ pound spinach, cooked and chopped
¼ teaspoon ground nutmeg
3 tablespoons chopped parsley
12 ounces ground veal
¼ cup bread crumbs
1 egg
¼ cup heavy cream
¼ cup skinned pistachio nuts
salt and freshly ground pepper

For Cooking the Veal Breast
3-pound boneless veal breast, with a pocket cut for stuffing
2 tablespoons vegetable oil
2 tablespoons butter
1 onion, sliced
1 rib celery heart, sliced
1 carrot, sliced
1 small imported bay leaf
¾ cup dry white wine
2½ cups chicken stock
Mustard and Herb Mayonnaise (page 195)

1. For the stuffing: Heat the olive oil and 1 tablespoon butter in a small skillet and soften the onion over low heat. Stir in the chopped garlic and cook for 2 minutes. Scrape the mixture into a mixing bowl. Beat in the spinach, nutmeg, and parsley. Cool. Beat in the ground veal, bread crumbs, egg, cream, and pistachio nuts. Season the stuffing with salt and pepper.

2. Fill the cavity of the veal breast with the stuffing, packing it in an even layer. Sew up the opening with a trussing needle and kitchen string, making sure that the stuffing cannot ooze out.

3. Heat the vegetable oil in a 12-inch casserole, which should accommodate the veal breast without any bends or buckles. Brown the veal breast on both sides, remove to a plate, and season well with salt and pepper.

4. Pour out the vegetable oil and add the 2 tablespoons butter. Add the sliced onion, celery, and carrot to the casserole and sauté until lightly browned. Add the bay leaf and wine. Bring the wine to a boil over moderately high heat, stirring. Pour in the chicken stock and lay in the veal breast. Bring the liquid to a boil, then regulate the heat so that the liquid simmers. Cover and simmer on the stove top or cook in the lower third of a preheated 325° F oven for 2 hours or until the veal tests tender.

To Store Cool the stuffed veal breast in the cooking liquid, then remove the piece from the casserole. Wrap in plastic wrap and aluminum foil and place in an airtight storage container. Refrigerate for up to 5 days.

To Serve Prepare the Mustard and Herb Mayonnaise. Remove all of the binding strings from the veal breast and cut into long slices to reveal a large strip of the filling. Arrange the slices on a serving dish and pass the mayonnaise separately.

NOTE: If you are doing the Smoked Sablefish Steaks with Tuna, Caper, and Anchovy Sauce (page 202) this week, you may not wish to do a mayonnaise with the veal breast, since the tuna sauce is mayonnaise-based. Instead, a fresh vegetable sauce could be used, such as one based on diced fresh tomatoes, onions, chopped oregano, and parsley in a light oil and vinegar dressing.

Menu Suggestion Begin the meal with Cold Cream of Tomato Soup (page 215); finish with Raspberries in Warm Framboise Sauce (page 310).

SHOPPING LIST
Meat: boneless veal breast, ground veal
Vegetables: onions, garlic, spinach, celery, carrot
Dairy: butter, eggs, heavy cream

Staples: olive oil, vegetable oil, bread crumbs, pistachio nuts, dry white wine, chicken stock
Herbs and spice: parsley, bay leaf, ground nutmeg

MUSTARD AND HERB MAYONNAISE

2 egg yolks, at room temperature
2 teaspoons prepared mustard
salt and freshly ground pepper
2 cups oil, half peanut, half olive

1 tablespoon chopped fresh tarragon
1 tablespoon chopped parsley
1 tablespoon chopped chives
2 tablespoons lemon juice

1. Place the egg yolks, mustard, salt, and pepper in a mixing bowl and beat for 2 minutes.

2. Beat in the oil by droplets at first until you have added ½ cup of the oil and the mixture takes on body and density. Add the remaining oil in a very thin stream, beating steadily as it is introduced into the egg yolks. (If the egg yolks turn into a watery, curdled state, you have added the oil too fast. Put a new, fresh egg yolk in a clean bowl, add ½ teaspoon of mustard, and beat for 2 minutes. Beat in the curdled mixture a teaspoon at a time until the mixture turns heavy and thick. After ½ cup of the curdled mixture has been added, add the remainder very slowly.)

(*continued*)

3. Beat in the chopped herbs and lemon juice. Correct the seasoning, adding more salt, pepper, and lemon juice as needed. You may wish to thin out the mayonnaise with a little light cream or boiling water to the consistency you like.

SHOPPING LIST
Fruit: lemon
Dairy: eggs

Staples: peanut oil, olive oil, prepared mustard
Herbs: fresh tarragon, parsley, chives

COUNTRY TERRINE

This country terrine is a handsome blend of some standard ingredients found in pâtés: pork, veal, chicken, chicken livers, and spices. It is easiest, it seems, to do this terrine by mixtures, as I have set forth below.

Mixture 1:
1 large whole chicken breast, split, boned, and cut into ½-inch-thick strips
2 small garlic cloves, minced

3 tablespoons brandy or port
¼ teaspoon ground allspice
salt and freshly ground pepper, to taste, but suggested proportions are ¼ teaspoon pepper and ¼ teaspoon salt

Combine all the ingredients in a bowl; store in the refrigerator until needed.

Mixture 2:
10 chicken livers
2 tablespoons vegetable oil

1 tablespoon port or brandy
salt and freshly ground black pepper, same proportions as above

Wash the livers, dry them, and trim away any fat or greenish spots. Heat the oil in a skillet and sauté the livers just until they firm up. Pour on the port or brandy and shake the pan so that it bubbles around the livers. Season with salt and pepper; cool.

Mixture 3:
½ pound ground veal
1 pound ground pork
½ pound ground pork fat
¾ teaspoon salt
¼ teaspoon ground allspice
2 eggs

½ teaspoon dried thyme, crumbled between the fingertips, or leaves from 4 full branches of thyme, chopped
¼ teaspoon peppercorns, finely cracked
½ cup cognac or port
½ pound salt pork, cut into strips

Combine the veal, pork, pork fat, salt, allspice, thyme, peppercorns, and cognac or port in a bowl. Add the salt pork strips and beat in the eggs, one at a time.

½ pound sheets of pork fat, for lining   1 imported bay leaf
    the terrine

1. Line the bottom and sides of a 1½-quart terrine with the sheets of pork fat, reserving some pieces for the top of the mixture.
2. Layer the terrine as follows:
    Half the ground pork mixture (Mixture 3)
    Half the chicken livers (Mixture 2)
    Half the chicken (Mixture 1)
    Remaining chicken livers
    Remaining chicken
    Remaining ground pork
3. Put the bay leaf on top and lay over the remaining pork fat sheets, tucking them in along the sides, trimming if necessary with a sharp knife or scissors.
4. Cover the whole terrine with a double thickness of aluminum foil and seal the edges well. Put on the lid. Set the terrine in a deep pan filled with enough warm water to rise at least one-third up the sides of the terrine. Bake in a preheated 350° F oven for 1 hour 55 minutes. Remove the terrine from the water bath, pour out the water from the baking pan, and put the terrine back into the pan. Put an equal level of weights (a few bricks or a board weighed down by some canned goods) on top of the terrine to press out the fatty liquid and consolidate the texture.

To Store   Cool the terrine to room temperature, clean off the outside of the casserole, and refrigerate with the weights. A few hours later, replace the foil with a double thickness of plastic wrap followed by a new sheet of foil. Refrigerate for up to 1 week.

To Serve   Peel off the top layer of pork fat sheets and cut slices directly from the casserole.

Menu Suggestion   With the terrine, Pepper Strips with Garlic (page 242) and Sliced Tomatoes with Mozzarella and Basil (page 244); finish the meal with a good, rich ice cream, such as Double-Rich Peach Ice Cream (page 296) or any other fruit variety.

SHOPPING LIST
Meat and poultry: chicken breast, chicken livers, salt pork, ground veal, ground pork, ground pork fat, pork fat sheets
Vegetable: garlic

Dairy: eggs
Staples: vegetable oil, brandy or port, cognac (or port)
Herbs and spices: thyme, bay leaf, ground allspice, peppercorns

CHICKEN IN MUSTARD AND HERB SAUCE

The use of good mustard is important if you are to achieve the tang in this dish, so do a little investigation to uncover a pungent one. Some mustards are bold, slightly sweet, and amber-colored, others hot and brown, and many are laced with the coarsely ground seeds of the plant. A zesty mustard can also double as a bread spread, but do avoid the mild, turmeric-colored variety (it always reminds me of bologna sandwiches on cotton fluff slices of bread that the mustard was slathered on in my childhood).

3½ tablespoons vegetable oil
2¾–3-pound whole chicken, cut into 8 serving pieces
½ cup all-purpose flour, in a shallow bowl
salt and freshly ground pepper
3 tablespoons butter
8 shallots, chopped

⅔ cup dry white wine
1⅓ cups chicken stock

To Serve

2 tablespoons finely chopped parsley
1 tablespoon chopped fresh chervil
1 tablespoon finely snipped chives
2 tablespoons spicy prepared mustard

1. Heat the vegetable oil in a 10-inch sauté pan. A few pieces at a time (as many as will fit in a single, comfortable layer in the pan), dredge the chicken lightly in the flour and brown in the hot oil. Remove the chicken pieces to a plate as they are browned and season them with salt and pepper.

2. Pour out the oil from the skillet and add the butter. Sauté the chopped shallots in the butter until they are soft. Pour in the wine and bring to a boil, stirring the small bits up from the bottom of the pan that may be clinging. Boil the wine for 1 minute. Pour in the chicken stock and put back the chicken pieces.

3. Baste the chicken pieces over with the liquid, then bring the contents of the pan to the simmer. Cover and simmer for 30 minutes or until the chicken is tender.

To Store   Remove the chicken to a storage container and boil down the liquid until it has reduced by a third; pour it over the chicken. Cool the chicken, then refrigerate tightly covered for up to 2 days or freeze for up to 2 weeks.

To Serve   Reheat the chicken in a covered casserole. When it is hot, remove it to a warm oven, and boil the liquid down further if it is not already syrupy. Stir in the parsley, chervil, chives, and mustard; correct the seasoning and simmer. Put the chicken on a warm serving platter, pour the herb sauce over it, and serve.

Menu Suggestion   Serve Eggplant, Zucchini, and Fennel Stew (page 236) as a first course, vegetable course, or right along with the chicken; for dessert, Apricot Fool (page 272).

✳ SHRIMP PANNED WITH CORN

"To pan" is my favorite expression for the process of passing food quickly through sweet butter and seasonings. In this recipe, shrimp and golden nuggets of corn are turned in butter, emerging from the sauté pan gleaming and juicy. The key to this dish is an uninterrupted cooking rhythm: all the components should be ready at stoveside so that cooking can move smoothly along.

4 tablespoons butter
1 tablespoon olive oil
1½ cups fresh corn kernels
1¼ pounds fresh shrimp, peeled, with the tails left on, and deveined
4 small garlic cloves, minced

¼ cup dry white wine
2 tablespoons lemon juice
2 tablespoons finely chopped parsley or a combination of parsley and chervil
salt and freshly ground pepper
lemon wedges

1. Put the butter and olive oil in a heavy sauté pan and set over moderate heat.

2. When the butter has melted, stir in the corn kernels and cook for 4–5 minutes. Raise the heat and add the shrimp; stir and cook for 1–2 minutes or until the shrimp just begins to turn opaque. Add the minced garlic; cook and stir for 30 seconds. Pour in the wine, add the lemon juice, and stir and cook for a few moments longer until the liquid bubbles up around and glazes the shrimp. Stir in the chopped herb(s) and season with salt and pepper. Turn the panned mixture out onto a serving plate and have extra lemon wedges at hand for each eater.

Menu Suggestion Green Beans, Summer Style, with Tomatoes and Tarragon (page 238), as a vegetable along with the shrimp, as a first course, or at room temperature as a vegetable-salad course; Spiced Compote of Cherries (page 278) for dessert.

❋ SCALLOPS WITH TOMATOES AND WHITE WINE

In this recipe, the pieces of tomato are added just about the same time as the scallops so that they will not cook down too much. This simplifies the recipe for minimal kitchen maneuvers and keeps all the brilliant, fresh flavors intact.

1½ pounds scallops
3½ tablespoons olive oil
3 garlic cloves, finely chopped
1 small hot pepper, cored, seeded, and finely chopped, or 3 pinches of crushed red pepper

2 red, ripe tomatoes, peeled, seeded, and cut into small cubes or thin wedges
½ cup dry white wine
2 tablespoons finely chopped parsley
salt and freshly ground pepper

1. Rinse the scallops quickly under a spray of cool water. Drain and dry. If you have large sea scallops, cut them in half.

2. Heat the olive oil in a skillet. Sauté the chopped garlic until lightly golden and stir in the hot pepper. Add the tomatoes and cook over moderate heat for 1 minute. Add the scallops, cook for 30 seconds, then pour in the wine. Sauté the scallops until they turn opaque and the wine, in turn, glazes the scallops. Fold in the chopped parsley and season to taste with salt and pepper.

Menu Suggestion   For dessert, any of the fruit ones baked or in compote, or a fool, such as Apricot Fool (page 272), in which you can substitute nectarines (poach them as you would the apricots).

SHOPPING LIST
Shellfish: scallops
Vegetables: hot pepper, tomatoes, garlic

Staple: olive oil
Herb: parsley

❋ COMPOSED SALAD OF NEW POTATOES, HAM, AND CHEESE

The creation of an enticing main-course salad does not always depend on a scrupulously strict set of ingredients. Play with a composed salad and vary the range of components at will, changing the texture according to the goods that crop up at market. Here, still observing a good balance, you might want to add two handfuls of fresh marbled-pink cranberry beans cooked until tender and tossed with the warm dressing along with the potatoes, or slivers of mildly hot red pepper, or, for a smooth richness, wedges of cooked artichoke heart.

2 pounds small new potatoes	freshly ground pepper
salt	¾ pound sliced lean cooked country
1 imported bay leaf	ham, cut into strips
13 tablespoons olive oil	½-pound piece Gruyère cheese, cut into
2 garlic cloves, crushed with the back of	strips
a knife and peeled	2 teaspoons lemon juice
4 tablespoons red wine vinegar	2 tablespoons finely chopped parsley
½ tablespoon prepared mustard	watercress or leaves of Boston lettuce
1 bunch scallions, pale green and white	12 black olives
parts only, minced	

1. Put the potatoes in a large pot and cover with water. Add 1½ teaspoons salt and the bay leaf. Bring the water to a boil, then simmer the potatoes until tender. Drain.

2. While the potatoes are cooking, place 12 tablespoons of the olive oil and the garlic in a small saucepan. Set over low heat to warm the oil and draw out the garlic flavor, about 10 minutes. Discard the garlic and beat in the vinegar, mustard, scallions, and salt and pepper to taste.

3. Cut the potatoes into quarters if large or in half if small. Toss the potatoes in the warm oil-scallion mixture. Add the ham and toss again.

4. Toss the strips of cheese in the remaining tablespoon of olive oil, lemon juice, and a little pepper. Combine the cheese with the potatoes and ham, along with folding in the chopped parsley. Line a platter or bowl with the watercress or lettuce. Place the salad on it and dot with the olives.

Menu Suggestion   Blueberries in Maple–Brown Sugar Syrup (page 275) for dessert.

SHOPPING LIST
Meat: cooked country ham slices
Vegetables and fruit: new potatoes, scallions, garlic, watercress or Boston lettuce, lemon
Dairy: Gruyère cheese

Staples: olive oil, red wine vinegar, prepared mustard, black olives
Herbs: parsley, bay leaf

✳ SMOKED SABLEFISH STEAKS WITH TUNA, CAPER, AND ANCHOVY SAUCE

Nicely moist sablefish can be cut to order at most well-stocked delicatessens. This delicious summertime preparation is served here with a mayonnaise sauce, and indeed, the only work here is in the sauce. It's a fast dish that depends on the quality of the smoked fish.

When buying sablefish, look out for the slabs that show no sign of drying around the edges. The skin side should be shiny and glossy but not slimy. Another variation on this concept is to do the sablefish in chunks, lightly bound with some of the mayonnaise. Add some greenery and vegetables to this, including, if you like, the thin strips of smoked sturgeon in addition to the salmon, tossed pick-up-stick fashion over the sablefish.

2 egg yolks
⅞ cup olive oil
juice of 1 lemon
salt and freshly ground pepper
3 ounces tuna fish packed in olive oil, drained
4 anchovy fillets
1 tablespoon capers, chopped
1 garlic clove, minced

4 smoked sablefish steaks, about ⅓ pound each
tiny black olives or thin slices of sour pickles (cornichons)
¼ pound smoked sturgeon slices, cut into strips
¼ pound smoked salmon slices, cut into strips
lemon wedges

1. Put the egg yolks in a mixing bowl. Using a hand-held beater, beat the olive oil into the egg yolks by droplets until a third of the oil has been added. Add the rest of the oil, beating it in by half-teaspoons to make a thick mayonnaise. Slowly blend in the lemon juice and season with salt and pepper.

2. Spin the tuna fish with the anchovy fillets in a food processor or blender to chop finely. Beat the tuna into the mayonnaise. Stir in the capers and minced garlic. Correct the seasoning. Thin out the sauce with a little boiling water if you do not like it quite so thick.

3. Place the sablefish steaks on a serving platter and spoon some of the mayonnaise on top of each steak. Garnish the fish with the olives or cornichons and the strips of smoked sturgeon and smoked salmon. Serve the remaining mayonnaise separately and offer lemon wedges on the side.

Menu Suggestion For dessert, Nectarines Steeped in Sweet Wine with Honey (page 293), or substitute any of the berries or melons for the nectarines—delicious!

Fish: smoked sablefish steaks, tuna fish, smoked sturgeon slices, smoked salmon slices
Vegetable and fruit: garlic, lemons

Dairy: eggs
Staples: olive oil, anchovies, capers, olives or sour pickles (cornichons)

PART TWO

ACCOMPANIMENTS TO THE SEASONAL MAIN COURSES

6
SOUPS

AUTUMN GARDEN SOUP

Fresh basil and thyme are absolutely essential to this soup, so switch over to another vegetable-type soup if you are not currently cultivating any plants or you cannot buy the herbs from a greengrocer. The herbs point up and contrast the vegetables, which must cook slowly in the stock. The appeal, for me, is the simple earthy tone to this soup. I often serve it in porcelain or earthenware bowls with a generous covering of cheese on top.

3 tablespoons butter
1 tablespoon olive oil
2 onions, sliced
4 leeks, white part only, sliced
4 carrots, sliced
4 ribs celery heart, sliced
2 small turnips, peeled and diced
2 small boiling potatoes, peeled and cubed
¾ cup tomato purée (homemade) or

chopped canned plum tomatoes
5 cups chicken stock
4 fresh basil leaves, shredded
leaves from 2 small branches of fresh thyme
salt and freshly ground pepper

To Serve

¼ pound Gruyère cheese, grated

1. Put the butter and oil in a soup pot. Stir in the onions and leeks; cook over moderate heat for 3 minutes. Stir in the carrots and cook 2 minutes. Stir in the celery and cook for 2 minutes. Add the turnips and potatoes, give the contents a few turns, and cook 2 minutes.

2. Pour in the tomato purée or canned tomatoes and chicken stock. Add the basil and thyme. Season the contents of the pot with salt and pepper to taste.

3. Bring the contents of the soup pot to a simmer, cover, and simmer for 1 hour or until the vegetables are tender. The soup should take on body.

To Store   Cool the soup to room temperature, ladle into a storage container, and refrigerate for up to 6 days or freeze for up to 1 month.

To Serve   Reheat the soup to piping hot and serve covered with a thick mantle of cheese atop each serving.

SHOPPING LIST
Vegetables: onions, leeks, carrots, celery, turnips, potatoes
Dairy: butter, Gruyère cheese

Staples: olive oil, tomato purée or canned plum tomatoes, chicken stock
Herbs: fresh basil, fresh thyme

BROCCOLI AND CELERY SOUP

The better the stock, the better the soup. And no better place for a good rich chicken stock than this soup of broccoli and celery, a soothing autumnal combination.

1 bunch (about ½ pound) fresh green broccoli
3 tablespoons butter
1 onion, diced
6 ribs celery heart, diced
1 teaspoon fresh thyme leaves

3 cups full-bodied chicken stock
salt and freshly ground pepper

To Serve

1 cup light cream, warmed
1½ tablespoons finely chopped parsley

1. Trim off any tough, woody stems from the broccoli and pare away a thin, outer layer from the stalks with a swivel-bladed vegetable peeler. Cut the broccoli into small pieces and blanch them in boiling salted water. Drain the broccoli in a colander and quickly refresh in cold water.

2. Put the butter in a soup pot, add the onion, and stew until soft. Stir in the celery and cook for 3–4 minutes or until the pieces have absorbed some of the butter and turn glossy and shiny. Stir in the broccoli and thyme. Cover and cook slowly for 15 minutes until the vegetables are soft. Purée this through a food mill, then return to the pan.

3. Pour the chicken stock over the puréed vegetables, season with salt and pepper, stir, and bring the contents to a simmer. Simmer, covered, for 40 minutes.

To Store   Cool the soup thoroughly and refrigerate in a covered container for up to 6 days or freeze for up to 4 weeks.

To Serve   Heat the soup over a low flame until very hot. Stir in the warmed cream, adjust the seasoning, and simmer for 3–4 minutes longer. Stir in the chopped parsley and serve.

SHOPPING LIST
Vegetables: broccoli, onion, celery
Dairy: butter, light cream

Staple: chicken stock
Herbs: fresh thyme, parsley

CAULIFLOWER AND POTATO SOUP WITH CHIVES

This is one of those vegetable-type soups that's nice to have on hand; without the final fillip of cream, this soup stores perfectly up to 6 days. It is also one which is enjoyably easy to assemble. Lightly creamy, it sparkles with a sprinkling of nutmeg and pinch of cayenne pepper.

3 leeks, white part only, sliced
3 tablespoons butter
3 ribs celery heart, diced
1½ cups cauliflower flowerets
3 boiling potatoes, peeled and cubed
4½ cups chicken stock
salt and freshly ground pepper

To Serve

½ cup light cream and ⅓ cup heavy cream, warmed together
cayenne pepper
freshly ground nutmeg
2 tablespoons snipped chives (if fresh chives are absolutely unavailable, just substitute finely chopped parsley and rename the soup)

1. In a soup pot, soften the sliced leeks in the butter over moderately low heat. Add the celery and cauliflower, stir, cover, and cook for 5 minutes. Stir in the potatoes and cook, uncovered, for 3 minutes.

2. Pour the chicken stock on the vegetables. Season with salt and pepper. Give the pot a few stirs, then cover and cook at a simmer for 1 hour.

To Store   Cool the soup and store in a covered container in the refrigerator for up to 6 days or freeze for up to 1 month.

To Serve   Bring the soup to a simmer in a saucepan. Stir in the warmed creams; season with a pinch of cayenne pepper and several gratings of nutmeg. Heat the soup until very hot throughout. Correct the seasoning, stir in the chives (or parsley), and serve.

SHOPPING LIST
Vegetables: leeks, celery, cauliflower, boiling potatoes
Dairy: butter, light cream, heavy cream
Staple: chicken stock

Herb and spices: chives, cayenne pepper, ground nutmeg

CHIVE-CORN CHOWDER

Although the onions and potatoes must cook in the chicken stock for 20 minutes (and then the corn is added and simmered until tender), this soup is very easy to do because the working time is minimal. It takes only a little time to soften the onions in the butter, cube the potatoes, and remove enough corn kernels from the cob to measure 1½ cups. And, like all soups, the flavor is as good as the stock is, as perfect as the smallest, sweetest corn kernels.

3 tablespoons butter
1 onion, chopped
2 small boiling potatoes
6 parsley stems tied with 1 small imported bay leaf
4 cups chicken stock
salt and freshly ground pepper

1½ cups fresh corn kernels

To Serve

¾ cup light cream, warmed
2 tablespoons snipped chives
2 teaspoons finely chopped parsley

1. Melt the butter in a soup pot or a heavy 2-quart saucepan. Stir in the chopped onion and sauté for 3 minutes. Stir in the potatoes and parsley bundle. Pour in the chicken stock and season lightly with salt and pepper.

2. Bring the contents of the pot to a boil, then reduce the heat so that the liquid simmers gently when the pot is covered. Simmer for 20 minutes. Add the corn and simmer, partially covered, for 10–12 minutes or until the corn is tender. Discard the parsley bundle.

To Store Cool the soup to room temperature, then refrigerate in a tightly covered container up to 5 days or freeze for up to 2 weeks.

To Serve Reheat the soup in a large saucepan. Stir in the cream and chives, and bring just to the simmer. Check the seasoning and stir in the chopped parsley before serving.

NOTE: ½ cup chopped bacon, sautéed until lightly browned, may be added along with the potatoes in Step 1.

SHOPPING LIST
Vegetables: onion, boiling potatoes, corn
Dairy: butter, light cream
Staple: chicken stock
Herbs: parsley, bay leaf, chives

CLAM SOUP WITH SHALLOTS AND WHITE WINE

I have adapted this recipe from the collection of a friend whose professional mainstay is in the field of solar energy. Among other talents, my friend is an outrageously good cook who loves to work with shellfish, especially in chowder and main-course stews, and came up with this recipe.

3 dozen littleneck clams, the smaller the better, well scrubbed
6 large shallots, chopped
½ onion, chopped
2 tablespoons butter
3 ribs celery heart, chopped

½ cup dry white wine
2 cups fish stock
salt and freshly ground pepper
1 cup light cream, warmed
1 tablespoon finely chopped parsley

1. Put the clams in a heavy saucepan, cover, and cook over high heat until they just open. Remove the clams from the shells, chop coarsely, and reserve. Strain the clam juice of any sandy sediment (a coffee filter works perfectly here) and set aside.

2. In a soup pot, soften the shallots and onion in the butter until translucent. Stir in the celery and cook for 3 minutes. Pour on the wine and fish stock, and add the strained clam broth. Season with salt and pepper. Put the lid on the pot askew and simmer steadily for 20 minutes.

3. Add the cream, stir once, and cover the pot. Simmer for 15 minutes. Add the clams, stir, and simmer for 5 minutes. Adjust the seasoning, stir in the parsley, and serve.

SHOPPING LIST
Shellfish: clams
Vegetables: shallots, onion, celery
Dairy: butter, light cream

Staples: dry white wine, fish stock
Herb: parsley

CLAMS, SERVED SOUP-STYLE, WITH WHITE WINE, LEEKS, AND CORIANDER

These clams are presented in their shells, in deep soup bowls, and ladled up with them is the white wine and coriander broth. Delicious with a cracking loaf of French bread to soak up the juices.

2 tablespoons olive oil
2 tablespoons butter
4 leeks, white part only, finely chopped
2 garlic cloves, finely chopped
1 small hot pepper, cored, seeded, and chopped (optional)
1 small imported bay leaf
2 tablespoons chopped parsley

3 tablespoons chopped fresh coriander leaves
salt and freshly ground pepper
½ cup dry white wine
3 dozen littleneck clams, well scrubbed (buy an extra dozen if the clams are unusually small)

1. Heat the oil and butter in a casserole large enough to accommodate all of the clams. Stir in the leeks and cook them slowly until tender and translucent.

2. Stir in the garlic and (optional) hot pepper. Stir and cook for 1 minute. Add the bay leaf, parsley, and coriander, and season lightly with salt and pepper.

3. Pour on the wine and bring to a rapid boil. Reduce the heat so that the liquid bubbles steadily and simmer for 5 minutes. Add the clams to the liquid, stir, cover, and raise the heat to high. Steam the clams open in the liquid, about 4 minutes, until the hinges of the shells open widely. Do not overcook, or the clams will toughen up.

4. Check the seasoning and distribute the clams, with the liquid, among 4 large bowls.

SHOPPING LIST
Shellfish: littleneck clams
Vegetables: leeks, garlic, hot pepper (optional)
Dairy: butter

Staples: olive oil, dry white wine
Herbs: bay leaf, parsley, fresh coriander

CREAM OF CARROT SOUP

Thin young carrots are best for this soup, which is flecked with fresh thyme leaves.

4 tablespoons butter
1 onion, chopped
5 fresh carrots, peeled and thinly sliced
¼ teaspoon granulated sugar
3¾ cups chicken stock
2 teaspoons fresh thyme leaves, chopped
salt and freshly ground pepper

6 parsley stems tied with kitchen string

To Serve

1 cup light cream, warmed
1 tablespoon chopped parsley or snipped chives

1. Put the butter and onion in a large saucepan or soup pot and soften over moderately low heat. Stir in the carrot slices and sprinkle with sugar. Cover tightly and cook over low heat for 20 minutes.

2. Uncover the saucepan, and stir in the chicken stock, thyme, and salt and pepper to taste. Add the parsley stems. Cover the saucepan and simmer for 20 minutes.

To Store Discard the parsley stems and purée the mixture through a food mill. Pour into a container and refrigerate covered for up to 3 days or freeze for up to 3 weeks.

To Serve Heat the soup in a large saucepan. When hot, stir in the cream and simmer slowly for 5 minutes. Correct the seasoning and stir in the parsley or chives.

SHOPPING LIST
Vegetables: onion, carrots
Dairy: butter, light cream

Herbs: fresh thyme, parsley, chives

COLD CREAM OF TOMATO SOUP

For a warm-weather soup to remain faithful to the principles of cold, it should keep its clear refreshing flavor even when parts of it are stored and chilled; its texture should not be too heavy (with the exception of some vegetable-laden soups), in direct contrast to rugged winter soups, and for the cook's convenience, the soup must store well in the refrigerator through certain stages. This cold tomato soup passes the test. Pure and simple, it is a soup in which the flavor of sweet, blushing summer tomatoes reigns, supported by some root vegetables, fresh basil, homemade stock, and pure cream.

1 onion, chopped
2 garlic cloves, peeled and halved
3 tablespoons olive oil
2 carrots, sliced
2 ribs celery heart, sliced
4 small fresh basil leaves
1 small imported bay leaf tied with 4
 parsley stems

8 ripe tomatoes, cored and quartered
salt and freshly ground pepper
pinch of cayenne pepper
pinch of granulated sugar

To Serve

3 cups cold light chicken stock
1 cup light cream
1 tablespoon finely chopped parsley

In a large nonmetallic saucepan or soup pot, sauté the onion and garlic in the oil until the onion is soft. Stir in the sliced carrot and celery and sauté for 1 minute. Add the basil, bay leaf bundle, tomato quarters, cayenne pepper, and sugar and cover. Simmer the tomatoes for 35 minutes or until the flesh is soft and melted down, stirring several times to break up the tomato pulp.

To Store   Discard the herb bundle and purée the soup base through a food mill, using the medium-coarse disk. Pour the purée into a storage container. When completely cool, cover and refrigerate for up to 5 days.

To Serve   Blend the cold chicken stock into the tomato base. Pour in the cream and chill until ready to serve. Correct the seasoning, swirl in the chopped parsley, and serve.

Shopping List
Vegetables: onion, garlic, tomatoes, carrots, celery   *Herbs and spice:* fresh basil, parsley, bay leaf, cayenne
Dairy: light cream   pepper
Staples: olive oil, sugar, chicken stock

CREAM OF MUSHROOM AND LEEK SOUP

This is a beautiful soup that takes the best of mushrooms, fresh and dried, for combining with the enticing flavor of cooked leeks. When I can locate fresh morels, I use a generous half pound in this recipe, making this soup very special and, taste-wise, intricate. And the final cream enrichment, stirred in on the day the soup is reheated, makes it at the same time lightly soft and completely full-bodied.

1½ ounces dried mushrooms, such as morels (if you find fresh morels, clean them well, trim, and finely chop)
4 tablespoons butter
3 leeks, white part only, thinly sliced
½ pound fresh mushrooms, sliced
4 cups chicken stock

salt and freshly ground pepper

To Serve

2 egg yolks
¾ cup *crème fraîche*
1 tablespoon snipped chives

1. Soak the dried mushrooms in warm water to cover for 35 minutes. Strain enough of the soaking liquid of all sand and dirt to measure ⅓ cup. Rinse the mushrooms under cool water, and chop into small pieces but not too fine. Reserve.

2. Put the butter in a soup pot and set over moderately low heat. Soften the leeks in

the butter. Stir in the fresh mushrooms, cover, and cook slowly for 5 minutes. Add the soaked dried mushrooms (or fresh wild mushrooms), the ⅓ cup mushroom soaking liquid, and chicken stock. Season with salt and pepper. Cover the saucepan and simmer the soup for 30 minutes.

To Store Cool completely. Refrigerate the soup in a covered container for up to 5 days or freeze for up to 1 month.

To Serve Reheat the soup until it is very hot. In a medium-size mixing bowl, whisk the egg yolks with the *crème fraîche*. Ladle ½ cup of the hot soup in the *crème fraîche* mixture, stirring very well. Off the heat, slowly return the *crème fraîche* mixture to the hot soup, whisking as you pour in a thin, steady stream.

Adjust the seasoning with salt and pepper. Bring the soup to the simmer, stirring, and simmer for 2 minutes. Blend in the chives and serve hot.

SHOPPING LIST
Vegetables: leeks, mushrooms (if available)
Dairy: butter, eggs, *crème fraîche*

Staples: dried mushrooms, chicken stock
Herb: chives

CREAM OF ONION SOUP

Some cream soups are gossamer preparations of shellfish, while others rely on a range of puréed vegetables. And some onion soups are heady brews of richly browned onions in beef stock under a thick tangle of cheese. This is a soup that is dense with onions, like a good dark onion soup, and is silkened with *crème fraîche* for a nicely rich creamy quality. It is as substantial as it is fragile.

4 tablespoons butter
5 onions, chopped
1 garlic clove, finely chopped
4½ cups chicken stock
salt and freshly ground pepper
1 small imported bay leaf

To Serve

½ cup *crème fraîche*
¾ cup light cream
2 egg yolks

1. Put the butter in a soup pot and let it melt over moderately low heat. Stir in the chopped onions; cook slowly for 3 minutes. Reduce the heat to low, cover the pot, and cook the onions until they soften completely and are tenderly translucent, for about 25 minutes.

2. When the onions are soft, stir in the chopped garlic and cook for 2 minutes. Pour in the chicken stock, season with salt and pepper, and add the bay leaf. Simmer the soup, covered, for 40 minutes.

To Store   Cool the soup to room temperature and refrigerate in a tightly covered container up to 5 days or freeze for up to 6 weeks.

To Serve   Slowly reheat the soup to a simmer. In a small mixing bowl, blend the *crème fraîche* and light cream, then whisk in the egg yolks. Add ½ cup of the hot soup to the mixture and blend it in well. Remove the soup from the heat source, and slowly blend in the *crème fraîche* mixture. Over low heat, bring the soup just to the simmer, stirring. Correct the seasoning and serve.

SHOPPING LIST
Vegetables: onions, garlic
Dairy: butter, *crème fraîche*, light cream, eggs

Staple: chicken stock
Herb: bay leaf

CREAM OF SORREL SOUP

Pleasantly tart, verdant sorrel leaves animate sauces for veal chops, are sensational in a topping when baking shellfish, and, shredded into minuscule strands, make a wine vinegar, mustard, and oil vinaigrette memorable. Sorrel imparts a special tang when a pile is reduced to a purée and added to iced soups, traditionally based on sour cream, flecked with chives and dill, garnished with hard-cooked eggs and cucumbers. In this soup, you will find the thin green strips in a hot cream soup, sturdied with potatoes and added after the main part of the soup has simmered for a while. And remember, when purchasing sorrel, to look out for the smallest, greenest leaves, without tough and woody stems. These are the choicest, most tender leaves.

2 onions, thinly sliced
3 tablespoons butter
3 small boiling potatoes, peeled and
   thinly sliced
1 carrot, sliced
4 cups chicken stock

salt and freshly ground pepper

To Serve

½ pound sorrel leaves
¾ cup light cream, warmed
1 tablespoon butter, softened

1. In a soup pot, soften the sliced onions in 3 tablespoons butter slowly over a low flame. The onions must be quite soft and should not take on any color; cover the pot after a few minutes and cook for about 20 minutes.

2. Stir in the potatoes and carrot slices; cook for 3 minutes. Pour in the chicken stock and season with salt and pepper. Simmer the soup base, covered, for 40–45 minutes or until the potatoes and carrots are very soft.

To Store   Purée this part of the soup through a food mill, cool to room temperature, and refrigerate in a covered container for up to 6 days or freeze for 1 month.

To Serve   Trim the sorrel leaves of the stems and cut into very fine shreds. If the stems appear very thick and coarse, you should remove the part of the stem that travels up the leaf, because that part is frequently tough and fibrous. Bring the soup base to a simmer in a large saucepan. Stir in the sorrel leaves and cream, cover, and cook the soup over low heat for 15 minutes. Check the seasoning and, off the heat, swirl in the tablespoon of softened butter.

SHOPPING LIST
Vegetables: onions, boiling potatoes, carrot, sorrel   *Staple:* chicken stock
Dairy: butter, light cream

CROOKNECK SQUASH SOUP WITH CHERVIL

To arrive at the nicest texture for this soup, by all means put it through your food mill fitted with the medium disk. The food processor tends to spin the soup into an airy indiscriminate liquid. And I like to purée the vegetables in with the soup once they are cooked, rather than purée them raw, which some recipes for this type of soup encourage. In this way the soup is smooth and fiberless, and the flavor is more fully developed when the vegetables are cooked in the stock.

4 tablespoons olive oil
1 onion, finely chopped
1 garlic clove, finely chopped
¾ pound yellow crookneck squash, cubed
3 cups chicken stock
salt and freshly ground pepper

dash of cayenne pepper or a few drops of Tabasco sauce

To Serve

1 cup heavy cream, warmed
1½ tablespoons chopped fresh chervil
½ tablespoon finely chopped parsley

1. Heat the olive oil in a soup pot or large heavy saucepan. Stir in the chopped onion and garlic, and soften both in the oil until translucent, slowly, over low heat.

2. Stir in the squash cubes and continue to cook slowly for 5 minutes. Pour in the chicken stock. Season with salt and pepper and add a sprinkling of cayenne pepper or

Tabasco. Bring the soup to a boil. Simmer, covered, until the squash is very tender, about 30 minutes.

To Store Cool the soup slightly, purée it through a food mill, then cool completely. Store the soup in a covered container in the refrigerator for up to 3 days.

To Serve Slowly reheat the soup base in a covered saucepan. Uncover, and stir in the warmed cream and chopped chervil. Bring the soup just to the simmer, heating the liquid until it is piping hot. Correct the seasoning and stir in the chopped parsley.

NOTE: This soup is also delicious served cold. To do so, stew the onions and garlic as outlined in Step 1. Add the squash and 2 tablespoons of water, cover the pot tightly, and cook slowly until the squash is tender, then purée the vegetables. Chill the purée, keeping it in a covered container in the refrigerator, for up to 2 days. On serving day, add the chicken stock (it must be very cold) and the heavy cream (very cold). Season with salt, pepper, cayenne or Tabasco, and chill again until serving time. Stir in the chopped parsley and chervil before serving.

SHOPPING LIST
Vegetables: onion, garlic, crookneck squash
Dairy: heavy cream
Staples: olive oil, chicken stock

Herbs and spice: fresh chervil, parsley, cayenne pepper or Tabasco

GARLIC SOUP

There are numerous ways to arrive at a bowl of garlic soup, the main drawing card being whole garlic cloves simmered in water and stock until they are soft and buttery, then puréed and sent back into the soup base. Some cooks finish off the soup creamily, blending in a supplement of egg yolks and cream or egg yolks and olive oil. I prefer the latter and have outlined the procedure for this last fillip below.

8 large or 12 small garlic cloves, unpeeled
1 tablespoon olive oil
leaves from 2 sprigs of fresh thyme
6 parsley stems tied with 1 small imported bay leaf
large pinch of ground cloves
4 cups chicken stock

salt and freshly ground pepper

To Serve

2 egg yolks
2½ tablespoons olive oil
cayenne pepper
1 recipe Crisp Bread Slices (page 154)
a bowl of freshly grated Gruyère cheese

1. Put the garlic cloves in a saucepan of boiling water and boil for 1 minute. Drain and peel.

2. In a soup pot, place the garlic cloves, 1 tablespoon olive oil, thyme, parsley bundle, and cloves. Pour on the chicken stock and season with salt and freshly ground pepper.

3. Bring the contents of the pot to a simmer. Cover and simmer for 50 minutes. Discard the parsley bundle and purée the garlic cloves with a little of the soup through a food mill. Stir the puréed mixture back into the soup.

To Store　Cool the soup thoroughly, then refrigerate, in a covered container, for up to 4 days or freeze for up to 1 week.

To Serve　Reheat the soup to piping hot. Beat the egg yolks and 2½ tablespoons olive oil in a mixing bowl until thick and sticky. Beat in a sprinkle or two of cayenne pepper. Pour two ladles of the hot soup into the egg yolk mixture and blend well.

Remove the soup pot from the heat and return the egg yolk mixture to the soup, stirring thoroughly. Put the soup pot back on the heat and bring just to below the simmer, slowly, stirring all the time.

Portion out the soup among bowls and top each with a few toasted bread slices. Pass the grated cheese for each person to sprinkle on top.

SHOPPING LIST
Vegetable: garlic
Dairy: eggs, Gruyère cheese
Staples: olive oil, chicken stock

Herbs and spices: fresh thyme, parsley, bay leaf, ground cloves, cayenne pepper
For serving: Crisp Bread Slices (see recipe)

LENTIL AND POTATO SOUP

Full-bodied soups revitalize, especially those built on lentils, white beans or split peas, and flavorsome homemade stock. It would be a pity to ruin soup makings with canned broth (the stagnant flavor is overwhelming). Make your stock, then make this soup.

¼ pound lean salt pork, rind removed, finely cubed
1 onion, chopped
2 tablespoons butter
1 small garlic clove, chopped
1 carrot, diced
2 small ribs celery heart, diced
¼ cup tomato purée (homemade) or chopped canned plum tomatoes

freshly ground pepper
6 parsley sprigs tied with 1 small imported bay leaf
5 cups beef stock
¾ cup lentils
2 small boiling potatoes, peeled and cubed
salt

1. Put the salt pork cubes in a soup pot and place over moderate heat. Sauté them in their own fat until lightly golden. Add the chopped onion and stir. Add the butter, garlic, carrots, and celery. Cook and stir for 5 minutes.

2. Stir in the tomato purée or canned tomatoes, and season with pepper. Simmer for 2 minutes. Add the parsley bundle, beef stock, and lentils. Bring the contents of the pot to a simmer, cover, and simmer steadily for 25 minutes.

3. Add the potato cubes and simmer until they are tender, about 20 minutes longer. Remove the bay leaf and parsley bundle. Season the soup with salt to taste.

To Store   Transfer the soup to a storage container, cool, and cover tightly. Refrigerate for up to 6 days or freeze for up to 8 weeks.

To Serve   Reheat the soup in a covered pot until piping hot throughout. (The stored soup may thicken on reheating. Thin it out with a little water or, if it is handy, a little extra beef stock.) Adjust the seasoning if necessary, and serve.

SHOPPING LIST
Meat: salt pork
Vegetables: onion, garlic, celery, carrot, tomato purée or canned plum tomatoes, boiling potatoes

Dairy: butter
Staples: lentils, beef stock
Herbs: parsley, bay leaf

MUSHROOM AND BARLEY SOUP

Mushroom soup with tiny pellets of barley is soothing, comforting food for cold, wind-swept days. And it is even more satisfying to know that a carton or two of the soup is safely tucked away in the refrigerator or freezer. Dried mushrooms are perfect for this kind of winter cookery because they lend a special deeply rounded aroma, and the barley gives forth its own mellow body.

1 ounce dried mushrooms
3 tablespoons butter
1 tablespoon vegetable oil
2 onions, chopped
⅔ cup pearl barley
salt and freshly ground pepper

4 cups chicken stock

To Serve

¾ cup light cream, warmed
2 tablespoons finely chopped parsley

1. Soak the dried mushrooms in ¾ cup warm water for 20 minutes.

2. While the mushrooms are soaking, heat the butter and oil in a soup pot or large saucepan. Stir in the chopped onions and sauté them slowly for 5 minutes.

3. Drain the mushrooms, saving the soaking liquid. Rinse the mushrooms under cool water, dry, and chop coarsely. Strain the mushroom juice through a filter: a coffee filter works perfectly for this.

4. Stir the mushrooms into the sautéed onions. Add the barley and season with salt and pepper. Pour in the filtered mushroom soaking liquid along with the chicken stock.

5. Bring the contents of the pot to a simmer. Cover and simmer for 45 minutes.

To Store   Cool the soup completely and store in a covered container in the refrigerator for up to 6 days or in the freezer for up to 6 weeks.

To Serve   Reheat the soup in a covered saucepan. Stir in the heated cream and chopped parsley. Correct the seasoning and simmer, uncovered, for 5 minutes before serving.

SHOPPING LIST
Vegetables: onions
Dairy: butter, light cream
Staples: dried mushrooms, vegetable oil, pearl barley,

chicken stock
Herb: parsley

POTATO AND LEEK SOUP

This soup will delight those who like the flavor of leeks in a creamy-rich potato base. The potatoes give the soup body and the dill is a tasty contrast against the subtle onion taste of the leeks.

3 tablespoons butter
1 bunch leeks (about 5), white part only, thinly sliced
½ pound potatoes, peeled and sliced
salt and freshly ground pepper
4 cups chicken stock

To Serve

¾ cup light cream
⅓ cup heavy cream
¼ cup fresh minced dill
1 tablespoon butter, softened

1. Put the 3 tablespoons butter in a heavy soup pot. Stir in the leeks to coat with the butter, then cover and cook over low heat for 20 minutes, or until very soft and translucent.

2. Stir in the sliced potatoes, season with salt and pepper, and pour in the chicken stock. Bring the contents of the pot to a simmer. Cover and simmer for 30 minutes.

To Store   Purée the liquid and vegetables through a food mill. When completely cool, store this part of the soup in a covered container in the refrigerator for up to 5 days or freeze for up to 1 month.

To Serve Slowly heat the soup in a covered pot until very hot throughout. Heat the creams and pour them into the soup. Stir in the dill and bring to the simmer. Cook slowly for 2–3 minutes longer to blend the flavors. Adjust the seasoning, swirl in the butter off the heat, and serve.

SHOPPING LIST
Vegetables: leeks, potatoes
Dairy: butter, light cream, heavy cream

Staple: chicken stock
Herb: dill

SHE-CRAB SOUP

This is not the usual vegetable-based crab soup, with green beans and tomatoes, with potatoes and celery. This recipe calls for some milk, some cream, and a few seasonings. If "blue" (fresh) female crabs are not available, just substitute a good 1½–1¾ cups of crabmeat, preferably with some of the roe included. The roe enriches the soup and makes it very tasty.

8 fresh she crabs, cleaned	2 teaspoons Worcestershire sauce
6 shallots, finely chopped	3 tablespoons dry sherry
2 tablespoons butter	large pinch of mace
2 teaspoons all-purpose flour	salt and freshly ground pepper
1½ cups light cream	1½ tablespoons finely chopped parsley
2½ cups milk	

1. Steam the crabs for 20 minutes. Cool, crack them open, and pick out the meat and roe.

2. In a heavy saucepan, sauté the shallots in the butter until they become soft. Stir in the flour and cook for 2 minutes, stirring. Remove the saucepan from the heat and pour in the cream and milk, stirring constantly. Season the liquid with the Worcestershire sauce, sherry, and mace. Add salt and pepper to taste.

3. Bring the soup base to a simmer over moderate heat, drawing a spoon around the bottom and sides of the saucepan as the soup heats up. Simmer the soup base, partially

covered, for 15 minutes. Add the crab roe and meat and simmer slowly until heated through. Correct the seasoning, swirl in the parsley, and serve very hot.

SPINACH AND LEEK SOUP

You will find this soup smoothly mellow, with more than a suggestion of nutmeg. Gratings of nutmeg, preferably freshly ground, unify the chopped spinach and thinly sliced leeks.

¾ pound young spinach leaves	salt and freshly ground pepper
4 leeks, white part only, finely sliced	4 cups chicken stock
2 tablespoons butter	
½ tablespoon flour	*To Serve*
gratings of ground nutmeg	¾ cup heavy cream

1. Wash the spinach leaves thoroughly; cut away the tough stems and any center vein that seems large and coarse. Put the spinach in a nonmetallic pot, cover tightly, and place over medium-high heat. Cook until the spinach is wilted down by its own moisture, about 4–5 minutes. Put the spinach in a colander, press out the water, and chop finely.

2. In a saucepan, soften the leeks in the butter over moderately low heat. Stir in the flour and cook on medium heat for 2 minutes. Stir in the nutmeg and season with salt and pepper. Pour in the stock. Cover the saucepan and cook at a gentle simmer for 30 minutes.

To Store   Cool the soup, then store in the refrigerator in a covered container for up to 5 days or freeze up to 1 month.

To Serve   Slowly bring the soup to a simmer, covered. Put the cream in a small mixing bowl, and when the soup is hot, stir in a few spoonfuls with the cream, then pour the cream-enriched mixture into the saucepan of soup. Heat the soup over a medium-low flame until it is quite hot. Correct the seasoning and serve.

SPRING VEGETABLE SOUP

Several weeks into the course of spring, you can compose this soup when the vegetables are especially prime. And if you pick and choose correctly, you'll end up with green peas, small and sweet, good and firm leeks and zucchini, and fresh young carrots for this soup.

4 tablespoons butter
3 leeks, white part only, diced
3 carrots, diced
2 small turnips, peeled and diced
2 slender, firm zucchini, diced
6 parsley stems tied with a piece of kitchen string
5 cups chicken stock, potent and flavorful

salt and freshly ground pepper

To Serve

1 pound fresh peas, shelled
1 tablespoon chopped fresh savory or, if unavailable, chopped parsley
¾ cup heavy cream, warmed

1. Heat the butter in a heavy soup pot. Soften the diced leeks in the butter. Stir in the diced carrots and turnips and turn them in the butter. Cook 2 minutes. Stir in the diced zucchini; cook 2 minutes.

2. Add the parsley stem bundle to the pot. Stir in the chicken stock and season to taste with salt and pepper. Bring the contents to a simmer, cover, and simmer slowly for 1 hour or until the vegetables are tender.

To Store   Discard the parsley stalks. When the soup has cooled, refrigerate it in a covered container for up to 5 days or in the freezer for up to 1 month.

To Serve   Reheat the soup in a covered pot. When the soup is hot, add the peas and savory or parsley. Simmer the soup until the peas are tender. Correct the seasoning. Stir in the warmed cream and heat for 3–4 minutes before serving.

SHOPPING LIST
Vegetables: leeks, carrots, turnips, zucchini, peas
Dairy: butter, heavy cream
Staple: chicken stock
Herbs: parsley, fresh savory

WHITE BEAN SOUP WITH BASIL AND CHEESE

This is one of those nourishing soups patterned with white beans, ideally fresh and newly snapped from the pods. Dried white beans, soaked overnight, are an acceptable exchange. But do not try to substitute any other ingredients, which would really obfuscate the identity of the soup. Fresh basil leaves are a must, as is the best-quality olive oil you can find. And if you were to put up a pot of this soup in summer, diced juicy ripe tomatoes and garden-fresh green beans would be most welcome here. Add these along in Step 2, just before you drop in the herb bundle.

¼ pound lean salt pork, diced
2 tablespoons olive oil
2 onions, diced
2 garlic cloves, chopped
2 carrots, diced
2 ribs celery heart, diced
2 cups fresh white beans or ¾ cup dried white beans, such as Great Northern, soaked overnight in cold water to cover, then drained
6 parsley stems tied with 5 basil leaves

and 1 bay leaf
5 cups chicken stock
salt and freshly ground pepper

To Serve

½ cup fresh basil leaves, torn into shreds
2 large garlic cloves, chopped
⅓ cup olive oil
½ cup loosely packed, freshly grated Parmesan cheese
a bowl of freshly grated Parmesan cheese

1. Put the salt pork in the bottom of a heavy soup pot and cook over moderate heat, stirring, until the fat has rendered out and the cubes turn a light golden. With a slotted spoon, remove the cubes to a plate and reserve.

2. Add the 2 tablespoons olive oil to the pot, add the onions, and sauté for 2 minutes. Stir in the garlic and carrots; sauté for 2 minutes. Add the celery and sauté another 2 minutes. Stir in the beans and add the herb bundle.

3. Pour in the chicken stock and season with a very small pinch of salt and freshly ground pepper to taste. Bring the contents of the pot to the simmer. Stir, cover, and simmer slowly for about 1 hour 40 minutes to 2 hours, until the beans are tender.

To Store   Discard the herb bundle, cool the soup to room temperature, then refrigerate in a covered container for up to 6 days or freeze for up to 1 month.

To Serve   Reheat the soup in a covered pot until piping hot. While the soup is heating, prepare the basil, garlic, and cheese addition. Put the basil shreds in a mortar and add the chopped garlic. Season with a pinch of salt. Begin to pound the basil and garlic until the ingredients become pastelike. Add a tablespoon of olive oil and a tablespoon of cheese and pound it in until blended. Continue to add the olive oil and the rest of the ½ cup cheese in this fashion until the mixture is combined.

You could facilitate this process by blending the basil, garlic, and oil in a blender or food processor until pasty, then beat in the cheese. I think that the time is well spent doing the basil and cheese addition by hand—the end product is the better for it—and I would urge you to try the by-hand method at least once.

Put the basil-oil mixture into a serving bowl or serve it directly from the mortar.

Serve the soup very hot and let each person swirl a little basil "sauce" into his or her serving. Pass, also, a bowl of freshly grated Parmesan cheese to sprinkle on top of each portion of soup.

SHOPPING LIST
Meat: salt pork
Vegetables: onions, garlic, carrots, celery, fresh or dried white beans

Dairy: Parmesan cheese
Staples: olive oil, chicken stock
Herbs: parsley, fresh basil, bay leaf

7
VEGETABLES

ARTICHOKES WITH CAPER AND FENNEL SAUCE

The sauce for these artichokes is one of chopped capers and fresh fennel bulb, finely diced, based on oil and vinegar, heightened by a few chopped anchovy fillets. Serve these artichokes warm, basted with spoonfuls of the sauce, as a vegetable course.

4 whole artichokes, trimmed; trimmed parts rubbed with the cut half of a lemon	½ fennel bulb, finely diced
	1 teaspoon capers, chopped
3 tablespoons wine vinegar	8 tablespoons olive oil
3 anchovy fillets, finely chopped	freshly ground pepper
	salt, as necessary

1. Bring a large kettle of salted water to the boil, add the artichokes, and allow the water to return to the boil. Cover and simmer the artichokes until tender when the base is pierced with a skewer or the tip of a knife.

2. While the artichokes are cooking, prepare the caper and fennel sauce. In a mixing bowl, whisk the vinegar and anchovy fillets together until the anchovies begin to disintegrate and blend in. Blend in the fennel bulb and capers. Beat in the olive oil, by tablespoons. Season the sauce with freshly ground pepper.

3. Drain the artichokes when they are tender. Turn them upside down on a wide plate so that all the water drains out.

4. While the artichokes are still quite warm, put them in a serving bowl, not too deep, not too shallow. Taste the sauce; add salt if necessary, or extra pepper. Pour equal parts of the sauce over each artichoke, spooning some between the leaves and around the base, and serve.

SHOPPING LIST
Vegetables: artichokes, fennel   *Staples:* wine vinegar, olive oil, anchovies, capers

ARTICHOKE STEW

Of the many artichoke dishes I have eaten, I am most partial to the kind that simmer the artichokes with vegetables and seasonings, so that the flavors can meld together. In that way, you don't need to offer a side dish of sauce for dipping the leaves into, the goodness comes right from the pan sauce. This recipe is a good example of the benefits of this method, and I have had variations of this kind served up as a vegetable course on large plates with abundant bread slices from a chewy loaf and a ramekin of sweet butter. It is an arrangement I heartily pass on.

3 tablespoons olive oil
1 onion, chopped
2 garlic cloves, chopped
3 ribs celery heart, chopped
¼ pound sliced lean cooked country ham, diced
3 tablespoons chopped parsley
1 tablespoon chopped fresh tarragon leaves

1 small imported bay leaf
⅓ cup dry white wine
1½ cups chicken stock
2 dozen tiny artichokes, trimmed and soaked in a large bowl of water containing the juice of 1 lemon
salt and freshly ground pepper
1 teaspoon lemon juice, or to taste

1. Put the olive oil and the chopped onion in a heavy 6-quart casserole and sauté for 3 minutes. Stir in the garlic and celery; stir and cook for 3 more minutes.

2. Over moderate heat, stir in the ham, parsley, and tarragon. Add the bay leaf and pour on the wine. Bring to the boil. Add the chicken stock and artichokes, drained; season with salt and pepper. Blend everything together.

3. Bring the contents of the casserole to a simmer, cover, and cook at a simmer until the artichokes are tender when the heart is pierced with a skewer or tip of a small knife, about 30 to 40 minutes for small artichokes. Stir occasionally.

4. If, when the artichokes are tender, the liquid has not turned into a light syrup, remove the artichokes and simmer the liquid down. Discard the bay leaf, correct the seasoning, and sprinkle on a little lemon juice to taste. Serve the artichokes, with the syrupy pan juices, heaped in a bowl.

SHOPPING LIST
Vegetables and fruit: artichokes, onion, garlic, celery, lemons
Meat: cooked country ham

Staples: olive oil, dry white wine, chicken stock
Herbs: parsley, fresh tarragon, bay leaf

WHOLE ARTICHOKES WITH GARLIC AND HERBS

In this recipe, a mixture of chopped herbs, garlic, and oil is spread in between the leaves of the raw, trimmed artichokes. Then the artichokes are cooked slowly in a little white wine and chicken stock until tender. I like to do this in one of those casseroles called a *doufeu*.

This pot, most likely found in enameled cast iron, has a cover the top of which is hollowed out for filling with ice cubes or cool water. So during cooking, by the process of condensation, little beads of moisture gather on the underside of the lid, which is riddled with small bumpy dots. The whole piece is a magnificent self-basting unit. I would recommend buying one with a capacity of 6 quarts, so that you can do any of my long-simmering beef, veal, lamb, or pork dishes in it, too.

4 artichokes, trimmed
½ lemon
5 tablespoons olive oil
1 onion, chopped
4 garlic cloves, finely chopped
1 teaspoon fresh thyme leaves, chopped
6 fresh basil leaves, chopped

⅓ cup chopped parsley
salt and freshly ground pepper
three ⅛-inch-thick slices prosciutto, cut
    into strips
½ cup dry white wine
1½ cups chicken stock

1. Trim the artichokes and rub the cut portions with the lemon half.

2. Heat 2 tablespoons of the olive oil in a casserole large enough to hold all of the artichokes, sitting on their bases. Depending on the size of the artichokes, one of your 10- or 12-inch casseroles should do nicely. Soften the chopped onion in the hot olive oil.

3. Combine the remaining 3 tablespoons olive oil, garlic, thyme, basil, parsley, and salt and pepper to taste in a small mixing bowl. Spread the mixture evenly between the leaves of the artichokes.

4. Stir the prosciutto strips into the softened onion, stir, and cook over moderate heat for 1 minute. Pour in the wine and chicken stock and bring to the boil. Season the liquid with salt and pepper.

5. Put the artichokes into the casserole and return the liquid to the boil, spooning some of the liquid over the artichokes as it approaches the boil. Cover the casserole tightly and simmer the artichokes until they are tender, about 45 minutes. A thin skewer plunged through to the base will easily glide past the choke into the heart.

6. Remove the cooked artichokes to a serving platter. Boil down the cooking liquid in the casserole until it is syrupy. Check the seasoning and pour the liquid over the artichokes. Serve them warm, tepid, or at room temperature.

SHOPPING LIST
Meat: prosciutto
Vegetables and fruit: artichokes, onion, garlic, lemon

Staples: olive oil, dry white wine, chicken stock
Herbs: fresh thyme, fresh basil, parsley

ASPARAGUS WITH CREAMY HERB DRESSING

Barely warm asparagus and the tangy soft sheen of an oil and vinegar dressing with cream of one sort, paired with an ideal mixture of fresh herbs, is a felicitous match. Even more, this recipe is one among the culinary lucre of dishes that can be brought to perfection while main courses are reheating.

1½ pounds firm asparagus	salt and freshly ground pepper
2 tablespoons lemon juice	1 tablespoon chopped fresh tarragon
1 teaspoon prepared mustard	leaves
6 tablespoons olive or walnut oil	1 tablespoon snipped chives
2 tablespoons *crème fraîche* or heavy	1 tablespoon chopped parsley
cream	1 teaspoon capers, chopped

1. Trim the asparagus spears and peel off a fine layer of flesh from the bottom of the tip to the base. Trim the base. Put the spears in a deep skillet of cold salted water, bring to the boil, then simmer uncovered until tender, but not limp and mushy (about 12 minutes).

2. Drain the asparagus and pour a few cupfuls of cold water over it to return the fresh green color and stop the cooking process. Drain and dry well.

3. In a mixing bowl, whisk the lemon juice with the mustard. Beat in the oil by tablespoons. Blend in the *crème fraîche* or heavy cream. Stir in the chopped herbs and capers. Season to taste with salt and pepper.

4. Put the asparagus on a serving platter and pour the dressing over the stems.

SHOPPING LIST
Vegetable and fruit: asparagus, lemon
Dairy: crème fraîche or heavy cream

Staples: prepared mustard, olive or walnut oil
Herbs: fresh tarragon, chives, parsley

EGGPLANT WITH FENNEL AND ONIONS

This is a vegetable combination cooked to develop all the full-bodied flavors before being topped off with cheese and baked briefly. This dish is particularly delightful when juicy ripe and brilliant red summer tomatoes become abundant. It is then that the freshest taste of the layerings comes forth; even stored homemade tomato purée is only second best.

2 eggplants

10 tablespoons olive oil

salt and freshly ground pepper

3 small fennel bulbs, trimmed and cut into slices

1 onion, chopped

4 ripe tomatoes, peeled, seeded, and diced

1 tablespoon chopped fresh basil

2 teaspoons chopped fresh oregano

2 tablespoons finely chopped parsley

½-pound piece of fresh mozzarella, shredded

½ tablespoon butter, cut into small pieces

1. Peel the eggplants and cut into long ¾-inch-thick slices. Salt the slices and let them drain in a colander for 20 minutes. Dry the slices on paper toweling and cut into cubes.

2. Heat 3 tablespoons of the oil in a heavy skillet and sauté half of the eggplant in the oil until golden. Remove the eggplant to a bowl; season with salt and pepper. Repeat with the remaining eggplant and another 3 tablespoons olive oil. Add the eggplant to the bowl and season with salt and pepper.

3. Put 3 more tablespoons olive oil in the skillet and stir in the fennel and onion; cook over moderately low heat for 5 minutes, stirring. Stir in the tomatoes, basil, oregano, and parsley. Add the eggplant. Cover and cook for 15 minutes.

4. Turn the vegetables into an ovenproof baking dish, such as a 10-inch oval one, and cover the top with the shredded mozzarella. Sprinkle the top with the remaining tablespoon of olive oil and dot with the pieces of butter.

5. Bake the vegetables in the upper third of a preheated 425° F oven for about 12 minutes, until the cheese is melted and lightly browned on top.

SHOPPING LIST

Vegetables: eggplants, fennel, onion, tomatoes

Dairy: mozzarella cheese, butter

Staple: olive oil

Herbs: fresh basil, fresh oregano, parsley

EGGPLANT WITH ONIONS AND CAPERS

Eggplant cubes, sautéed until golden, with a placement of capers, olives, and a good splash of red wine vinegar make a beautiful side dish that is equally delicious served lukewarm or at room temperature. Some people like to offer it cold, but I feel that the flavors are numbed then. In addition to being a good accompaniment to beef salads, it is a fine first course (when I often add in some roasted peppers) with crusty wedges of bread.

3 firm eggplants
10 tablespoons olive oil
3 onions, diced
4 ribs celery heart, diced
4 fresh tomatoes, peeled, seeded, and chopped (save all the juices)

salt and freshly ground pepper
1 tablespoon tiny nonpareil capers
½ teaspoon red wine vinegar, or more, to taste
8 green olives, thinly sliced
1 tablespoon finely chopped parsley

1. Peel the eggplants and cut each into long slices. Salt the slices and leave them in a colander to drain for 20 minutes. Drain and dry on paper toweling. Cut into large cubes.

2. In a large skillet, heat 3 tablespoons of the olive oil and sauté half the eggplant cubes until lightly golden. Repeat the process with another 3 tablespoons oil and the rest of the eggplant; remove the eggplant.

3. Put the remaining 4 tablespoons oil in the skillet and sauté the onions and celery for 3 minutes. Stir in the tomatoes and season with salt and pepper. Stir in the eggplant, capers, vinegar, and olives. Cover tightly and simmer until the vegetables are tender. Fold in the chopped parsley. Serve warm, tepid, or at room temperature.

To Store   Place the eggplant mixture in a tightly covered container and refrigerate for up to 4 days.

Shopping List
Vegetables: eggplants, onions, celery, tomatoes
Staples: olive oil, capers, red wine vinegar, green olives

Herb: parsley

EGGPLANT, ZUCCHINI, AND FENNEL STEW

Here is a vegetable stew that is a kaleidoscope of colors: putty-toned eggplant and green-skinned zucchini surrounding creamy white flesh, set against the soft mild green of fennel and red tomato flecked with basil. Each vegetable is sautéed briefly in a modest amount of olive oil to lock in its exclusive flavor before all the ingredients are simmered together. The different textures blend, but the stew does not cook long enough to produce a pulpy, puréelike mass.

salt
2 firm eggplants, peeled and cubed
3 slender zucchini, cubed
11 tablespoons olive oil
2 fennel bulbs, trimmed and sliced
2 onions, thinly sliced
3 sweet peppers, a combination of red
   and green, by choice, cored, seeded,
   and cubed

5 ripe tomatoes, peeled, seeded, and
   cubed
3 garlic cloves, minced
2 tablespoons chopped parsley
5 fresh basil leaves, torn into small pieces
freshly ground pepper
1 small imported bay leaf
lemon wedges (optional)

1. Salt the eggplant cubes lightly and place them in a colander. Let them sit for 20 minutes to draw out any bitter juices. Salt the cubes of zucchini lightly and let them drain in a colander as well, for about 20 minutes. Have a large skillet handy.

2. Dry the eggplant and zucchini cubes separately on paper toweling. Sauté the eggplant cubes in two batches: for each batch, heat 3 tablespoons of the olive oil and sauté the cubes until lightly golden. Remove to a bowl and season with salt and pepper. Heat 2 tablespoons of the oil and toss the zucchini cubes in the oil until very lightly browned; add to the bowl and season with salt and pepper.

3. Add 2 tablespoons oil to the skillet and sauté the fennel and onions for 3 minutes. Add this to the bowl and season with salt and pepper.

4. In the remaining tablespoon of oil, sauté the sweet peppers for 3 minutes. Add the tomatoes, garlic, parsley, and basil. Cook for 1 minute longer, add to the bowl, and season with salt and pepper. Add the bay leaf.

5. Turn all the vegetables into a large casserole—a 6-quart one should do fine—and bring to the simmer. Cover and simmer for 25 minutes. Uncover and simmer until the vegetables are tender, about another 20–25 minutes longer, stirring from time to time. Discard the bay leaf.

To Store   Refrigerate the stew, once cooled to room temperature, in a covered storage container for up to 6 days.

To Serve   Serve cool or at room temperature, with lemon wedges on the side, if you like.

Shopping List
Vegetables and fruit: eggplants, zucchini, fennel, onions, peppers, tomatoes, garlic, lemons (optional)

Staple: olive oil
Herbs: parsley, fresh basil, bay leaf

ENDIVES, GLAZED AND BAKED

For this recipe, the pale cream-colored heads of endive are cut into manageable slices and steamed in butter. In goes some hot heavy cream that seeps into the vegetable and enriches it before the whole is turned into a baking dish, topped with cheese, and finished off in the oven until golden.

8 fat heads of Belgian endive, sliced into
   1-inch pieces
1 tablespoon lemon juice
2½ tablespoons butter
salt and freshly ground pepper
½ cup heavy cream, warmed

¼ pound Gruyère cheese, grated
3 tablespoons freshly grated Parmesan
   cheese
2 tablespoons butter, cut into small
   cubes

1. Toss the endive slices in the lemon juice. Heat the 2½ tablespoons butter in a skillet, stir in the endive, and season with salt and pepper. Cover tightly and simmer until the endive is just tender.

2. Stir the warmed cream into the endive and transfer the contents of the skillet to a 7–8-inch baking dish.

3. Combine the grated cheeses and sprinkle evenly over the top of the endive. Dot the surface with the butter cubes. Bake the endive in the upper third of a preheated 400° F oven until golden on top and bubbly within, about 10 minutes.

Shopping List
Vegetable and fruit: endives, lemon
Dairy: butter, heavy cream, Gruyère cheese, Parmesan cheese

GREEN BEANS, SUMMER STYLE, WITH TOMATOES AND TARRAGON

Two special delights of summer, besides the excellent vegetables, are the luxuriant growths of the very greenest and pungent fresh herbs. You don't need much more, save a recipe which is not too ornate for combining them together, such as this one. It all has a lively taste and is good with simple fish sautés or any kind of chicken dish that is not laced with tomatoes.

1½ pounds slender green beans
3½ tablespoons olive oil
1 onion, sliced
4 shallots, chopped
1 small imported bay leaf

4 firm ripe tomatoes, peeled, seeded, and
  cut into large cubes
1 tablespoon chopped fresh tarragon
salt and freshly ground pepper
1 tablespoon finely chopped parsley

1. Cook the green beans in a large pot of boiling salted water until they are partially cooked. Drain them in a colander, refresh with sprays of cold water, drain again, and dry. Trim the ends off the beans and, if they are very long, halve them or slice them into thirds.

2. Heat the olive oil in a sauté pan and cook the onion and shallots until they are soft. Add the bay leaf, tomato cubes, tarragon, the beans, and salt and pepper to taste. Stir once and bring the contents to a simmer. Cover and simmer until the tomatoes reduce down slightly and the beans are tender. Adjust the seasoning, stir in the chopped parsley, and serve.

Shopping List
Vegetables: green beans, onion, shallots, tomatoes   *Herbs:* bay leaf, fresh tarragon, parsley
Staple: olive oil

GRATIN OF FENNEL AND LEEKS

This fast-and-tasty gratin may be prepared with great ease while the white beans are cooking for the main course, Brisket of Beef with White Beans (p. 41). Use the gratin as a vegetable course or serve sections of it right along with the meat.

3 tablespoons butter
5 tablespoons olive oil
8–10 leeks, white part only, cut into 1-
  inch slices
3 shallots, finely chopped
4 fennel bulbs, trimmed and cut into ½-
  inch slices

2 teaspoons lemon juice
salt and freshly ground pepper
¼ pound Gruyère cheese, grated
2 tablespoons freshly grated Parmesan
  cheese
1 tablespoon bread crumbs
1 tablespoon butter, cut into small cubes

1. In a large, heavy nonmetallic saucepan or 4-quart casserole put the 3 tablespoons butter, 4 tablespoons of the oil, and leeks. Set over moderately low heat, cover, and cook 5 minutes, stirring often. Uncover, stir in the shallots, and cook for 3 minutes.

2. Add the fennel and lemon juice and season with salt and pepper. Cover tightly and cook about 25 minutes until the fennel is tender.

3. In a small bowl, combine both cheeses with the bread crumbs. Turn the vegetables into a baking dish, along with all the good buttery juices, and level the top. Sprinkle on the cheese and bread crumb mixture. Dot with the butter cubes and dribble the remaining tablespoon of olive oil on top.

4. Put the gratin under a preheated broiler until the topping is golden and serve.

SHOPPING LIST

Vegetables and fruit: leeks, shallots, fennel, lemon   *Staples:* olive oil, bread crumbs
Dairy: butter, Gruyère cheese, Parmesan cheese

LEEKS, GLAZED AND BAKED

This recipe is a good example of one vegetable's ambidextrous quality. Leeks, cooked in butter and stock, are glazed before they are covered with cheese and baked to make the topping golden. On their own, a vegetable course. With a main course, a savory addition. I also like to change the recipe around slightly, replacing the butter with olive oil, cooling the leeks completely, and steeping them in a vinaigrette dressing with plenty of fresh herbs (and so omitting the final baking).

10–12 leeks
4 tablespoons butter
salt and freshly ground pepper
2 cups chicken stock

To Serve

2½ tablespoons butter
¾ cup grated Gruyère cheese
1 tablespoon dry bread crumbs
pinch of cayenne pepper
1 tablespoon olive oil

1. Trim the roots and the green part from the leeks, leaving the white length. Wash the leeks thoroughly under cold running water to remove the surface dirt. With a small sharp knife, make a slit on the top of each leek, opposite the root end. Flush out any pockets of dirt that cling in the leaves with cool water. Dry the leeks.

2. Melt the 4 tablespoons butter in a casserole large enough to accommodate the leeks in one layer. Add the leeks, turn them in the butter, and season with salt and pepper. Pour

on the chicken broth, bring to a simmer, and cover the saucepan tightly. Cook the leeks at a steady simmer until tender to the tip of a sharp knife, about 30 minutes.

To Store   Cool the leeks in the liquid, which should be lightly reduced and syrupy. Store the leeks with the liquid in a tightly covered container and refrigerate for up to 2 days.

To Serve   Bring the leeks to a simmer in a casserole. Smear 1 tablespoon of the butter on the inside of an 8-inch baking dish. Arrange the leeks in two layers and pour over all the syrupy cooking juices. Combine the grated cheese, bread crumbs, and cayenne pepper and scatter this on top of the leeks. Divide the remaining 1½ tablespoons butter into small cubes and strew on top of the bread crumbs and cheese. Dribble on the olive oil. Bake the leeks in the upper third of a preheated 375° F oven until they are heated through to very hot and the topping is golden, about 35 minutes.

Shopping List
Vegetable: leeks
Dairy: butter, Gruyère cheese

Staples: chicken stock, bread crumbs, olive oil
Spice: cayenne pepper

GRATIN OF BRAISED ONIONS

The large white onions called "silverskins" are fat and mildly sweet, my first choice for this sort of preparation. The outer papery covering of these large globes has a silvery metallic glow and the inside is pearl white. Braised onions take on a glassy sheen from simmering in beef stock and butter, ending with an overlay of cheese.

4½ tablespoons butter
2 tablespoons olive oil
3 pounds onions, sliced
salt and freshly ground pepper
1 cup beef stock

1 cup grated Gruyère cheese
2 tablespoons bread crumbs
1½ tablespoons butter, cut into small
  cubes

1. Heat 4 tablespoons of the butter with the olive oil in a large saucepan or casserole and set over moderate heat.

2. When the butter has melted, stir in all of the sliced onions and cook until they have reduced in volume somewhat, about 2–3 minutes.

3. Season the onions with salt and pepper and pour on the beef stock. Stir to combine

all of the additions and bring the liquid to a simmer. Cover the pot and simmer the onions until tender, about 20 minutes.

4. To assemble the gratin, spread the ½ tablespoon butter on the inside of an 8–9-inch baking dish. Add the onions and all the cooking liquid. Level the top.

5. Combine the cheese and bread crumbs and sprinkle that evenly over the top. Dot the surface with the butter cubes.

6. If the onions are still quite hot at this stage, you need only to put the gratin under a preheated broiler to brown the top and make the onions and juices bubble gently. Otherwise, bake the onions in the upper third of a preheated 400° F oven until golden and bubbly, about 10 minutes.

Shopping List
Vegetable: onions
Dairy: butter, Gruyère cheese

Staples: olive oil, beef stock, bread crumbs

PEPPER STRIPS WITH GARLIC

This is a recipe of crisply sautéed peppers seasoned with chopped garlic. Right before serving, add a dash of wine vinegar or even lemon juice to cut the edge of the olive oil.

8 large sweet peppers, a mixture of red
   and green
⅓ cup olive oil
4 garlic cloves, finely chopped

3 tablespoons finely chopped parsley
salt and freshly ground pepper
red wine vinegar or lemon juice

1. Core, seed, and derib the peppers. Slice into strips.

2. Heat the olive oil in a large skillet and sauté the pepper strips for 4 minutes or until they *just* begin to turn crisply tender. Stir in the chopped garlic and half the chopped parsley. Cook 1–2 minutes longer, stirring, until the strips are tender but still retain their shape.

3. Season the pepper strips with salt and pepper. Splash in some wine vinegar or lemon juice to taste, and stir in the remaining parsley. Serve tepid or at room temperature.

Shopping List
Vegetables: red and green peppers, garlic
Staples: olive oil, red wine vinegar (lemon juice may

be substituted)
Herb: parsley

SPINACH GRATIN WITH NUTMEG

I like to sort out the small, tender spinach leaves and use them in this gratin. Once the spinach is cooked, it is combined with chicken stock and a little cream. The topping is mostly cheese, so it is important, as always, that the cheese be freshly grated. In that way, it does not have a chance to dry out and the flavor is intense.

3 pounds spinach, trimmed and washed well
4 tablespoons butter
salt and freshly ground pepper
¼ teaspoon freshly ground nutmeg
1 cup chicken stock

⅓ cup light cream
¼ cup grated Gruyère cheese
¼ cup freshly grated Parmesan cheese
1 tablespoon bread crumbs
1½ tablespoons butter, cut into small cubes

1. Cook the trimmed spinach leaves in boiling salted water for 4 minutes. Drain well, squeezing all of the water out (it is easiest to do this between two large plates). Chop the spinach.

2. Heat the 4 tablespoons butter in a skillet. Stir in the chopped spinach. Season with salt, pepper, and nutmeg. Pour on the chicken stock and bring to the simmer. Stir in the cream.

3. Turn the spinach into a 9-inch oval baking dish (or use a square dish if you do not own an oval one). In a small bowl, combine the two cheeses with the bread crumbs and sprinkle this evenly over the top of the spinach. Dot the top with the butter cubes.

4. Bake the spinach in a preheated 400° F oven until it is bubbly within and golden on top, about 15–20 minutes. Run the gratin under a hot broiler if the inside is ready and the top is pale.

Shopping List
Vegetable: spinach
Dairy: light cream, Gruyère cheese, Parmesan cheese, butter

Staples: chicken stock, bread crumbs
Spice: ground nutmeg

SLICED TOMATOES WITH MOZZARELLA AND BASIL

For some sultry weeks in summer, artificial gas-ripened tomatoes are replaced with immaculate home-growns. And the best salad treatment is not to tamper with the just-off-the-vine flavor. The addition of basil, a natural companion, and some soft mild mozzarella blends well with the sunny tomato taste. A good, dark green olive oil fits in, but wine vinegar would vie, so reserve it for those seasonal greens.

4 large ripe tomatoes	8 small fresh basil leaves
salt and freshly ground pepper	4–6 tablespoons good olive oil
½ pound piece of mozzarella	

1. Slice the tomatoes a scant ½ inch thick. Arrange the slices, one overlapping the next, on a serving platter. Season the tomatoes with salt and pepper.

2. Cut the mozzarella into cubes or thin slices and scatter them over the tomatoes. Tear the basil into pieces and sprinkle over all.

3. Spoon the olive oil evenly over all so that the tomatoes and mozzarella glisten.

Shopping List
Vegetable: tomatoes　　　　　　　　　　*Staple:* olive oil
Dairy: mozzarella cheese　　　　　　　　*Herb:* fresh basil

BAKED ZUCCHINI AND TOMATOES

When you find yourself with a small pile of zucchini and some fresh tomatoes, turn them into this irresistible dish. The vegetables are cooked briefly with some sliced onion, then baked under a simple covering of bread crumbs and a sprinkling of olive oil. Choose very young, thin zucchini, and if they are indeed small, toss in a few extra. Scrub them well to take off the surface grit, then trim the ends.

6 zucchini, sliced	½ tablespoon chopped oregano leaves
¼ cup olive oil	4 basil leaves, torn into small pieces
1 onion, sliced	salt and freshly ground pepper
2 peppers, red or green, cored, seeded, deribbed, and sliced into thin strips	4 tablespoons bread crumbs
	1 teaspoon finely chopped parsley
3 tomatoes, peeled, seeded, and cubed	1½ tablespoons olive oil

1. Sprinkle the zucchini slices with salt and leave in a colander to drain for 15 minutes.

2. In a skillet, heat the ¼ cup olive oil and sauté the onions until soft. Stir in the sliced peppers and sauté for 3 minutes. Drain the zucchini slices well on paper toweling. Add them to the peppers and onions and sauté for 4 minutes.

3. Stir in the tomatoes, oregano, and basil. Cook over moderate heat for 5 minutes. Season the vegetables with salt and pepper.

4. Turn the vegetable mixture into an ovenproof baking dish, 9–10 inches. Combine the bread crumbs and parsley, and sprinkle the mixture over the vegetables. Sprinkle evenly with the 1½ tablespoons olive oil.

5. Bake the vegetables on the upper level of a preheated 375° F oven until they are cooked through and the topping is golden, about 20 minutes. If the vegetables are done but the top is still pale, run the dish under a hot broiler for a few seconds before serving.

Shopping List
Vegetables: zucchini, onions, peppers, tomatoes   *Herbs:* fresh oregano, fresh basil, parsley
Staples: olive oil, bread crumbs

GRATIN OF ZUCCHINI WITH ONIONS AND HERBS

If you muse on what makes compilations of vegetables so appealing, you may concede that it really only takes a few ingredients to create a nice dish: good cheese, sweet unsalted butter, snippets of fresh herbs, and of course, the fresh vegetables. That's all there is to it. Here is an example of what I mean.

5 tablespoons butter
2 tablespoons olive oil
3 onions, thinly sliced
8 slender zucchini, cut into rounds, lightly salted, left to stand in a colander for 15–20 minutes, drained, and dried

1½ teaspoons fresh thyme leaves, chopped
5 fresh basil leaves, shredded
salt and freshly ground pepper
⅓ cup chicken stock
1 cup grated Gruyère cheese
3 tablespoons bread crumbs
1 tablespoon butter, cut into cubes

1. Heat the 5 tablespoons butter and olive oil in a heavy skillet. Add the onions and cook them until soft and translucent. Stir in the zucchini and cook over moderate heat until they just begin to give up their firmness.

2. Stir in the thyme and basil; season with salt and pepper. Cook for 1 minute. Turn the vegetables into a 9–10-inch baking dish and pour on the chicken stock.

3. Stir the bread crumbs into the grated cheese and sprinkle this over the top of the vegetables. Dot the top with the butter cubes. Bake the vegetables in the upper third of a preheated 400° F oven until tender and hot all through and the topping is golden.

SHOPPING LIST

Vegetables: onions, zucchini
Dairy: butter, Gruyère cheese

Staples: olive oil, chicken stock, bread crumbs
Herbs: fresh thyme, fresh basil

8

POTATOES, GRAINS, AND NOODLES

WARM POTATO SALAD WITH OREGANO AND RED ONION

This is a lovely variation of the potato salad theme. Like the others that follow, it uses freshly cooked potatoes—old, cold, previously simmered potatoes have no luster—and it is reinforced with thin slices of red onion. Remember to soak the onion slices in ice water to dispel any harsh flavors.

2 pounds small boiling potatoes
salt
1 small red onion, thinly sliced
7 tablespoons olive oil

leaves from 3 sprigs of oregano, about 1½ tablespoons, chopped
2½ tablespoons wine vinegar
freshly ground pepper

1. Put the potatoes in a large pot. Add several healthy pinches of salt and enough cold water to comfortably cover the potatoes. Bring the water to a boil, then simmer the potatoes until they are tender at the piercing of a metal skewer, about 15 minutes, depending on the size of the potatoes.

2. As the potatoes cook, soak the slices of red onion in ice water for 15 minutes, then drain and blot them dry on paper toweling.

3. Drain the potatoes in a colander, peel them, and cut into thick slices or cubes. Turn the potatoes and onion slices into a mixing bowl and coat with the olive oil. Fold in the chopped oregano and vinegar. Season with salt and pepper, and serve.

SHOPPING LIST
Vegetables: boiling potatoes, red onion
Staples: olive oil, wine vinegar

Herb: oregano

WARM POTATO SALAD WITH SAVORY

The key to a lovely warm salad is to cook the potatoes until tender in their jackets and dress them right after they are peeled.

2½ pounds small boiling potatoes
1 small imported bay leaf
salt
8 tablespoons olive oil
1 tablespoon chopped fresh summer savory

2 small garlic cloves, peeled and sliced in half
2½ tablespoons white wine vinegar, or to taste
freshly ground pepper
1½ tablespoons finely chopped parsley

1. Put the potatoes in a large pot. Add the bay leaf and several good pinches of salt; pour in enough cold water to cover the potatoes. Bring the potatoes to a boil and simmer

until tender. A thin skewer should pierce the potatoes easily, but they must not lose their shape or turn mushy.

2. Drain the potatoes in a colander and peel them. Cut each into cubes or thick slices. In a bowl, gently toss the warm potatoes with the oil, savory, garlic, and vinegar. Let the potatoes sit to absorb all the flavors, at least 10 minutes.

3. Sprinkle over the vinegar and toss. Discard the garlic clove halves and season the potatoes with salt and pepper to taste. Fold in the chopped parsley, toss again, and serve.

SHOPPING LIST

Vegetables: boiling potatoes, garlic
Staples: olive oil, white wine vinegar

Herbs: bay leaf, fresh summer savory, parsley

WARM POTATO SALAD WITH WHITE WINE

Warm potatoes, just boiled and peeled, are delicious when tossed in white wine along with some other ingredients that seep in and blend in a piquant way. A big bowl of potatoes prepared in this fashion has changed the loyalty of many I know from the variation which is often brashly overloaded with mayonnaise and onions. One thing you must remember, if the potato salad is to be savored at its best, is to serve this dish while the potatoes are still warm.

1¾ pounds small boiling potatoes
3 tablespoons dry white wine
1 tablespoon white wine vinegar
2 teaspoons prepared mustard, such as a coarse-grained variety

salt
6–8 tablespoons good olive oil
freshly ground pepper
2 tablespoons finely chopped parsley

1. Put the potatoes in a large saucepan of cold water, bring to the boil, and simmer until just tender. Drain the cooked potatoes in a colander and peel them while they are still hot.

2. Cut the potatoes into thick slices or large chunks, as you like. Transfer the potatoes, as they are prepared, to a mixing bowl. Toss the potatoes in the wine.

3. Whisk the vinegar, mustard, and salt to taste in a small mixing bowl. Blend in the

olive oil, tablespoon by tablespoon, adding 6 tablespoons at first. Season with pepper. Pour this over the potatoes and toss well. Add the remaining 2 tablespoons of olive oil if the potatoes seem dry (this will depend on the age and type of the boiling potatoes).

4. Scatter the chopped parsley over the potatoes, taste for additional salt and pepper, and serve while warm.

SHOPPING LIST
Vegetables: boiling potatoes
Staples: dry white wine, white wine vinegar, prepared
mustard, olive oil
Herb: parsley

BUCKWHEAT KERNELS WITH SAUTÉED ONIONS

The small brown and white kernels of buckwheat (kasha) have a definite nutty flavor, which for some is an acquired taste. The kernels, or groats, are available in three textures, medium, coarse, and whole. For me, the choicest varieties are coarse and whole because the composition of the cooked grains is assertive and textural.

4 tablespoons vegetable oil
1 onion, chopped
2 cups whole or coarse buckwheat groats
2 eggs, beaten
2 garlic cloves, finely chopped

3 tablespoons chopped parsley
1 teaspoon salt, or to taste
freshly ground pepper
4 cups boiling stock or water

1. Heat the vegetable oil in a 4-quart casserole. Stir in the chopped onions and cook them until soft and translucent. Raise the heat slightly and sauté the onions until golden.

2. While the onions are sautéing, heat the buckwheat groats in a wide skillet over a moderately high flame for 3 minutes, or until you begin to smell the nutty aroma of the grains. Stir once or twice as the grains begin to heat up. Remove the skillet from the heat, pour on the beaten eggs, and stir the eggs through thoroughly to coat all the grains.

3. Stir the chopped garlic into the onions; sauté for 1 minute. Stir in the chopped parsley, salt, and pepper to taste. Fold in the buckwheat groats. Pour the boiling stock or water into the casserole. Stir once to combine.

4. Bring the contents of the casserole to a simmer, cover tightly, and simmer over low heat for 20–30 minutes or until the buckwheat groats have absorbed the entire amount of liquid and are tender-soft. If serving immediately, turn out into a warm serving bowl.

(continued)

To Store   Cool the groats completely, turn into a storage container, and cover. Refrigerate for up to 3 days in advance of serving.

To Serve   Place the groats in a lightly oiled casserole, cover tightly, and heat in a 300° F oven until hot throughout, about 25–30 minutes.

Shopping List
Vegetables: onion, garlic
Dairy: eggs
Staples: vegetable oil, buckwheat groats, stock or

water
Herb: parsley

CRACKED WHEAT WITH PECANS

Coarse cracked wheat grains (bulghur) are delicious when cooked in homemade chicken stock, which the angles of the grains absorb so well. In this recipe, the cracked wheat is embroidered with butter-toasted chopped pecans. I hope you will try this along with stuffed cabbage leaves and consider what a pleasant change it is from potatoes or rice.

2 onions, peeled and chopped
1 tablespoon vegetable oil
2 tablespoons butter
1½ cups coarse cracked wheat
½ teaspoon salt

freshly ground pepper to taste
3 cups hot chicken stock
⅓ cup chopped pecans, sautéed until lightly golden in 1 tablespoon butter
2 tablespoons finely chopped parsley

1. In a heavy casserole (4-quart is a convenient size), soften the onions in the oil and butter over moderately low heat.

2. Stir in the cracked wheat, season with salt and pepper, and pour on the stock. Stir once.

3. Bring the liquid to a simmer, cover the casserole closely, and cook over low heat about 15–20 minutes until the grains are tender and the chicken stock is absorbed. Fold in the sautéed pecans and chopped parsley and serve the cracked wheat from a warm bowl.

Shopping List
Vegetables: onions
Dairy: butter
Staples: vegetable oil, coarse cracked wheat, chicken

stock, pecans
Herbs: parsley

BUTTERED NOODLES

Noodles pick up the perfectly seasoned pan sauce that is part of many main courses done in advance. Bring a large pot of water to the boil while your entrée is heating up; boil the noodles as the main course is nearly ready, and once the noodles are dressed, never let them linger.

Possible additions to buttered noodles are 1 teaspoon poppy seeds; 1 tablespoon lightly toasted sesame seeds; 3 tablespoons pine nuts browned lightly in 2 teaspoons butter. Be careful not to pair the seed or nut additions with main courses that would conflict with or repeat the flavor. Also, noodles with nuts should not appear in a menu that includes nuts in the dessert.

¾ pound broad egg noodles (or fine noo-
    dles, for a change)

3½ tablespoons butter, softened
salt and freshly ground pepper to taste

1. Cook the noodles in a large pot of boiling salted water until cooked, but still slightly firm to the bite, not at all mushy, as you would any good-quality pasta. Taste a noodle from time to time to judge the right stage.

2. Drain the noodles in a colander and quickly transfer them to a warm bowl, to which you have added half the butter. Toss, add the remaining butter and seasonings, and toss again.

SHOPPING LIST
Dairy: butter

Staple: egg noodles

9
SALADS

BIBB LETTUCE SALAD

4 heads of Bibb lettuce (fewer if they are large)
1½ tablespoons lemon juice
salt

4½ tablespoons olive or walnut oil
3 tablespoons minced celery leaves
2 teaspoons finely chopped parsley

1. Detach the leaves from the central core of the lettuce. Wash the leaves under cool water and dry thoroughly. Tear the leaves into manageable pieces; place in a bowl.

2. In a small mixing bowl, blend the lemon juice with salt to taste. Beat in the oil, tablespoon by tablespoon. Mix in the celery leaves. Pour the dressing over the greens and toss. Sprinkle on the chopped parsley and toss again.

SHOPPING LIST
Vegetables and fruit: Bibb lettuce, celery leaves, lemon

Staples: olive or walnut oil
Herb: parsley

ENDIVE AND BEET SALAD

1 tablespoon lemon juice
½ tablespoon wine vinegar
salt
½ teaspoon prepared mustard
4½ tablespoons olive oil

1 tablespoon finely chopped parsley
freshly ground pepper
4 heads of endive
3 cooked beets, peeled and shredded or cubed

1. In a small mixing bowl, beat together the lemon juice, vinegar, and salt to taste. Blend in the prepared mustard. Beat in the olive oil slowly, whisking constantly. Mix in the parsley and pepper to taste.

2. Cut the endive heads into 1-inch-thick pieces and place in a bowl with the beets. Pour over the dressing, toss, and serve.

SHOPPING LIST
Vegetables and fruit: endive, beets, lemon
Staples: wine vinegar, olive oil, prepared mustard

Herb: parsley

SALAD OF ENDIVE AND CELERY HEART

4 firm, tight heads of endive
2 ribs celery heart, thinly sliced
1½ tablespoons red wine vinegar
salt

½ teaspoon prepared mustard
1 teaspoon dry sherry
4½ tablespoons olive oil
freshly ground pepper

1. Trim the endive and cut into 1-inch-thick slices. Combine with the celery in a mixing bowl.

2. In a bowl, whisk the vinegar with salt to taste. Blend in the mustard and sherry. Beat in the olive oil by tablespoons and season with pepper to taste. Pour the dressing over the endive and celery, toss, and serve.

SHOPPING LIST
Vegetables: endive, celery heart

Staples: red wine vinegar, prepared mustard, dry sherry, olive oil

GREEN BEAN SALAD WITH SHALLOTS AND MIXED HERBS

For this green bean salad, I like to use a vinegar other than the standard red wine type, such as a sherry wine vinegar or that deep balsamic kind. It has a deep, full flavor, not at all thin. I would also use a supply of fresh herbs, mixed, but you could get by with just chopped parsley if you are not fostering any tarragon or marjoram.

1 pound thin fresh green beans
2 tablespoons sherry wine vinegar or another vinegar, your choice
2 anchovy fillets, minced
5 shallots, minced
salt

6 tablespoons olive oil
freshly ground pepper
1 tablespoon finely chopped parsley
2 teaspoons chopped fresh tarragon
2 teaspoons chopped fresh marjoram or oregano

1. Cook the green beans in plenty of boiling salted water until crisply tender. Drain in a colander, pour cold water over them to cool thoroughly, drain well, and dry.

2. Trim off the two ends of the beans with a sharp paring knife, then cut the beans into manageable pieces.

3. In a small mixing bowl, whisk the vinegar with the anchovy fillets and shallots. Season with salt to taste. Beat in the olive oil, one tablespoon at a time. Season with pepper to taste.

4. Put the beans in a mixing bowl, and toss with the dressing until they glisten. Add the herbs, toss again, and serve.

SHOPPING LIST

Vegetables: green beans, shallots
Staples: sherry wine or other vinegar, anchovies, olive oil

Herbs: parsley, fresh tarragon, fresh marjoram or oregano

SALAD OF LENTILS WITH BASIL

Lentils are enticing in salad form, blended with celery, wine vinegar, some dense olive oil, and small pieces of fresh basil. I think that lentils prepared in this fashion are just as good as they are in thick winter soups.

1 pound lentils
1 small imported bay leaf
1 small carrot, cut into thirds
11 tablespoons olive oil
4 ribs celery heart, diced
½ small red onion, diced
3 tablespoons red wine vinegar

1 teaspoon good-quality prepared mustard
freshly ground pepper
6 fresh basil leaves, torn into small pieces
2 tablespoons finely chopped parsley
salt

1. Put the lentils, bay leaf, and carrots in a large pot. Pour in enough cold water to cover the goods by 3 inches. Bring the water to a boil, then reduce the heat so that the lentils simmer slowly about 35 minutes until they are tender. Do not add any salt at this point or the lentils will toughen.

2. When the lentils are tender, drain them in a colander. Discard the bay leaf and carrots. Place the lentils in a mixing bowl and dribble over 2 tablespoons of the olive oil, then shake the bowl to draw in the olive oil.

3. In a small mixing bowl, whisk the vinegar with the mustard. By tablespoons, beat

Salads   259

in the remaining 9 tablespoons olive oil. Add the basil and parsley. Season with pepper to taste. Fold the dressing into the lentils. Just before serving, season with salt.

SHOPPING LIST
Vegetables: carrot, celery, red onion
Staples: lentils, olive oil, red wine vinegar, prepared mustard
Herbs: fresh basil, parsley, bay leaf

SALAD OF RED LEAF LETTUCE WITH HERBS

1 head red leaf lettuce, trimmed
1½ tablespoons lemon juice
1 teaspoon wine vinegar
¼ teaspoon prepared mustard
salt

5½ tablespoons olive oil
1½ tablespoons chopped mixed fresh herbs, such as tarragon, chervil, and parsley
freshly ground pepper

1. Wash the lettuce leaves well in cool water. Dry. Tear the leaves into manageable pieces and put them in a bowl.

2. In a small mixing bowl, whisk the lemon juice, vinegar, mustard, and salt to taste. Add the olive oil slowly, beating well. Blend in the chopped herbs and season with pepper to taste.

3. Pour the dressing over the greens and toss.

SHOPPING LIST
Vegetable: red leaf lettuce
Staples: lemon juice, wine vinegar, prepared mustard, olive oil
Herbs: fresh mixed herbs (tarragon, chervil, parsley, or your own combination)

WATERCRESS AND BIBB LETTUCE SALAD

2 heads Bibb lettuce
2 bunches watercress
1½ tablespoons wine vinegar
½ teaspoon nonpareil capers, finely chopped

salt
4½ tablespoons olive oil
freshly ground pepper

1. Wash the lettuce and watercress well. Dry thoroughly and tear the greens into pieces. Finely chop part of the more tender stems to make 3 tablespoons.

2. In a small mixing bowl, whisk the vinegar with the capers and salt to taste. Beat in the olive oil by tablespoons. Blend in the watercress stems and pepper to taste.

3. Pour the dressing over the greens, toss, and serve.

SHOPPING LIST
Vegetables: Bibb lettuce, watercress   *Staples:* wine vinegar, capers, olive oil

SALAD OF WATERCRESS AND ENDIVE

2 bunches crisp watercress
3 firm, tight heads endive
1½ tablespoons lemon juice

1 teaspoon wine vinegar
5 tablespoons olive oil
salt and freshly ground pepper

1. Trim the watercress, discarding the thicker stems. Wash and dry. Break off the small clusters of leaves into bite-size pieces. Place the watercress in a bowl.

2. Cut the endive into 1-inch pieces and add to the watercress.

3. Whisk the lemon juice and vinegar in a mixing bowl. Beat in the olive oil a tablespoon at a time. Season with salt and pepper to taste. Pour the dressing over the watercress and endive. Toss and serve.

SHOPPING LIST
Vegetables and fruit: watercress, endive, lemon   *Staples:* wine vinegar, olive oil

WATERCRESS SALAD WITH LEMON VINAIGRETTE

3 bunches watercress
2 tablespoons lemon juice
½ teaspoon prepared mustard
salt
6 tablespoons olive oil

freshly ground pepper
2 teaspoons chopped parsley
2 teaspoons chopped fresh chervil or tarragon

1. Wash the watercress leaves well. Dry. Detach the tougher central stems and discard. Tear the sprigs into small pieces and put them into a bowl.

2. In a small mixing bowl, whisk the lemon juice with the mustard and salt to taste. Beat in the olive oil by tablespoons. Season with pepper to taste. Blend in the chopped herbs.

3. Pour the dressing over the greens, toss, and serve.

WATERCRESS SALAD WITH MUSTARD AND HERBS

2–3 bunches watercress, depending upon size
1½ tablespoons wine vinegar
salt
¾ teaspoon good-quality prepared mustard

4½ tablespoons olive oil
freshly ground pepper
2 teaspoons finely chopped parsley
2 teaspoons finely chopped fresh chervil
2 teaspoons finely chopped fresh tarragon

1. Wash the watercress well under cool water and dry thoroughly. Trim into tiny branches, removing the tougher and longer stems. Place the watercress in a bowl.

2. In a small mixing bowl, blend the vinegar with salt to taste. Whisk in the mustard, and add the olive oil by tablespoons. Season with pepper to taste.

3. Pour the dressing over the watercress, scatter over the chopped herbs, and toss well.

SALAD OF WATERCRESS AND RED LEAF LETTUCE

1 head red leaf lettuce
1 bunch crisp watercress
1½ tablespoons wine vinegar
salt

4½ tablespoons olive oil
freshly ground pepper
1 tablespoon snipped chives
2 teaspoons finely chopped parsley

1. Wash the lettuce and watercress thoroughly under cool water, dry, then trim and break into manageable pieces. Put the lettuce and watercress into a bowl.

2. Whisk the vinegar with salt to taste in a small mixing bowl. Beat in the olive oil by tablespoons and season with pepper to taste. Blend in the chives and parsley. Pour the dressing over the greens, toss, and serve.

SHOPPING LIST
Vegetables: red leaf lettuce, watercress
Staples: wine vinegar, olive oil

Herbs: chives, parsley

WATERCRESS AND WALNUT SALAD

3 bunches crisp watercress
1½ tablespoons wine vinegar
salt
2 pinches dry mustard or ½ teaspoon prepared mustard
5 tablespoons walnut oil

12 walnut halves, lightly toasted and coarsely chopped
freshly ground pepper
1 tablespoon finely chopped parsley (optional)

1. Break off the thicker central stems of the watercress leaves and discard. Separate out the smaller branches and rinse them in cool water. Dry thoroughly. Place the watercress in a bowl.

2. Whisk together the vinegar, salt to taste, and mustard. Blend in the walnut oil by tablespoons, then the chopped walnuts. Season with pepper to taste. Blend in the parsley, if you like.

3. Pour the dressing over the watercress and toss lightly but thoroughly.

SHOPPING LIST
Vegetable: watercress
Staples: wine vinegar, dry or prepared mustard, wal-

nut oil, walnut halves
Herb: parsley (optional)

VINAIGRETTE OF ZUCCHINI

A simple vegetable dish that needs best-quality olive oil and characterful vinegar. You could also turn this into a sautéed salad by salting cut-up zucchini cubes and leaving to drain in a colander for 20 minutes. After they are dried, cook them until tender-crisp without browning in hot olive oil. Season while still hot and serve warm.

8 slender, firm zucchini, washed well	salt
8 tablespoons olive oil	freshly ground pepper
1 garlic clove, peeled and sliced in half	1½ tablespoons chopped fresh marjoram
2 tablespoons sherry vinegar or red wine	or savory
vinegar	1 tablespoon finely chopped parsley

1. Cook the whole zucchini, uncovered, in rapidly boiling water until tender but not limp, about 15–20 minutes. Drain in a colander and refresh under cold water.

2. Trim off the top and bottom from each zucchini and cut into cubes. Put the cubes into a mixing bowl, pour in 2 tablespoons of the olive oil, and add the garlic. Toss carefully and let sit until serving time.

3. At serving time, drain off the oil and discard the garlic pieces. In a small mixing bowl, whisk the vinegar with salt to taste. Blend in the remaining 6 tablespoons olive oil by tablespoons and season with pepper to taste. Fold in the chopped herbs and pour the dressing over the zucchini. Toss carefully. Correct the seasoning and serve.

Shopping List
Vegetables: zucchini, garlic

Herbs: fresh marjoram or savory, parsley

Staples: olive oil, sherry vinegar or red wine vinegar

10
DESSERTS

APPLE-APRICOT CUSTARD WITH CURRANTS

This is a fine dessert for using the first crop of crisp cooking apples. The apricot preserves (which, by the way, should be a good quality that includes chunks of the fruit) lend a sweet-sharpness that blends well with the apples and cream.

5 teaspoons butter	1 cup heavy cream
2 tablespoons moist, dried currants	salt
4 firm cooking apples, peeled, cored, thinly sliced, and tossed in the juice of ½ lemon	3 whole eggs
	2 egg yolks
	¾ cup granulated sugar
4 tablespoons pure apricot preserves	1½ teaspoons vanilla extract
1½ cups light cream	confectioners' sugar

1. Smear the inside of a 10-inch baking dish with 2 teaspoons of the butter. Scatter over the currants.

2. Heat the remaining 3 tablespoons butter in a skillet, stir in the apple slices, and sauté until they are no longer firm but tender-crisp. Stir in the apricot preserves. Spoon and scrape the apple-apricot mixture into the bottom of the prepared baking dish.

3. Pour both creams into a heavy saucepan and add a pinch of salt. Scald the creams.

4. While the creams are heating, beat the whole eggs and egg yolks together in a mixing bowl. Beat in the granulated sugar.

5. Pour ¼ cup of the scalded cream through a sieve into the beaten eggs and sugar. Mix well. Add the remaining cream in this fashion. Stir in the vanilla extract and pour the cream over the apples.

6. Put the baking dish in a larger pan and fill the pan with enough warm water to reach halfway up the sides of the dish holding the custard. Place the whole unit in the lower third of a preheated 350° F oven and bake until the custard has delicately set, 40–50 minutes. A knife inserted about 2 inches from the edge of the dish should withdraw clean.

7. Remove the custard from the oven and water bath. Cool on a rack, but serve warm, sprinkled with confectioners' sugar. The custard, sprinkled with sugar, may be glazed under a preheated broiler.

SHOPPING LIST
Fruits: apples, currants
Dairy: butter, light cream, heavy cream, eggs

Staples: granulated sugar, confectioners' sugar, apricot preserves
Flavoring: vanilla extract

APPLE FOOL

To make a proper fool, you must make a quality sweetened fruit purée in which the fruit is simmered slowly then passed through a food mill. This process done, the apple "sauce" should chill completely before being combined with thick heavy cream whipped and sweetened.

Think of a fool as a gelatin-free mousse, but more seasonally oriented. The same method for apples can be used for rhubarb (add more sugar, leave out the water, and flavor with cinnamon) and summer's nectarous ripe apricots.

2 pounds tart, firm cooking apples, peeled, cored, roughly sliced, and tossed in the juice of 1 lemon
finely grated rind of 1 lemon
½ cup water
⅔ cup granulated sugar (or more, to taste)

3 inches of vanilla bean, split down the middle, and the tiny seeds scraped out
2 cups heavy cream, very cold
4 tablespoons confectioners' sugar, sifted
4 egg whites, beaten to firm peaks
¼ cup chopped walnuts, toasted (optional)

1. Put the apples, lemon rind, water, granulated sugar, and vanilla into a heavy nonmetallic saucepan with a tight-fitting lid. Place the saucepan over moderately low heat, cover, and simmer the apples until they are very tender.

2. Purée the apples, with all of the juices, through a food mill, using the medium disk, or through a medium-coarse sieve (nonmetallic). Cool the purée to room temperature. Cover and refrigerate for 1 day.

3. To finish the fool, whip the cream until soft peaks are formed. Beat in the sifted confectioners' sugar. Stir several spoonfuls of the sweetened whipped cream into the apple purée, pour this over the bulk of the remaining whipped cream, and fold the two together, lightly and quickly. Fold in the egg whites.

4. Pour the fool into a serving bowl and refrigerate at least 1½ hours before serving. Just before serving, if you like, sprinkle the border of the fool with chopped walnuts that have been lightly toasted.

SHOPPING LIST
Fruits and nuts: cooking apples, lemons, walnuts (optional)
Dairy: heavy cream

Staples: granulated sugar, confectioners' sugar
Flavoring: vanilla bean

BAKED SPICED APPLE SLICES

Apple slices turned in cinnamon, nutmeg, and sugar, covered over by a mantle of brown sugar and nut crumbs.

1 tablespoon butter
2¾ pounds apples, peeled, cored, sliced, and tossed in the juice of 1 large lemon
⅓ cup granulated sugar
¾ teaspoon ground cinnamon
¼ teaspoon ground nutmeg

3 tablespoons fine dry bread crumbs
½ cup all-purpose flour
⅔ cup light-brown sugar
¾ cup pecans, chopped
6 tablespoons butter, cut into rough cubes
whipped cream or *crème fraîche*

1. Grease the inside of a 5–6-cup baking dish with the 1 tablespoon butter and set aside.

2. Put the apple slices in a large mixing bowl. Add the granulated sugar, cinnamon, and nutmeg, toss to combine, then turn into the prepared baking dish and level the top without mashing down the apple slices.

3. In a mixing bowl, combine the bread crumbs, flour, brown sugar, and pecans. Add the butter cubes and reduce them to small lentil-size bits with a round-bladed knife. Cover the apples with the mixture, spreading it evenly over the top with a spatula.

4. Bake the apples in a preheated 375° F oven for 45 minutes or until the apples are tender and the topping is golden. Serve warm, with a bowl of whipped cream or *crème fraîche* for spooning on each serving.

SHOPPING LIST
Fruits: cooking apples, lemon
Dairy: butter, whipping cream or *crème fraîche*

Staples: sugar, bread crumbs, light-brown sugar, pecans
Spices: ground cinnamon, ground nutmeg

GRATIN OF APPLES WITH BROWN SUGAR AND PECANS

This dessert is similar to Baked Spiced Apple Slices (preceding recipe), but here, tablespoons of heavy cream are added to the apples for a smoother, slightly silkier finish to the baked apples.

1 tablespoon butter

2½ pounds firm, tart cooking apples, peeled, cored, cut into thin slices, and tossed in the juice of 1 large lemon

⅓ cup granulated sugar blended with ¼ teaspoon freshly ground nutmeg

4 tablespoons heavy cream

½ cup all-purpose flour, preferably un-bleached

⅓ cup brown sugar, firmly packed

¼ cup granulated sugar

1 teaspoon ground cinnamon

6 tablespoons butter, cut into cubes

⅔ cup chopped pecans

heavy cream

1. Spread the 1 tablespoon butter on the inside of a 6-cup baking dish.

2. In a large bowl, toss the apple slices in the sugar-nutmeg blend. Fold in 4 tablespoons cream. Transfer the apples to the prepared baking dish, making sure that the top is level.

3. In a mixing bowl, stir together the flour, both sugars, and cinnamon. Scatter in the butter cubes and reduce them to very small bits with a round-bladed knife. Lightly and quickly stir in the chopped pecans. Cover the top of the apples with this mixture. Spread the topping evenly to conceal all of the apples.

4. Bake the gratin on the middle level of a preheated 375° F oven for 40 minutes or until the apples are tender and the topping is golden. If the topping begins to brown too quickly, loosely cover the top with a sheet of aluminum foil.

5. Place the gratin on a rack to cool slightly. Serve warm with heavy cream, plain or whipped and lightly sweetened.

SHOPPING LIST

Fruits: cooking apples, lemon

Dairy: butter, heavy cream

Staples: granulated sugar, brown sugar, flour, pecans

Spices: ground nutmeg, ground cinnamon

WARM APPLE SPICE PUDDING

One of the simplest coverings for fruit that is to be baked is a light, butter-enriched shortcake, the kind that mixes up slightly sticky and bakes into puffy mounds. It is a good formula to know because so many juicy sweet types of seasonal fruit can be baked in this way—peaches, cherries, and blackberries react well to this treatment, and you can sift different ground spices into the flour for the topping to harmonize with the fruit.

For the Apples

1 tablespoon butter

2½ pounds crisp, tart cooking apples, peeled, cored, sliced, and tossed in the juice of 1 large lemon

⅔ cup granulated sugar blended with ½ teaspoon ground cinnamon, ¼ teaspoon ground nutmeg, and ¼ teaspoon ground cloves

2 teaspoons all-purpose flour, sifted

3 tablespoons butter, melted and cooled

For the Shortcake

1 cup all-purpose flour, preferably unbleached

large pinch of salt

1 teaspoon baking powder

½ teaspoon baking soda

5 tablespoons butter, cut into cubes

1 tablespoon solid shortening, cut into cubes

1 tablespoon granulated sugar

⅓ cup light cream

2½ tablespoons sour cream

1. Butter the inside of a deep 9-inch round or square baking dish with the tablespoon of butter. Set aside.

2. Toss the apples in the sugar and spice blend. Dust the flour over and fold it in. Blend in the melted butter. Turn the apples into the prepared baking dish and level the top.

3. For the shortcake topping, sift the flour, salt, baking powder, and baking soda into a mixing bowl. Drop in the butter and shortening cubes and blend them into the flour with a round-bladed knife until both are reduced to fine shreds. Sprinkle the sugar over the flour and stir it in quickly. Combine the light cream and sour cream. Make a well in the center of the flour, add both creams, and mix the liquid and flour together until a soft, slightly sticky dough is formed. Give the dough a few turns in the bowl.

4. Cover the top of the apples with heaping tablespoons of the shortcake mixture, leaving small gaps between the mounds. Bake the pudding on the middle-level rack of a preheated 425° F oven for 10 minutes, reduce the heat to 400° F, and continue baking until the apples are tender and the topping is golden, 25–35 minutes longer. If the topping begins to brown too fast before the apples begin to soften, cover the top with a loose sheet of aluminum foil.

5. Remove the pudding to a rack to cool, but serve warm.

Shopping List

Fruits: cooking apples, lemon

Dairy: butter, light cream, sour cream

Staples: granulated sugar, flour, salt, baking powder, baking soda, shortening

Spices: ground cinnamon, ground nutmeg, ground cloves

APRICOT FOOL

Fools are good desserts to think about when you have extra ripe fruit that is in need of immediate attention. You can prepare the fruit, transforming it into a purée, and store it in the refrigerator to stay very cold until whipped cream is folded in. This fool is delicate and very good; it's also one of those cozy, old-fashioned desserts that makes you feel comforted and well satisfied.

double recipe of the poached apricots in
Fresh Apricot Compote with Vanilla
and Cinnamon (following recipe)

2 cups very cold heavy cream
chopped nuts (optional)

Purée the poached apricots in a food mill set over a bowl. Beat in as much of the poaching liquid as it takes to lighten the purée so that it will mound in a spoon. Add the liquid by tablespoons; the mixture should not be loose, nor too stiff. A very thick purée will not fold into the whipped cream, but a very thin purée will water down the cream.

To Store   Place the purée in the refrigerator, tightly covered, for up to 3 days.

To Serve   Whip the cream until firm peaks are formed. Stir several spoonfuls of the whipped cream into the purée to make it less dense at first. Transfer the mixture to a large bowl. Fold in the rest of the purée, swiftly but thoroughly. Turn the fool into a serving bowl and chill well. Garnish the edges, if you like, with chopped nuts.

SHOPPING LIST
Fruit: the poached apricots in Fresh Apricot Compote (see recipe)

Dairy: heavy cream
For serving: nuts (optional)

FRESH APRICOT COMPOTE WITH VANILLA AND CINNAMON

So infrequently can we savor fresh apricots. Since the dried variety is always available season in, season out, we come to rely on packaged apricots. But when the fruit appears, ripe and fresh, it is then that you should add them to lamb (see Lamb with Ripe Apricots and

Cinnamon, page 163), eat them out of hand, or, as in this recipe, cook them for compote. Here, if the apricots are very small, leave them whole; if they are larger, ten apricots are sufficient: halve and stone each large apricot and use a pan wide enough so that the halves can sit flat side down. In this way, the larger apricots have a chance to cook evenly and absorb the flavorful syrup rather than pile up on each other.

I do like to serve a bowl of whipped cream along with the compote. The cream can be prepared just before serving the dessert, for it only takes several minutes to whip up and flavor. Serve the apricots plain if the main course features cream. Or serve with a Vanilla Custard Sauce (page 282) flavored with some freshly ground ginger or nutmeg.

1½ cups dry white wine	4-inch length of vanilla bean, split down
¾ cup water	the middle
¾ cup granulated sugar	juice of 1 lemon
¼ cup honey, not a very strong one	16 small, fresh, ripe, unblemished apri-
3-inch piece of cinnamon stick	cots

1. In a heavy casserole, such as an enameled one, place the wine, water, sugar, honey, cinnamon stick, and vanilla bean. Cover and cook the mixture over low heat until the sugar has completely dissolved.

2. Uncover the casserole, add the lemon juice, and boil the liquid for 6 minutes. Add the apricots and simmer slowly, basting the fruit with some of the cooking liquid frequently, until the apricots are tender but not mushy or falling apart, about 15 minutes.

3. Transfer the apricots to a bowl with a slotted spoon. Boil down the liquid until it is a medium-heavy syrup, then strain the syrup over the apricots. At this point, you may serve the dessert warm. Leave in the cinnamon stick if you like. (The vanilla bean, washed off and dried well, can be buried in a small container of granulated sugar to flavor it.)

To Store When the apricots are cool, transfer the container, covered, to the refrigerator and store up to 3 days.

SHOPPING LIST
Fruit: lemon, apricots
Staples: dry white wine, sugar, honey

Spices: cinnamon stick, vanilla bean

BLACKBERRIES IN NUT-LACE CRISP

Blackberries are especially good in a deep-dish pie, with a tender cloak of pastry on top, or sweetened and spiced, all covered over with mounds of shortcake. You could follow the directions for the batter in my recipe for Pears Under Shortcake (page 301), sugaring the berries with ¾ cup granulated sugar blended with 3 tablespoons flour, ½ teaspoon ground cinnamon, and ¼ teaspoon ground nutmeg. Cover the berries with the soft dollops of shortcake and bake at 425° F until the berries are bubbly and the topping is totally cooked and golden. But this recipe is the easiest of them all to put together. Two kinds of sugar, flour, nuts, and butter are blended together to form a crunchy topping that you scatter over the prepared fruit, covering it all up. Serve this crisp with Vanilla Custard Sauce (page 282), Vanilla Whipped Cream Sauce (page 280), or good vanilla ice cream.

1½ tablespoons butter	⅓ cup sifted all-purpose flour
4 cups blackberries	½ teaspoon ground ginger
¾ cup granulated sugar	⅔ cup chopped pecans
1½ tablespoons all-purpose flour	5 tablespoons butter, cut into small
juice of ½ lemon	cubes
¼ cup light-brown sugar	

1. Smear the 1½ tablespoons butter on the inside of a 9-inch round or oval baking dish.

2. In a large mixing bowl, combine the blackberries, ½ cup of the granulated sugar, 1½ tablespoons flour, and lemon juice. Place the mixture into the buttered baking dish.

3. Combine the remaining ¼ cup white sugar, the brown sugar, ⅓ cup flour, ginger, and pecans in a medium-size mixing bowl. Drop in the butter cubes and cut them up in small bits with a round-bladed knife or spatula. Cover the top of the blackberries with the mixture, spreading it all over the fruit in one even layer.

4. Bake the crisp on the middle level of a preheated 375° F oven for 35–40 minutes or until the topping is golden and the fruit is tender. Cool the crisp on a rack but serve warm.

SHOPPING LIST
Fruit: blackberries, lemon
Dairy: butter

Staples: granulated sugar, light-brown sugar, flour, pecans
Spice: ground ginger

BLUEBERRIES IN MAPLE AND BROWN-SUGAR SYRUP

This is a recipe for poached blueberries, a method not all that common to this fruit, although the dessert is delicious in its own homey way, especially when all decked out with whipped cream. The one thing that you should remember is that the blueberries, in cooking, should remain whole and not burst open into an indiscriminate mass. Keep the syrup at a gentle simmer and you will have perfect results. Serve the berries with a cream-based sauce, a vanilla custard or whipped cream one. As an aside: the poached blueberries, should any be left over, are delicious as a breakfast fruit.

¼ cup light-brown sugar
¼ cup pure maple syrup
1 cup water
6 strips of lemon peel
1 cinnamon stick

3-inch piece of vanilla bean, slit down
    the middle to reveal the tiny seeds
2 pints fresh, plump blueberries, picked
    over and washed well

1. Combine the light-brown sugar, maple syrup, water, lemon peel, cinnamon stick, and vanilla bean in a large heavy saucepan. Cover the pan and set over low heat to dissolve all of the sugar. When every last bit of sugar has dissolved, uncover the pot and boil the liquid for 5 minutes.

2. Add the blueberries to the syrup and simmer slowly until they absorb the syrup and yield slightly, but have not become mushy. Stir the berries carefully as they cook; here I use a sturdy rubber spatula so that I do not mash the berries.

3. Transfer the contents of the pot to a storage bowl. When cool, discard the lemon peel and vanilla bean. (Remember, you can wash and dry the vanilla bean and use it to flavor a few cups of sugar.) Leave in the cinnamon stick if you enjoy a spicy cinnamony flavor. Otherwise, discard it, too. Chill the berries briefly before serving.

SHOPPING LIST
Fruit: blueberries, lemon
Staples: light-brown sugar, maple syrup

Spices: cinnamon stick, vanilla bean

BREAD PUDDING WITH DATES AND WALNUTS

The revival of good, solid homey food calls to mind all those ambrosial desserts based on cream and eggs. The fruits mingling between the bread and custard are raisins and dates; coconut and walnuts ornament the pudding, too. The method is not involved—the two main tasks are buttering the bread and heating up the cream. The pudding may be accompanied by a bowl of lightly sweetened heavy cream flavored with a pinch of ground cinnamon, to spoon over each portion.

1 tablespoon butter

8–10 ⅓-inch-thick slices of French bread, or 5–6 large slices of top-quality white bread (crusts trimmed, slices halved)

3 tablespoons butter, softened

2 tablespoons dark raisins, soaked in boiling water for 10 minutes, drained, and dried

½ cup chopped pitted dates

¼ cup chopped walnuts

4 tablespoons shredded coconut

4 cups light cream

pinch of salt

5 whole eggs

3 egg yolks

1⅓ cup granulated sugar

2 teaspoons vanilla extract

confectioners' sugar

1. Smear the tablespoon of butter on the inside of a baking dish measuring at least 10 inches long and 1¾ inches deep.

2. Butter the slices of bread on one side only with the 3 tablespoons of softened butter. Arrange the bread on the bottom of the baking dish, overlapping slightly as necessary. Scatter on the raisins, dates, walnuts, and coconut.

3. Pour the cream into a heavy saucepan. Add the salt and scald the cream over moderate heat. While the cream is heating, beat the whole eggs and egg yolks together in a mixing bowl. Beat in the granulated sugar.

4. Strain a fourth of the hot cream into the egg-sugar mixture and quickly stir it in. Strain in the remaining liquid in small lots, stirring after each portion is added. Blend in the vanilla.

5. Strain the egg-cream mixture over the bread. Place the dish in a larger baking pan and fill with enough warm water to rise halfway up the sides of the dish holding the pudding.

6. Put the whole unit in the lower third of a preheated 350° F oven and bake the pudding for 50–55 minutes or until a knife inserted 2 inches from the edge emerges clean.

7. Carefully remove the dish of pudding from the pan of water and place it on a rack to cool. Sprinkle confectioners' sugar over the top before serving.

Sʜᴏᴘᴘɪɴɢ Lɪsᴛ
Dairy: butter, cream, eggs
Staples: bread, dark raisins, dates, walnuts, coconut,

granulated sugar, confectioners' sugar
Flavoring: vanilla extract

CANTALOUPE WITH CASSIS, WHITE WINE, AND HONEY

Let me tell you how I have had this treatment of cantaloupe as one part of a dessert. It was very unusual and, for that reason, noteworthy. A kind of jam was made with pieces of cantaloupe, sugar, lemon, and spices, cooked down until nice and thick, in the old-fashioned way. Having been stocked in the larder, part of the jam was used on the day when ripe cantaloupe was marinated in the following syrup of honey, white wine, and cassis. Then a crisp pastry tart shell was covered over with some of the thick jam, over which was a layer of pastry cream, more jam, and the cantaloupe (drained and assembled on top). The jam, by the way, is good on hot breads; I made the jam and this whimsy of a dessert once and liked it very much. Here is one part of the dessert which is delightful alone, even without the jam and pastry conceit. Garnish it with fresh mint leaves, if available. It is good with macaroons and whipped cream on the side.

1 cup dry white wine
½ cup black-currant liqueur (crème de cassis)
⅓ cup honey
4 whole cloves
3-inch piece of vanilla bean, split down

the middle with a sharp knife

To Serve

2 ripe cantaloupes, cut into cubes
⅓ cup chopped, toasted walnuts or pecans

In a heavy nonmetallic saucepan, place the wine, liqueur, honey, cloves, and vanilla bean. Cover, place over moderately low heat, and cook until the honey has dissolved. Uncover the saucepan, bring the contents to the boil, and boil for 6 minutes.

To Store   Cool the syrup to room temperature. Discard the cloves and pour the syrup into a storage container. Refrigerate, covered, for up to 6 days.

To Serve   Put the cantaloupe in a bowl. Stir the chopped nuts into the syrup and pour over the fruit. Turn the fruit in the syrup and leave at room temperature to marinate for at least 20 minutes, or up to 1 hour.

Sʜᴏᴘᴘɪɴɢ Lɪsᴛ
Fruit: cantaloupes
Staples: dry white wine, black-currant liqueur, honey,

walnuts or pecans
Spices: whole cloves, vanilla bean

SPICED COMPOTE OF CHERRIES

Cherries, the practical pie fruit, are especially pleasing when poached. This poaching syrup is pointed up with a dose of red wine and sharpened with slivers of lemon peel and whole spices. The syrup could also glamorize small purple beach plums, which plump up in the syrup just as the cherries do. Serve this compote with a pitcher of cold heavy cream or a custard sauce.

1½ pounds Bing (sweet red) cherries	3-inch piece of cinnamon stick
¾ cup granulated sugar	6 strips of lemon peel
1¼ cups water	6 whole cloves
¾ cup dry red wine	1 teaspoon vanilla extract

1. Wash and pit the cherries and set aside.

2. Put the sugar, water, and wine in a wide, nonmetallic saucepan. Set the saucepan over low heat, cover, and cook until every grain of sugar has dissolved. Uncover the pot; add the cinnamon stick, lemon peel, and whole cloves. Bring the liquid to a boil and boil for 6 minutes, until syrupy and slightly dense.

3. Add the cherries to the syrup, turn down the heat to moderately low, and simmer for 5 minutes or until the cherries remain whole but are cooked through without bursting. Baste the cherries with some of the poaching liquid from time to time.

4. Remove the saucepan from the heat and lift out the cherries with a slotted spoon. Boil down the syrup over moderately high heat to thicken somewhat, about 3–4 minutes. Stir in the vanilla and strain the syrup over the cherries. Transfer the cinnamon stick to the cherries if you like a prominent cinnamon flavor in your compote. Serve the cherries warm at this point, or store.

To Store   Cool the compote to room temperature, then refrigerate for up to 3 days in a covered container.

SHOPPING LIST
Fruit: cherries, lemon
Staples: granulated sugar, dry red wine

Flavoring: vanilla extract
Spices: cinnamon stick, whole cloves

CHOCOLATE AND ORANGE VELVET

Chocolate and orange is sleek and slick. The vigorous freshly grated rind offsets the chocolate flavor which the liqueur intensifies, and the butter binds all together creamily. The top of the velvet can be garnished with whipped cream pressed through a pastry bag fitted with a star tip and swirled around the edges and dotted with candy coffee beans, or served with a bowl of fresh orange segments, or presented plain, with a bowl of lightly whipped cream on the side.

1 pound bittersweet chocolate, cut into pieces	1 tablespoon vanilla extract
⅓ cup plus 2 tablespoons superfine sugar	1½ tablespoons orange liqueur
⅓ cup water	grated rind of 2 oranges
5 egg yolks	4 egg whites
11 tablespoons butter, softened at room temperature	pinch of cream of tartar or salt
	2 cups heavy cream, very cold
	2 tablespoons confectioners' sugar

1. Melt the chocolate with the superfine sugar and water in a heavy enameled saucepan over a low flame or in the top of a double boiler over barely simmering water. Stir frequently. When the chocolate is quite smooth, remove it from the heat and cool, stirring, for a few seconds.

2. Beat in the egg yolks, one at a time, and the tablespoons of butter, chunks at a time, beating well to keep the chocolate mixture smooth and glossy.

3. Blend in the vanilla extract, liqueur, and grated orange rind. Cool the chocolate mixture.

4. In a clean dry bowl, beat the egg whites until frothy, add a pinch of cream of tartar or salt, and continue beating until the whites peak softly when the beaters are lifted. In another bowl, whip the cream until it mounds lightly, sift the confectioners' sugar over it, then continue to beat the cream until it holds its shape in a spoon or leaves soft peaks behind when the beating device is lifted.

5. Stir a large spoonful of the beaten whites into the chocolate base. Fold in the remaining whites. Add the whipped cream and fold it in until the streaks of white are blended into the chocolate. Do this carefully so that you do not diminish the volume of the velvet, keeping everything light. Carefully pour the cream into a 7-cup serving bowl and smooth over the top.

To Store   Place the velvet in the refrigerator and, after an hour or so, cover the top with plastic wrap. Refrigerate 1 day.

SHOPPING LIST
Fruit: oranges
Dairy: butter, eggs, heavy cream
Staples: bittersweet chocolate, confectioners' sugar, superfine sugar, orange liqueur, cream of tartar or salt
Flavoring: vanilla extract

VANILLA WHIPPED CREAM SAUCE

1½ cups cold heavy cream
2½ tablespoons sifted confectioners'

sugar, or more to taste
1½ teaspoons vanilla extract

1. Pour the cream into a chilled bowl. Begin beating it (either manually or with a portable electric beater) slowly at first, then faster as the cream begins to thicken. Beat in the confectioners' sugar.

2. Continue to whip the cream until very soft peaks are formed when the beaters are lifted. Stir in the vanilla extract. Turn the flavored cream into a serving bowl and use straightaway.

NOTE: I use the heavy-duty cream that is not ultrasterilized and is available at health-food stores.

SHOPPING LIST
Dairy: heavy cream
Staple: confectioners' sugar

Flavoring: vanilla extract

SUGAR-CRUST CUSTARD WITH RASPBERRY COMPOTE

You will recognize this as a variation of a thick cream and egg yolk dessert that had its English roots at Kings College in Cambridge, England. It is known as crème brulée, or burnt custard, not because, by some error, you have scorched the custard and tinged it brown. Rather, the name speaks of the crackling browned sugar coating on top of the custard that is done after the custard rests and sets in the refrigerator overnight. The procedure for making the custard is not complicated, but you should take care to stir the mixture carefully and cook it slowly over low heat so that the egg yolks do not curdle. Once the cream and egg yolk mixture has thickened, it is poured into a shallow heatproof dish—I use a fluted porcelain baking dish that measures 9 inches in diameter and is about 1½ inches deep. Then I slip the custard into a preheated oven so that a skin forms over the top. That little trick helps to set the custard before the overnight refrigeration.

The Custard

2½ cups heavy cream (preferably the type that is not ultrasterilized)

5 egg yolks

½ cup superfine sugar (I use vanilla-flavored sugar which I make by putting a split vanilla bean into a jar of the sugar)

2 teaspoons vanilla extract

about ¼ cup light-brown sugar

1. Put the heavy cream into a saucepan and scald it.

2. Beat the egg yolks until sticky and beat in the superfine sugar slowly, a little at a time, until the mixture is light and there are no traces of sugar granules present; the texture should not be gritty.

3. Strain ¼ cup of the hot scalded cream into the egg yolks and stir it in quickly. Strain in the remaining cream in a thin stream, blending after quarter-cups are added. Transfer the mixture to a clean heavy saucepan (preferably an enameled cast-iron one) and stir over low heat with a wooden spoon until thickened. The custard will coat a spoon lightly. As the custard begins to thicken, you will notice that the foam over the top subsides—do not rush the procedure by raising the heat, or the egg yolks will curdle.

4. When the custard is thick enough to coat a spoon, quickly strain it directly into a baking dish. Place the custard in the middle of a preheated 350° F oven for exactly 3½ minutes: this procedure sets the custard.

To Store　Cool the custard completely, then refrigerate for 1 day, or overnight.

To Serve　Cover the top of the custard with the brown sugar put through a medium-mesh sieve. Use enough sugar to cover the top completely. Place the dish under a preheated broiler for a minute or long enough to brown the top. Watch carefully to avoid burning the sugar! Chill the custard briefly until serving time.

This custard is wonderful with a fresh red raspberry compote that adds just the correct fruity balance to the richly smooth dessert.

The Raspberry Compote

1 pint red raspberries

superfine sugar to taste

2 tablespoons raspberry brandy (framboise) or lemon juice

1. Place the raspberries in a wide mixing bowl or baking dish. Sprinkle on enough sugar to sweeten the berries and let them stand until the sugar has dissolved.

2. After several minutes, shake the dish to toss the berries. Sprinkle on the brandy or lemon juice, and toss lightly again.

3. When the juices begin to appear, taste the berries and add additional sugar and

brandy (or lemon juice) to taste. Turn the berries into a bowl and serve along with the custard.

SHOPPING LIST

Fruit: red raspberries, lemon (if brandy is not used)
Dairy: heavy cream, egg yolks
Staples: superfine sugar, light-brown sugar, raspberry

brandy (framboise)
Flavoring: vanilla extract

VANILLA CUSTARD SAUCE

1¼ cups light cream
3 egg yolks
superfine sugar

pinch of salt
1¼ teaspoons arrowroot
1½ teaspoons vanilla extract

1. Pour the cream into a saucepan and heat slowly until a skin forms over the top and small bubbles appear around the sides of the pan.

2. While the cream is heating, place the egg yolks in a mixing bowl. Beat in a scant ¼ cup superfine sugar, salt, and arrowroot. Whisk the mixture until it is thick and pale yellow in color. Pour ¼ cup of the hot cream through a sieve into the beaten yolk mixture and whisk well. Add the remaining cream in this way.

3. Pour the cream mixture into a clean heavy saucepan (preferably enameled cast iron) and set over a low flame. With a wooden spoon or whisk, cook the sauce over low heat, stirring all the time, until it coats the back of a spoon and is no longer a very thin, liquidy mixture. Do not allow the sauce to approach the simmer or it will curdle.

4. Remove the saucepan from the heat and stir in the vanilla extract. Strain the sauce into a container or serving bowl. Dust the top with superfine sugar to prevent a skin from forming over the top. Stir the sauce once before serving.

NOTE: For Orange Custard Sauce, stir in the grated rind of 1 orange, 2 teaspoons orange brandy (or more to taste), and a few drops of vanilla extract.

SHOPPING LIST

Dairy: light cream, eggs
Staples: superfine sugar, arrowroot

Flavoring: vanilla extract

FIGS IN BLACK-CURRANT SYRUP

I like choice, sweet fresh figs without any further embellishment save a pour of thick heavy cream over the split halves. But I also like a little pomp and ceremony for the full-formed fruit, like adding a flavorsome syrup based on cassis and spices. Making the syrup is child's play, easily accomplished while other foods are cooking, and it can rest safely in the refrigerator until the day you slice the figs and immerse them in this aromatic brew.

1 cup water
¾ cup granulated sugar
4 whole allspice berries
3 whole cloves
juice of 1 lemon
½ cup black-currant liquer (crème de cassis)

To Serve

1 cup cold heavy cream or 1 recipe Vanilla Custard Sauce (preceding recipe)

1. Put the water, sugar, allspice berries, and cloves in a heavy nonmetallic saucepan. Cover, place over low heat, and cook the liquid until every granule of sugar has dissolved.

2. Uncover the saucepan, raise the heat to moderately high, and boil the liquid for 5 minutes. Add the lemon juice and boil another 3 minutes. Pour in the black-currant liqueur and boil an additional 2 minutes.

To Store Cool the syrup, discard the whole spices, and pour into a storage container. Cover and refrigerate for up to 6 days.

To Serve Stem the figs, slice them thickly or leave them whole, and arrange them in a serving dish with a slight lip to hold in the syrup. Pour over the prepared syrup and pass the heavy cream or custard sauce separately.

SHOPPING LIST
Fruit: figs, lemon
Staples: granulated sugar, black-currant liqueur
Spices: allspice berries, whole cloves

For serving: heavy cream or Vanilla Custard Sauce (see recipe)

FIGS IN HONEY-SPICE SYRUP

Without a doubt, the best honey I have used with the figs in this recipe is Mt. Hymettus Thyme. It is a deep amber color with a well-rounded, intensely rich flavor. The kind I like comes in one-pound jars from Pittas Company, Limited, in Athens. The honey is also very good "straight," that is, on biscuits and homemade tea breads.

1½ cups dry white wine	1 cinnamon stick
⅓ cup plus 1 tablespoon honey	3-inch length of vanilla bean, slit down
3 whole allspice berries	the middle with a sharp knife
3 whole cloves	8 ripe figs

1. Place all the ingredients except the figs in a casserole which can hold all the figs in one upright layer (a 4-quart one should work unless the figs are jumbo).

2. Cover the casserole and place over low heat to dissolve the honey. When the honey is all blended in, raise the heat to high and boil the liquid for 9 minutes.

3. Stand the figs in the syrup, base side down, and spoon over some of the wine-honey syrup. Simmer the figs until they begin to absorb syrup and soften ever so slightly, about 5–6 minutes.

4. When the figs are cool enough to handle, carefully transfer them to a not-too-shallow bowl. Boil down the syrup until it is dense, then pour it over the figs. The spices are pretty when left to mingle with the syrup. Serve the figs at room temperature or cool.

SHOPPING LIST
Fruit: figs
Staples: dry white wine, honey

Spices: allspice berries, vanilla bean, whole cloves, cinnamon stick

COMPOTE OF SPICED FIGS

In late fall and through the first part of winter, an array of dried fruit appears as a foretoken of holiday baking. But aside from fruitcakes and bar cookies, it seems that we make all too little use of supple and sweet dried fruit. Put soft chunks of them into stuffings or prepare one (or a colorful collection) as you might poach fresh fruit, in a spicy red wine syrup. This recipe highlights figs, but look into my Stuffed Prunes and Whole Apricots Steeped in Wine and Spices (page 307) for another kind of approach (the prunes are stuffed with pecans and the apricots with dates).

½ cup honey, or more to taste
6 whole cloves
1 piece of dried ginger
3-inch piece of cinnamon stick
4 black peppercorns

1½ cups dry red wine
¼ cup water
1 pound dried whole figs
crème fraîche (optional)

1. Put all the ingredients except the figs and *crème fraîche* into a 2-quart nonmetallic saucepan. Cover the pan, set over low heat, and cook slowly to dissolve the honey. Taste the syrup and add more honey if you like a sweeter syrup for the figs. Cook a little longer, covered, if you add more honey.

2. When the honey has dissolved completely, uncover the pot, raise the heat to moderately high, and boil the liquid for 5 minutes, to make a light syrup.

3. Add the figs to the pan and baste over with the syrup. Cover the pan and cook the figs at a simmer until they are tender, basting again from time to time with some of the syrup.

4. With a slotted spoon, transfer the figs to a bowl. Boil the syrup down further for 3–4 minutes. Discard the spices and pour the warm syrup over the figs. Serve the figs tepid, at room temperature, or cold. Nice with a small mound of *crème fraîche* on each serving.

To Store   Place the figs with the syrup into a storage container. Cool completely, cover, and refrigerate for up to 5 days.

SHOPPING LIST
Fruit: dried figs
Dairy: crème fraîche (optional)
Staples: honey, dry red wine

Spices: whole cloves, dried ginger, cinnamon stick, peppercorns

FRUIT LAYERED IN CARAMEL SYRUP

The caramel syrup that shines over this fruit mélange is thin and clear. As some of the fruit gives up the natural juices, the syrup blends in and mingles in a sweet-tart way. For a change, sprinkle ½ cup coarsely chopped moist dates between one layer of fruit, or assemble another range of fruit—cubed melon, mango slices, grapes, grapefruit wedges, ripe pear wedges—in colorful textural bands.

2 cups granulated sugar
¾ cup water
1 teaspoon white corn syrup
¼ cup boiling water

To Serve

4 large, juicy oranges, peeled and cut into thin round slices

3 kiwi fruit, peeled and sliced
3 bananas, peeled, cut into 1-inch diagonal slices, and tossed in the juice of ½ lemon
1 bunch grapes, left whole if seedless, or halved and seeded if necessary
¼ cup walnuts, lightly toasted and chopped

1. Put the sugar, ¾ cup water, and corn syrup in a heavy 1-quart saucepan. Cover and place over low heat until the sugar granules have completely dissolved. Uncover, raise the heat to moderately high, and boil the syrup until it turns a rich brown color.

2. Quickly remove the saucepan from the heat and add the boiling water *all at once.* Take care—the syrup will boil up vigorously. Stir well.

To Store Cool the syrup to room temperature, then transfer to a storage container. Cover and refrigerate for up to 6 days.

To Serve Marinate each fruit in a little of the caramel syrup. Layer the fruit in a bowl (a glass one will show off the the colorful layers) along with all of the juices. Sprinkle the chopped nuts over the top and serve.

Shopping List
Fruit: oranges, kiwis, bananas, lemon, grapes   *Staples:* granulated sugar, white corn syrup, walnuts

BAKED KIWI CUSTARD

This custard is quickly put together if you deal with the kiwis as the cream scalds, and in a matter of minutes, the custard base is ready to pour over the fruit. The dessert may be baked in advance and chilled, but is even more intriguing warm from the oven, allowing the proper length of time for the custard to settle and mellow.

3 tablespoons butter	3 whole eggs
4 kiwi fruit, peeled and sliced	2 egg yolks
1 tablespoon granulated sugar blended with ¼ teaspoon ground cinnamon	¾ cup, less 1 tablespoon, granulated sugar
2¼ cups light cream, scalded	¼ cup light-brown sugar
pinch of salt	¼ cup coconut

1. Smear 1 tablespoon of the butter on the inside of a 9-inch baking dish. Sauté the kiwi slices in the remaining 2 tablespoons butter for 2 minutes and while they are still quite hot, turn them into the baking dish and sprinkle over the sugar and cinnamon blend. Reserve.

2. Have the scalded cream handy. In a small mixing bowl, put the salt, whole eggs, and egg yolks. Whisk until the eggs are broken up. Beat in the granulated sugar and brown sugar. Pour the hot cream through a sieve into the eggs, stirring well after the cream has been added.

3. Pour the egg and cream mixture over the kiwi slices and sprinkle with the coconut. Put the baking dish in a larger pan and fill with enough warm water to rise halfway up the side of the custard dish.

4. Put the custard in its water bath in the lower third of a preheated 350° F oven to bake for 45–50 minutes or until set.

5. Remove the baking dish from the water bath and cool. Serve warm, or prepare one day in advance and chill.

SHOPPING LIST
Fruit: kiwis
Dairy: butter, light cream, eggs

Staples: granulated sugar, light-brown sugar, coconut
Spice: ground cinnamon

KIWI FRUIT WITH GRAPES AND MANGO SLICES

Before it is time to adjust the seasonal worktable to summer fruit, we can take great pleasure in arranging translucent green sections of kiwi against halved grapes, against the orange-yellow flesh of mango slices, all of them splashed with rum and the juice of citrus fruit. You could present these three kinds of fruit in a plain glass cylinder, into which you have poured a cold vanilla sauce before arranging the fruit. Or arrange the fruit on a flat platter and garnish with a fresh flower. Pass a bowl of softly whipped heavy cream, lightly sweetened and sharp-pointed with rum.

4 tablespoons dark rum, or to taste
juice of 2 oranges
juice of 1 lime
superfine sugar or honey, to taste
1 bunch grapes, halved and seeds removed
2 mangoes, peeled and cut into long

slices or cubed
4 kiwi fruit, peeled and sliced
⅓ cup toasted walnuts or toasted skinned hazelnuts, chopped
1 cup cold heavy cream, whipped and flavored with confectioners' sugar and a little dark rum to taste

1. In a small mixing bowl, stir together the rum, orange juice, and lime juice. Sweeten to taste.

2. Put the grapes in a bowl and pour in a third of the sweetened juice. Put the mango cubes in another bowl and marinate in another one-third of the juice mixture. Do the same with the kiwi fruit.

3. Upon serving, arrange the three fruits in a serving dish, adding all of the fruity juice as well. Sprinkle the chopped toasted nuts in a ring around the fruit (or if you are serving the fruit in a glass cylinder, amid one of the layers) and serve with a bowl of whipped cream on the side.

SHOPPING LIST
Fruit: oranges, lime, grapes, mangoes, kiwis
Dairy: heavy cream

Staples: dark rum, superfine sugar or honey, walnuts or hazelnuts, confectioners' sugar

GRATIN OF KIWI AND PAPAYA

In this recipe kiwi and papaya are combined with apricot jam and orange juice, then layered into a baking dish. An overlay of macaroons and pecans, crushed and chopped, along with a few other ingredients, covers up the fruit while it bakes. Serve this in sections, with some kind of cream.

3½ tablespoons butter

3 papayas, peeled, seeded, and cut into short slices

4 kiwi fruit, peeled and sliced

grated rind of 1 orange

½ cup fresh orange juice

¼ cup apricot jam

¼ cup light-brown sugar

1 tablespoon sweet white wine or rum, or

an extra tablespoon of orange juice

¼ teaspoon vanilla extract

6 crisp macaroons, crushed

¾ cup chopped pecans

1 tablespoon all-purpose flour

2 tablespoons granulated sugar

½ teaspoon ground cinnamon

4 tablespoons butter, cut into cubes

1. Smear ½ tablespoon of the butter on the inside of a 9-inch baking dish and set aside.

2. Melt the 3 tablespoons butter in a skillet, add the papaya slices, and sauté them for 4–5 minutes or until lightly glazed. Transfer the papaya to a mixing bowl, add the kiwi slices, orange rind, orange juice, apricot jam, light-brown sugar, wine, rum, or extra orange juice, and vanilla extract. Carefully toss all together and turn into the prepared baking dish, layering the fruit so that the top is smooth.

3. Combine the crushed macaroons, pecans, flour, granulated sugar, and ground cinnamon. Scatter over the butter cubes and reduce them to small bits with a round-bladed knife. Cover the top of the fruit with the macaroon-nut mixture.

4. Bake the gratin in the upper third of a preheated 400° F oven until the topping is lightly golden and the fruit is bubbly, about 20 minutes. Remove to a rack to cool, but do serve it warm.

NOTE: You could also do the fruit, as a variation, in a rich cream cheese and egg custard. Beat ½ pound cream cheese, softened, ½ cup *crème fraîche*, 2 whole eggs, and 1 egg yolk in a mixing bowl. Beat in ½ cup granulated sugar, ¼ cup sifted cake flour, and 2 teaspoons vanilla extract. Prepare the kiwi and sauté the papaya as above; toss with the apricot jam and orange rind. Put the fruit in the baking dish and pour over the cream cheese mixture. Bake this in a water bath (as you would a custard) at 350° F or until set, about 50 minutes.

SHOPPING LIST

Fruit: papayas, kiwis, oranges

Dairy: butter

Staples: apricot jam, light-brown sugar, sweet white wine or rum, pecans, flour

Bakery: macaroons

Flavoring: vanilla extract

Spice: ground cinnamon

HOT LEMON SPONGE PUDDING

Hot lemon sponge must be the ultimate of all the pleasurable childhood sweet remembrances. Lemony sauce on the bottom and a cakelike sponge that rises to the top. This version has more eggs than the standard recipe, replaces milk with light cream, and uses more lemon rind. It's richer, especially if presented with a bowl of lightly whipped cream.

1 tablespoon butter, for the baking dish	3 tablespoons all-purpose flour
4 tablespoons butter, softened	juice of 2 lemons
finely grated rind of 2 lemons	1 cup light cream
⅔ cup granulated sugar	confectioners' sugar
3 eggs, separated	

1. Spread the 1 tablespoon of butter on the inside of a 1-quart baking dish. Beat the 4 tablespoons softened butter in a mixing bowl until light. Beat in the lemon rind and continue to whip the butter for another 2 minutes.

2. Add the granulated sugar in two parts, beating well after each addition. Add the egg yolks, one at a time, scraping down the sides of the bowl after each addition to keep the mix even. Sift over half the flour, blend it in, then sift and combine the remaining flour.

3. Beat in the lemon juice and cream. Whisk the egg whites until firm peaks are formed. Stir a spoonful of the whites into the egg mixture. Fold in the remaining beaten whites, lightly and quickly.

4. Pour the pudding mixture into the prepared dish. Place the dish in a larger baking pan and pour in enough warm water to reach halfway up the sides of the pudding pan.

5. Place this whole unit in a preheated 350° F oven and bake for 50 minutes to 1 hour or until the pudding has set and the sponge topping is golden.

6. Remove the pudding from the water bath and let it rest on a cooling rack until serving time. Sprinkle the confectioners' sugar over the top and serve warm.

SHOPPING LIST
Fruit: lemons
Dairy: butter, eggs, light cream

Staples: granulated sugar, confectioners' sugar, flour

MANGO CREAM

Another one of those fruit, egg yolk, and cream summaries to a meal. Another way to finish off this dessert, instead of sprinkling the baked cream with confectioners' sugar, is to top the cream with fine, dry macaroon crumbs and drizzle over a little melted butter. Glaze under a preheated broiler to make the topping sizzle.

3½ tablespoons butter
2 mangoes, peeled, seeded, and cubed
1 cup heavy cream
1 cup light cream
2 whole eggs
3 egg yolks

⅔ cup granulated sugar blended with ¼ teaspoon ground ginger, ¼ teaspoon ground cinnamon, and ⅛ teaspoon freshly ground nutmeg
1 teaspoon vanilla extract
confectioners' sugar

1. Smear ½ tablespoon of the butter on the inside of a 9-inch ovenproof baking dish and set aside.

2. Sauté the mango cubes in the remaining 3 tablespoons butter for 4 minutes. Transfer them to the bottom of the prepared baking dish.

3. While the mango cubes are sautéing, pour both creams into a saucepan and scald. Put the whole eggs and extra egg yolks into a mixing bowl. Beat the eggs, add the spiced sugar, and beat for 3 minutes.

4. Strain a fourth of the hot cream into the beaten egg-sugar mixture and stir it in. Add the remaining cream in this way, in two parts. Blend in the vanilla extract, and pour this over the mangoes.

5. Set the baking dish in a larger pan and fill the pan with enough warm water to rise halfway up the sides of the baking dish. Place the whole unit in the lower third of a preheated 350° F oven for 50–55 minutes or until set.

6. Remove the baking dish from the water bath and cool. Serve the cream tepid or at room temperature. Dredge the top with confectioners' sugar before serving, and, if you like, glaze the top under a preheated broiler.

SHOPPING LIST
Fruit: mangoes
Dairy: butter, heavy cream, light cream, eggs
Staples: granulated sugar, confectioners' sugar

Flavoring: vanilla extract
Spices: ground ginger, ground cinnamon, ground nutmeg

FROZEN MAPLE CREAM WITH PECANS

Here is a creamy-rich dessert based on pure maple syrup, eggs, and whipped cream, which could be bracketed with fingers of sponge cake layered into the dessert. I have also had remarkably good results replacing a few tablespoons of granulated sugar with free-flowing maple sugar, to strengthen the flavor of the dessert even more.

⅞ cup granulated sugar
½ cup less 2 tablespoons water
2 teaspoons white corn syrup
5 egg yolks, taken from extra-large eggs
pinch of salt
1 teaspoon vanilla extract
⅓ cup pure maple syrup

1½ cups very cold heavy cream
4 egg whites
½ cup chopped pecans

To Serve

whole or chopped pecans, to garnish

1. Put the sugar, water, and corn syrup in a heavy saucepan, preferably enameled cast iron. Cover and place over low heat until the sugar dissolves completely. Uncover the pan, raise the heat to moderately high, and insert a candy thermometer into the syrup on the side of the saucepan. Boil the liquid until it reaches a temperature of 240° F.

2. While the mixture is boiling—and do keep a careful eye on it—beat the egg yolks with a pinch of salt in a large mixing bowl for 5 minutes. When the syrup is ready, quickly remove the thermometer and pour the hot syrup into the egg yolks, beating as it is added. Continue to beat until the mixture is thoroughly cool; placing the bowl in a larger bowl filled with some ice cubes helps. Beat in the vanilla extract and maple syrup.

3. Put the cream base into the freezer for 10–15 minutes to get it very cold. Stir several times. Beat the heavy cream until soft peaks are formed. Beat the egg whites until peaks of the whites stand upright when the beaters are lifted, but do not beat until the stiff peak stage. Fold the whipped cream into the cold maple base, then fold in the egg whites along with the chopped pecans.

To Store Turn the cream into a 7-cup serving bowl, place the bowl in a large storage container, cover, and place in the freezer overnight, or for up to 3 days.

To Serve Garnish the maple cream with whole or chopped pecans.

SHOPPING LIST
Dairy: eggs, heavy cream
Staples: granulated sugar, white corn syrup, maple
syrup, pecans
Flavoring: vanilla extract

NECTARINES STEEPED IN SWEET WINE WITH HONEY

Many beautiful fruit desserts can be made with nectarines, since they substitute well for peaches: in pies and tarts, in homemade chutneys and jams. And you could also exchange ripe peaches here. For our purposes, the best nectarines are plump, with a smooth skin that shows no sign of shriveling. One piece of advice for storing the fruit, which also applies to peaches, is that nectarines should not be stacked in the refrigerator; it is best to use ripe fruit right away.

In this simple marinated fruit dessert, I am calling for freshly ground ginger. Dried Jamaican ginger may be ground on a nutmeg grater or on the tiny holes of a small straight-sided grater. The ginger is available bottled in 1¼-ounce jars in the spice section of your market. Ginger, much like nutmeg, is best when freshly grated. The ginger goes in with the honey and wine and all is poured over the slices of fruit. For this, you need gorgeous fruit and a deep, rich honey. Serve this dessert plain, with *crème fraîche,* or against a wedge of good spice cake.

6 tablespoons honey, or to taste
juice of 2 limes
1½ cups sweet white wine

¼ teaspoon freshly ground ginger
6–8 nectarines
¼ cup chopped toasted pecans

1. In a small mixing bowl, blend the honey with the lime juice, wine, and ginger.
2. Cut each nectarine in half, remove the seed, and cut the halves into neat ½-inch-thick slices. Place the fruit in a bowl and pour over the honey-wine mixture. Carefully toss the fruit in this liquid.
3. Just before serving, fold in the chopped nuts.

SHOPPING LIST
Fruit: limes, nectarines
Staples: honey, sweet white wine, pecans

Spice: ground ginger

ORANGES AND GRAPES IN HOT ORANGE SAUCE

A fitting tribute to those heavy, juicy winter seedless oranges is a hot, foamy orange sauce. The thick, airy sauce is egg yolk–based, and so a bit frail. No matter, use a double boiler arrangement, and serve the sauce the moment it is prepared. This recipe will serve you well because it builds a special dessert so speedily, and without tedious backup work for the cook.

6 seedless oranges, peeled and cut into segments	5 egg yolks
1 bunch grapes, stemmed, halved, and seeded	5 tablespoons granulated sugar
superfine sugar or honey, to taste	freshly grated rind of 2 oranges (grated before you peel the oranges, above)
2 teaspoons lemon juice	⅓ cup orange liqueur

1. Toss the orange segments and grapes in superfine sugar or honey to sweeten them. Sprinkle on the lemon juice, and toss again.

2. Arrange the fruit on a serving platter or on individual plates. Lining the platter or plates with fresh grape or ti leaves is very attractive and simple to execute in addition to being festive. Or, put the fruit in large glass goblets.

3. To prepare the hot orange sauce, put the egg yolks, granulated sugar, and orange rind in the top of a double boiler or a large bowl. Beat until well blended and thickly sticky. Place the top of the double boiler into the bottom, which contains a few inches of simmering water, or if you are using the mixing bowl arrangement, put the mixing bowl over a smaller saucepan of simmering water. The top unit holding the egg yolks should never touch the simmering water.

4. Begin to beat the eggs and sugar, slowly at first, then faster as the yolks begin to mound and swell in volume. After several minutes, add the orange liqueur in a thin stream, always beating the mixture. Continue to beat the mixture several minutes longer until it is quite thick and inflated at least fourfold.

5. Pour the sauce into a serving bowl and spoon a very thick band of it over each portion of fruit.

SHOPPING LIST
Dairy: eggs
Fruit: seedless oranges, grapes, lemon

Staples: superfine sugar or honey, granulated sugar, orange liqueur

ORANGES AND KIWIS IN ORANGE CUSTARD SAUCE

I admit that, for me, the real glory and delight of crafting (and enjoying) fruit desserts begins right about the time when the first flush of heat ripens local strawberries. Until we can shift into gathering baskets of sparkling berries, we can always rely on winter citrus and a small range of tropical fruit. It is then that a few special dessert sauces can work their special way, creamy and rich in texture, to ennoble some fruit, such as oranges, that are mainly eaten out of hand or by the wedge or slice. The custard sauce is immensely pleasing with oranges alone, in case you find yourself gifted with a large case of oranges, and is simple to prepare.

5 seedless oranges, peeled and sliced
3 kiwi fruit, peeled and sliced
3 tablespoons orange liqueur
juice of 1 lime

superfine sugar or honey
1 recipe Orange Custard Sauce (see
  Note, page 282)

1. Put the orange and kiwi slices in separate mixing bowls. Sprinkle 2 tablespoons of the orange liqueur over the oranges and 1 tablespoon over the kiwi slices.

2. Dribble two-thirds of the lime juice over the kiwi fruit and the rest over the orange slices. Sweeten the orange slices with superfine sugar or honey, to taste, and if you like, the kiwi slices, too. (I happen to prefer the kiwi without sugar, but it is a matter of personal taste.)

3. Allow the fruit to marinate in the liqueur, lime juice, and sweetener until you are ready to assemble the dessert. Overlap the fruit in an attractive pattern on a serving plate. Pour over all the delicious juices that may have accumulated.

4. Let each person help himself to a serving of fruit. Over each helping pour a belt of custard sauce.

<small>SHOPPING LIST</small>
Fruit: seedless oranges, kiwis, lime
Staples: orange liqueur, superfine sugar or honey

For serving: Orange Custard Sauce (see recipe)

DOUBLE-RICH PEACH ICE CREAM

This is a sumptuous ice cream, which is clearly stated in the ingredients: light cream, heavy cream, and egg yolks.

1 cup light cream	2½ cups heavy cream
3 egg yolks	1 tablespoon vanilla extract
pinch of salt	2 large firm but ripe peaches
½ cup plus 2 tablespoons granulated sugar	2 teaspoons lemon juice
	½ tablespoon granulated sugar

1. Pour the light cream into a heavy saucepan. Put the saucepan over moderate heat and heat the liquid to the scalding stage.

2. In a mixing bowl, beat the egg yolks, salt, and ½ cup plus 2 tablespoons sugar until thick and creamy. Strain the hot cream into the egg-sugar mixture and stir well. Put the egg-cream mixture in a heavy saucepan and cook the custard base over low heat, stirring, until it coats a spoon.

3. When the custard base has become lightly thickened and smooth, remove it from the heat and stir for a few moments to cool. Pour in the heavy cream, stir well, and blend in the vanilla extract.

4. Transfer the ice cream base to a storage bowl, cool completely, then refrigerate overnight, or up to 2 days, covered.

5. Shortly before the ice cream is to be churned, prepare the peaches: peel, halve, pit, and cut them into rough cubes. Toss the peaches in the lemon juice and the ½ tablespoon of sugar. Crush the peaches very lightly with the back of a spoon to get the juices going; refrigerate covered.

6. Scrape the ice cream base into the can of an ice cream machine, preferably one that you pack with cracked ice and rock salt, for the most superior of textures. Process the ice cream according to the directions supplied by the manufacturer. Halfway through the freezing time, stir in the crushed peaches and complete the freezing process. Let the ice cream mellow before serving.

SHOPPING LIST
Fruit: peaches, lemon
Dairy: light cream, heavy cream, eggs

Staple: granulated sugar
Flavoring: vanilla extract

PEACH SLICES BAKED WITH WALNUTS AND SPICES

Shapely peaches, round and juicy, are particularly enchanting when baked with a mantle of sugar, flour, and spices, sprayed with nuts. I do have an old-fashioned fondness for this type of dessert. Its roots may be homespun, but the peaches taste so good when baked in this way, especially when they have been snatched straight from the tree.

1½ tablespoons butter, for the baking dish
4 cups sliced peeled peaches
½ cup granulated sugar
finely grated rind of 1 lemon
juice of 1 large lemon
½ cup sifted all-purpose flour, preferably unbleached
½ cup chopped walnuts
pinch of salt

¼ cup dark-brown sugar
¼ cup granulated sugar
1 teaspoon ground cinnamon
pinch of ground cloves
5 tablespoons butter, cut into small cubes
vanilla ice cream, Vanilla Custard Sauce (page 282), or Vanilla Whipped Cream Sauce (page 280)

1. Smear the 1½ tablespoons butter on the inside of a 10-inch baking dish, 2 inches high.

2. Toss the peach slices in the ½ cup granulated sugar, lemon rind, and lemon juice.

3. Combine the flour, walnuts, salt, brown sugar, granulated sugar, cinnamon, and cloves in a mixing bowl. Scatter the butter cubes over the mixture and work it in with a round-bladed knife so that it becomes distributed into small shreds. Be careful not to overwork the mixture or it may become oily and dense instead of light.

4. Layer half the peaches in the prepared baking dish and sprinkle on 4 tablespoons of the butter-flour mixture. Cover with the rest of the peaches and all of the remaining butter-flour mixture. Make sure that the top layer of crumbs is even and fully covers the peaches.

5. Bake the peaches in a preheated 375° F oven for about 40 minutes, or until the peaches are tender and the topping is golden. If the topping begins to brown too quickly before the peaches are tender, cover the top loosely with a sheet of aluminum foil.

SHOPPING LIST
Fruit: peaches, lemon
Dairy: butter
Staples: granulated sugar, dark-brown sugar, flour, walnuts
Spices: ground cinnamon, ground cloves

STEWED SPICED PEACHES

If I am not tossing peach slices in sugar, lemon, and a little flour mixed with spices for a deep-dish pie, I am prone to simmer them briefly in a red wine and sugar liquid. For a deep-dish pie, plunge the peaches quickly in boiling water to make removing the skin easier; then halve and pit the peaches as usual. But for this kind of recipe, I tend to leave the skin on, for color and texture.

My absolutely favorite choice of peaches is the fat, juicy freestone variety which makes sectioning the slices so much easier. I usually bring home tubs of these very sweet peaches during the later part of the summer, gathered straight from the tree at a local orchard. I use part for this recipe, most of the peaches for jam, and some for chutney or another type of condiment.

This compote is good with homemade pound cake. Or flavor some *crème fraîche* with a little ground allspice and honey to sweeten, and serve in a separate bowl along with the peaches.

1½ cups granulated sugar
1½ cups dry red wine
½ cup water
3-inch piece of cinnamon stick
6 peppercorns
3 whole cloves

3 whole allspice berries
6 strips of lemon peel
8 large ripe but firm peaches, preferably freestones
juice of 1 lemon

1. Combine the sugar, wine, water, cinnamon stick, peppercorns, cloves, allspice berries, and lemon peel in a heavy casserole, such as a 6-quart one. Place the casserole over low heat, cover tightly, and cook until the sugar has dissolved.

2. Uncover the pot, raise the heat to high, and boil the liquid for 8 minutes. While the syrup is cooking, prepare the peaches by cutting them in half, removing the pit, and cutting each half into slices. Toss the peach slices in the lemon juice.

3. Add the peach slices to the syrup and regulate the heat so that the syrup simmers gently. Simmer the peaches for 6–10 minutes or until they are tender but have not lost their shape. Baste the slices with the syrup from time to time.

4. Remove the casserole from the heat and *carefully* remove the peach slices to a bowl with a slotted spoon. Boil down the liquid until it takes on some body—reduce it by about a third. Strain the liquid over the peaches. Put back the cinnamon stick, for extra added flavor, if you wish.

To Store   Place the stewed peaches and all the poaching liquid into a storage container, cover, and refrigerate up to 1 day in advance of serving.

To Serve   Serve the peaches cool or cold with some of the syrup.

SHOPPING LIST
Fruit: peaches, lemon
Staples: granulated sugar, dry red wine

Spices: cinnamon stick, peppercorns, whole cloves, allspice berries

PEAR AND GINGER BREAD PUDDING

I have a passion for all kinds of custards. To my mind, they are both rich and light, and the most fanciful ones are ornamented with bread and fruit. The plainer puddings are good with a fruit sauce (try sweetened puréed raspberries for a very elegant treat) or serve this one, in which the fruit is part and parcel of the dessert, with a bowl of pure whipped cream.

6 tablespoons butter

2 large pears, peeled, cored, sliced, and tossed in 1 teaspoon lemon juice

1 tablespoon granulated sugar

½ teaspoon ground ginger

10 ⅓-inch-thick slices of top-quality white bread, crusts removed and sliced

in half

3½ cups light cream

5 whole eggs

3 egg yolks

1⅓ cup granulated sugar

2 teaspoons vanilla extract

1. Smear 1 tablespoon of the butter on the inside of a 10-inch baking dish, at least 1½ inches deep.

2. Sauté the pears in 2 tablespoons butter, in a heavy skillet, until they are no longer firm, about 4–5 minutes. Sprinkle the tablespoon of sugar and the ginger over the pears, and fold both into the slices. Reserve.

3. Butter the bread slices on one side only with the remaining 3 tablespoons butter and arrange the slices in the bottom of the prepared baking dish. Cover the slices with the sautéed pears.

4. Scald the light cream in a saucepan. While the cream is scalding, beat the whole eggs and egg yolks together in a mixing bowl. Beat in 1 cup sugar. Strain a little of the hot cream onto the egg-sugar mixture, stir it in, and blend in the remaining cream. Stir in the vanilla extract.

5. Pour the custard mixture over the bread and fruit. Put the baking dish in a larger

baking pan and fill the pan with warm water to rise halfway up the sides of the pudding dish. Transfer the whole assembly into the lower third of a preheated 350° F oven to bake for 50 minutes, or until set.

6. Remove the pudding from the water bath and cool on a rack. Serve warm.

NOTE: Currants are a possible addition to this pudding: scatter 2 tablespoons plump ones on the bottom of the baking dish before the bread slices are added. If you happen to have some extra slices of gingerbread on hand, a delightfully unusual bread pudding can be made by substituting gingerbread slices for the white bread. Delicious.

SHOPPING LIST
Fruit: pears, lemon
Dairy: butter, light cream, eggs
Staples: bread, granulated sugar

Flavoring: vanilla extract
Spice: ground ginger

GRATIN OF PEARS WITH MAPLE SYRUP AND NUTMEG

Sometimes I tire of poaching pears in wine and flavorings. It is then that I turn to layering the fruit with maple syrup and nutmeg, and topping the whole construction with a mixture of walnuts, macaroon crumbs, and butter. Be sure to use an oval baking dish for this gratin. Somehow, and this may be my imagination, I think that the pears bake more evenly and the whole dish takes on a better shape (and flavor) in this type of dish. Serve this warm gratin with a bowl of *crème fraîche* flavored with a little maple syrup and a few gratings of nutmeg.

1 tablespoon butter, for the baking dish
2¾ pounds ripe pears, peeled, cored, sliced, and tossed in the juice of 1 large lemon
⅓ cup granulated sugar blended with ¼ teaspoon freshly ground nutmeg and ⅓ teaspoon ground cinnamon

½ cup pure maple syrup
6 dry macaroons, crushed into coarse crumbs
1 cup finely chopped walnuts
4 tablespoons butter, cut into cubes
2 tablespoons all-purpose flour

1. Smear the 1 tablespoon of butter on the inside of a 9-inch oval baking dish, at least 1¾ inches deep.

2. In a large mixing bowl, combine the sliced pears with the nutmeg-cinnamon-sugar

mixture. Put half the pear slices in the prepared baking dish and pour on half the maple syrup. Layer on the remaining pear slices and maple syrup.

3. In a small bowl, mix the macaroon crumbs and walnuts. Add the butter cubes and reduce them to small bits with a round-bladed knife. Stir in the flour. (If you have a food processor, put the whole macaroons, unchopped walnuts—a heaping 1⅓ cups—and butter in the work bowl fitted with the steel knife. Process, with quick on-off turns, until the ingredients are chopped. Stir in the flour.)

4. Cover the top of the pears with the butter-macaroon-nut crumbs in an even layer, but keep the topping light—do not pack it down.

5. Bake the gratin in the upper third of a preheated 375° F oven until the pears are cooked and the topping is golden, about 35 minutes. Do not be surprised if the baking time extends to 50 minutes for some pears to reach perfect tenderness. Cover the top of the gratin with a sheet of aluminum foil if the crumb topping begin to brown too fast.

6. Cool the gratin on a rack. Serve warm.

SHOPPING LIST
Fruit: pears, lemon
Dairy: butter
Staples: granulated sugar, maple syrup, walnuts, flour

Bakery: macaroons
Spices: ground nutmeg, ground cinnamon

PEARS UNDER SHORTCAKE

This is a deep layer of winter pears baked in a blend of sugar and cinnamon and partially hidden by a covering of shortcake mounds spiced with ginger.

The Pears

1 tablespoon butter, for the baking dish
2¾ pounds pears, peeled, sliced ½ inch thick, and tossed in the juice of 1 lemon
1 cup granulated sugar blended with ½ teaspoon ground cinnamon, ¼ teaspoon ground nutmeg, and 1½ tablespoons all-purpose flour
2 tablespoons butter, cut into cubes

The Shortcake

1 cup all-purpose flour
1 teaspoon baking powder
large pinch of salt
¼ teaspoon ground ginger
1 tablespoon solid shortening, cut into cubes
4 tablespoons butter, cut into cubes
1½ tablespoons granulated sugar
½ cup light cream, well chilled

1. Smear the tablespoon of butter on the inside of a deep 9-inch baking dish. Toss the pears in the sugar-spice-flour blend. Put half the pears in the prepared baking dish, and

scatter over half of the cubed butter (taken from the 2 tablespoons). Top with the remaining pears.

2. To make the shortcake: In a mixing bowl, sift the flour, baking powder, salt, and ginger together. Add the shortening and butter cubes and reduce them to very small bits with a round-bladed knife. Stir in the sugar. Make a well in the center of the flour mixture, pour in the cream, and stir the liquid and flour together to form a soft and lightly sticky dough. Beat the dough with a few swift strokes.

3. Drop the dough by heaping tablespoon mounds on top of the pears, allowing some of the fruit to show through. Place the baking dish in a preheated 425° F oven for 30 minutes or until the pears are tender and the topping turns golden. If, after 20 minutes, the topping is brown and the pears have not started to soften, reduce the oven temperature to 400° F and bake until the pears are tender.

4. Put the baked dessert on a cooling rack until serving time. Serve warm.

SHOPPING LIST
Fruit: pears, lemon
Dairy: butter, light cream
Staples: granulated sugar, flour, baking powder, short-ening
Spices: ground cinnamon, ground nutmeg, ground ginger

PEARS IN SWEET WINE WITH VANILLA

The tiny grains enclosed in the whole vanilla pod are especially welcome in poached pears. Such vanilla is a luxurious dessert addition, with a rich and intense flavor. As the sweet wine bubbles around the pears and spices, all three coax flavorful exchanges.

6 small ripe pears
a large bowl of cold water into which the juice of 1 large lemon has been squeezed
¾ cup granulated sugar
1½ cups sweet white wine
4-inch piece of vanilla bean, split down the center with a sharp knife
3-inch piece of cinnamon stick

4 whole cloves

To Serve

1 recipe Vanilla Custard Sauce (page 282), or Vanilla Whipped Cream Sauce (page 280), or 1½ cups plain heavy cream
2 tablespoons toasted slivered almonds or chopped walnuts (optional)

1. Peel the pears, cut them in half, and remove the core. As you prepare each pear, drop it into the large bowl of water.

2. Put the sugar and wine into a 10- or 12-inch casserole. Cover and cook over low heat until the sugar is dissolved. When every granule of sugar has melted, add the vanilla bean, cinnamon stick, and whole cloves. Raise the heat to moderately high and boil the liquid and spices slowly for 5 minutes.

3. Add the pear halves, flat side down, and regulate the heat so that the liquid simmers gently. Poach the pears until they are tender (about 30 minutes), basting them several times with the wine syrup.

To Store   Cool the pears in the syrup, then carefully remove them to a wide, flat storage container. If the syrup is not already lightly condensed, boil it down further. Strain the syrup over the pears. Cool completely, cover, and refrigerate for up to 2 days.

To Serve   Transfer the pears to a shallow bowl and spoon over the syrup. Serve with any of the sauces or plain cream. If you like, sprinkle the toasted nuts evenly over the pears just before serving.

SHOPPING LIST
Fruit: pears, lemon
Staples: granulated sugar, sweet white wine, almonds or walnuts (optional)

Spices: cinnamon stick, whole cloves, vanilla bean
For serving: Vanilla Custard Sauce or Vanilla Whipped Cream Sauce (see recipes) or heavy cream

WHOLE SECKEL PEARS IN SPICED WINE

As the leaves change from green to gold, small Seckel pears begin to pile up, pyramid-fashion, at produce stands and farm markets. I like to treat this pear as I would any of the larger varieties, by poaching in a spicy red wine syrup with lots of citrus peel. Seckels are very good poached, but the time-consuming part is trimming off the peel, neatly, to preserve the shape of the fruit. Then simmer them at a gentle bubble and enjoy. (I have also tried poaching the pears in their jackets, which seemed like a good idea at first, but turned out as an awful mess. The skins collapsed, even at the slowest simmer, and the flavor really did not penetrate the fruit. So remove the peel carefully enough to keep the contour of each pear.)

8 ripe Seckel pears, peeled and immersed
   in a bowl of water combined with the
   juice of 1 lemon
1 cup granulated sugar
½ cup water
2 cups red wine
6 strips orange peel
4 strips lemon peel

6 whole cloves
3-inch piece of cinnamon stick
juice of 1 lemon

To Serve

3 tablespoons sliced or slivered almonds,
   lightly toasted (optional)
whipped cream (optional)

1. Have the pears peeled, immersed, and handy.

2. Prepare the poaching syrup. Place all of the ingredients, except the pears, almonds, and whipped cream, in a 6-quart casserole or any other cooking vessel roomy enough for all the pears to sit on their bases without touching. Cover and cook the sugar, liquid, and spices over low heat until the sugar has dissolved completely.

3. When every granule of sugar has dissolved, uncover the casserole, raise the heat to moderately high, and bring the syrup to a boil. Boil the syrup for 5 minutes.

4. Arrange the pears, stem side up, in the spiced syrup. Simmer the pears, covered, over a low flame until tender (about 50–60 minutes), basting often.

To Store   Cool the pears in the liquid, then transfer them to a storage container that can hold them in one layer. Cook the syrup down until lightly condensed over moderately high heat, about 4–5 minutes. Strain the syrup and pour it over the pears. Cool completely, cover, and refrigerate for up to 2 days.

To Serve   Transfer the pears to a serving dish and pour over all of the syrup. Sprinkle almonds over the pears, if you wish, and serve. A side bowl of whipped cream is nice.

Shopping List
Fruit: Seckel pears, orange, lemon
Dairy: whipping cream (optional)
Staples: granulated sugar, dry red wine, sliced or sliv-
ered almonds (optional)
Spices: whole cloves, cinnamon stick

PERSIMMON ICE CREAM

Good ice cream is not only synonymous with summer and its intense heat. One of the silkiest and softly fruity ones I know is this autumn delight, done with the flesh of very ripe persimmons. First you make a custard base, which can (and must) be done in advance before the ice cream is churned. Once the ice cream is halfway frozen, the persimmon purée is added, then the freezing process may continue. Top off the scoops with a buttery ginger sauce or a drizzling of liqueur, chopped nuts, and candied ginger.

1½ cups light cream
⅔ cup plus 2 tablespoons granulated
    sugar
pinch of salt
4 egg yolks

2 cups heavy cream
3 teaspoons vanilla extract
2 softly ripe persimmons, to make ⅔ cup
    purée

1. Scald the light cream in a saucepan. While the cream is heating, beat the sugar, salt, and egg yolks together until thick. Strain in a few tablespoons of the hot cream and stir well. Strain in the rest of the cream and blend.

2. Pour the cream-egg yolk mixture into a clean, heavy saucepan. Cook the mixture over a low flame, stirring all the while, until it covers the spoon in a smooth, velvety mantle. Do not rush the procedure by raising the heat, or the custard will curdle, forming nasty egg yolk clumps.

3. When the mixture coats the spoon, remove it from the heat and cool by stirring for a few minutes. Stir in the heavy cream and 2 teaspoons vanilla extract. Cool the ice cream mixture to room temperature, then refrigerate in a tightly covered storage container. Chill for 8 hours or overnight.

4. The next day, churn the custard mixture in an ice cream freezer, according to the directions supplied by the manufacturer. In the meantime, peel the persimmons and purée the flesh through a food mill; stir in the tablespoon of vanilla extract. Cover and refrigerate until needed.

5. When the ice cream mixture is about halfway through the freezing stage, add the cold persimmon purée and finish processing. Pack the ice cream in a container (if you are using an electric machine that fits into the freezer comaprtment) and mellow, or leave to mellow in the machine of the hand-cranked or power-cranked variety.

SHOPPING LIST
Fruit: persimmons
Dairy: light cream, heavy cream, eggs

Staple: granulated sugar
Flavoring: vanilla extract

PINEAPPLE IN PORT WITH PECANS

While a flawlessly ripe pineapple alone is a refreshing dessert, a glistening port-strengthened syrup also does fine things for the fruit. The syrup, underlined with citrus parings and cinnamon stick, soaks into the fibery nap of the pineapple magnificently.

⅓ cup plus 2 tablespoons granulated sugar
¾ cup port
3 strips lemon peel
3 strips orange peel
3-inch stick of cinnamon

¼ cup golden raisins
4 cups pineapple wedges or fingers (about 2 ripe pineapples), tossed in the juice of ½ lemon
⅓ cup toasted chopped pecans

1. For the syrup, put the sugar, port, lemon peel, orange peel, and cinnamon stick in a heavy 1-quart saucepan. Cover the pan and place over low heat. Heat the contents until the sugar has dissolved completely.

2. When every granule of sugar has melted, uncover the pan, raise the heat, and boil the liquid for 4 minutes. Add the raisins and remove from the heat. Cool the syrup to room temperature, then refrigerate in a covered container for up to 6 days.

3. On serving day, put the pineapple in a serving bowl. Pour over the syrup and scatter on the pecans. Carefully fold the syrup and nuts through the fruit.

SHOPPING LIST
Fruit: lemon, orange, pineapples
Staples: granulated sugar, port, golden raisins, pecans

Spice: cinnamon stick

PRUNE PLUMS STEWED IN WHITE WINE

These tiny dark purple plums are delicious when cooked slowly in a sweet wine syrup. I like to add 2 tablespoons of plum brandy to the liquid because I think it brings out the flavor of the fruit. The proportion of sugar for sweetening the plums can be adjusted according to the natural sweetness of the fruit, and you can also add a small amount of lemon juice to correct the flavor after the prunes have simmered. This is good served with whipped cream flavored with ground cinnamon, vanilla extract, and a little sugar.

½ cup granulated sugar
1½ cups sweet white wine
¼ cup fresh orange juice, strained
6 thin strips of lemon peel
6 whole cloves

3-inch piece of cinnamon stick
2 tablespoons plum brandy (mirabelle) (optional)
1⅓ pounds small prune plums

1. Put the sugar, wine, and orange juice in a large heavy pot. Add the lemon peel, cloves, and cinnamon stick. Cover the pot and cook the liquid over low heat until the sugar has completely dissolved.

2. Pour in the plum brandy (if you wish to use it), bring the liquid to a boil, and boil for 5 minutes. Add the plums, cover, and simmer them slowly until tender but still whole, without any of the fruit collapsing, about 12 minutes, depending upon the ripeness of the fruit. Baste the plums several times with the pan liquid.

3. With a slotted spoon, carefully transfer the plums to a storage container. Boil down the cooking liquid until it is glossy, lightly thickened, and reduced by at least a third. Strain the syrup over the fruit.

To Store   Cool completely, cover, and refrigerate for up to 3 days in the refrigerator.

To Serve   May be served cold from the refrigerator, at room temperature, or warm.

SHOPPING LIST
Fruit: prune plums, orange, lemon
Staples: granulated sugar, sweet white wine, plum

brandy (optional)
Spices: whole cloves, cinnamon stick

STUFFED PRUNES AND WHOLE APRICOTS IN WHITE WINE AND SPICES

I often put up these prunes and apricots during the holiday season, when they turn into something like a confection, alongside my usual overwhelming supply of bakery goods. And together, in alternating layers, these fruits make lovely personal gifts from the kitchen, packed in hinged canning jars. As dried fruits go, this is a luxurious dessert that is best served with a bowl of whipped cream, enhanced with some freshly grated nutmeg, which melds nicely with the honey-flavored syrup.

1 pound prunes, pitted
½ cup pecans, toasted
1 pound whole dried apricots
about ½ cup dates, pitted and cut in half
4 cups fruity white wine
⅔ cup honey

6 strips lemon peel
4 whole cloves
3-inch piece of cinnamon stick
3-inch piece of vanilla bean, split down
   the middle with a sharp knife
a few gratings of nutmeg

1. Stuff the pitted prunes with a pecan half each. Stuff the whole apricots with a date half.

2. In a large nonmetallic saucepan or 4-quart casserole, combine the wine, honey, lemon peel, cloves, cinnamon stick, vanilla bean, and nutmeg. Cover and simmer over low heat until the honey has dissolved. Uncover the saucepan, raise the heat to moderately high, and boil the liquid for 5 minutes.

3. Pour half of the wine syrup into another casserole or saucepan, leaving some of the spices in each. Put the prunes in one saucepan and the apricots in another. Bring the contents of both pans to a gentle simmer and simmer slowly for 10 minutes, until each fruit is tender but not mushy. Let the fruit linger in the syrup until cool.

To Store   Discard the lemon peel and cloves from the syrup and put the fruit in different storage containers with the aid of a slotted spoon. Allow the fruit to cool completely in the syrup and refrigerate up to 3 weeks.

To Serve   Layer the fruit in a serving bowl along with the syrup.

SHOPPING LIST
Fruit: dried prunes, dried apricots, dates, lemon
Staples: fruity white wine, pecans, honey

Spices: whole cloves, cinnamon stick, vanilla bean, nutmeg

RASPBERRY CREAM

This dessert, decadent as it may be, is for the special days when you want to indulge in raspberries and cream. It is quite artless, with egg yolks and fruit purée which is vibrantly red but, when combined with the heavy cream and egg whites, turns the whole bowlful a light pink color. Good plain, or decorated with a few extra fresh raspberries, whipped cream, and slivered nuts, or with a puddle of sweetened raspberry purée underneath each serving.

1½ cups fresh ripe raspberries
⅞ cup granulated sugar
1 tablespoon white corn syrup
½ cup, less 1 tablespoon, water
5 egg yolks
pinch of salt

1 teaspoon vanilla extract
1 tablespoon raspberry brandy (framboise)
4 egg whites
1¾ cups heavy cream (preferably the kind that is not ultrasterilized)

1. Purée the raspberries in the blender, ½ cup at a time, or do the full amount in a food processor fitted with the steel knife. Strain the purée of all the seeds and store in the refrigerator.

2. Place the sugar, corn syrup, and water in a heavy saucepan. Cover and cook until every granule of sugar has dissolved. Uncover the saucepan and bring the liquid to a boil. Put in a candy thermometer and cook the syrup until the temperature registers 240° F.

3. As the syrup cooks, beat the egg yolks with a pinch of salt in a large mixing bowl until lightly thick, using a hand-held electric beater. When the syrup reaches 240° F, lift out the thermometer and slowly pour the hot syrup into the egg yolks, beating constantly.

4. Continue beating the syrup until it is cool. You can set the bowl into a larger bowl filled with ice water to speed up the process. In any event, the mixture must be cool. Beat in the vanilla extract and raspberry brandy. Beat in the cold fruit purée.

5. Place the raspberry mixture into the freezer for about 20 minutes, stirring several times, to chill it thoroughly before the cream and egg whites are added.

6. Beat the egg whites until soft mounds are formed, adding a pinch of salt or cream of tartar as the eggs begin to foam up.

7. Beat the cream until soft peaks are formed when a whisk or beaters are lifted. Fold the egg whites into the cold raspberry base, using a rubber spatula and an over and under folding technique. Fold in the whipped cream.

To Store Turn the raspberry cream into a 7-cup bowl and smooth over the top. Put the bowl into a larger storage container, cover, and freeze overnight or up to 2 days.

SHOPPING LIST
Fruit: raspberries
Dairy: heavy cream, eggs

Staples: granulated sugar, white corn syrup
Flavorings: raspberry brandy, vanilla extract

RASPBERRIES IN WARM FRAMBOISE SAUCE

Sterling raspberries with a mound of warm sauce. Taste a berry and sweeten the rest with a haze of superfine sugar if you think they need it; shake the berries around gently to dissolve the sugar before preparing the sauce. (I never find this to be necessary during the peak season.)

2 pints beautiful ripe red raspberries (or black ones)

5 egg yolks

5 tablespoons superfine sugar

4 tablespoons raspberry brandy (framboise)

3 tablespoons orange brandy

1. Pick over the berries for any stems or leaves.

2. Put the egg yolks in the top of a double boiler (or any other double boiler arrangement). With an electric beater (or by hand, with a wire whisk and a good, powerful arm), beat the yolks until they are thick and sticky.

3. Beat in the sugar by tablespoons. Set the pot over gently simmering water, adjusting the water level so that the water never touches the bottom of the top saucepan or bowl.

4. Beat the egg yolks until they begin to swell and take on volume, about 4 minutes. The water should be regulated so that it stays at a lazy bubble. Beat in the raspberry brandy by tablespoons, then add the orange brandy in the same way. Continue beating until the mixture is quite thick and holds its shape in a large mound. Transfer the warm sauce to a serving bowl and serve spoonfuls of it along with each portion of fruit.

SHOPPING LIST
Fruit: raspberries
Dairy: eggs

Staples: fine granulated sugar, raspberry brandy, orange brandy

RHUBARB BAKED WITH BROWN SUGAR AND CINNAMON

As rhubarb bakes with sugar, it intensifies into a deep raspberry-red color, tasting at once sweet and tart. The spicy adjunct is cinnamon, and the topping is riddled with nuts, one of the delightful textures to this dessert. Serve the rhubarb with *crème fraîche* or whipped cream, if you like.

1 tablespoon butter, for the baking dish
4½ cups 1½-inch rhubarb segments
1 cup granulated sugar
1 heaping cup chopped walnuts or pecans

4 tablespoons all-purpose flour
1 teaspoon ground cinnamon
¼ teaspoon ground cloves
½ cup brown sugar
6 tablespoons butter, cut into cubes

1. Smear the tablespoon of butter on the inside of a 9-inch baking dish. Set aside.

2. In a mixing bowl, toss the rhubarb with the granulated sugar and turn the sugared fruit into the prepared baking dish.

3. Combine the nuts, flour, cinnamon, cloves, and brown sugar in a small mixing bowl. Add the butter cubes and cut them into very tiny bits with a round-bladed knife.

4. Cover the top of the rhubarb with the nut-sugar-butter crumbs to conceal all of the fruit. Bake the rhubarb in the middle of a preheated 375° F oven until it is tender and the topping is crisply golden, about 40–45 minutes. Cool on a rack and serve warm.

SHOPPING LIST
Fruit: rhubarb
Dairy: butter
Staples: granulated sugar, brown sugar, walnuts or pecans, flour
Spices: ground cinnamon, ground cloves

RHUBARB COMPOTE

This baked compote, warm or chilled, is a lovely plain dessert suited to follow a lively, full-bodied main course. But you could also make the compote, chill it thoroughly, purée it, and fold in 2 cups of lightly whipped cream and come up with the classic rhubarb fool.

2 pounds bright red rhubarb, cut into 2-inch lengths
1¼ cups granulated sugar blended with 1 teaspoon ground cinnamon and ¼ teaspoon ground cloves

3-inch length of vanilla bean, split down the center, or 2 teaspoons vanilla extract
heavy cream

1. In a heavy casserole with a tight-fitting lid—a 4-quart one will do nicely—put one-fourth of the rhubarb. Sprinkle on a fourth of the sugar mixture.

2. Continue to layer the sugar and rhubarb, a fourth at a time, burying the vanilla bean midway (if you are using it) and ending with a layer of sugar.

3. Cover the casserole with the lid and bake the rhubarb in the middle of a preheated 325° F oven until tender (about 40 minutes), or simmer slowly on the stove top.

4. Remove the casserole from the heat. If the vanilla bean was not used, stir in the vanilla extract now. Discard the whole vanilla bean.

5. Serve the cooked rhubarb warm or chilled, with a pitcher of heavy cream.

SHOPPING LIST
Fruit: rhubarb
Dairy: heavy cream
Staples: granulated sugar

Flavoring: vanilla bean or vanilla extract
Spices: ground cinnamon, ground cloves

DEEP-DISH RHUBARB PIE

Fresh fruit and pastry dough are special soul-mates. Fragile, buttery dough can hold glowing summer fruit or act as a natural lid for fruit to be cooked under its canopy. Here, the pastry covers a deep dish of sugared rhubarb, and the pie, warm from the oven, is ethereal.

If the fancywork of pastrymaking indeed makes you bristle for fear of turning a mass of dough into a rubbery lump, and the whole experience nurses outbursts of rage and frustration, a delicious dessert can be made by covering the prepared fruit with a shortcake topping, like the one in Pears Under Shortcake (page 301), and forget about pastry dough for a little while. But if you, like I, think that digging a spoon past a brittle golden crust and coming up with warm baked fruit and a sheath of that pastry atop is just short of intoxicating, do this pie, and give this rich shortcrust pastry a go.

Pastry Dough
1½ cups flour
pinch of salt
1 egg yolk
3 tablespoons cold water
7 tablespoons cold butter
2 tablespoons cold solid shortening
1 tablespoon granulated sugar
1 tablespoon butter, for the baking dish
5 cups rhubarb chunks, about 1½ inches

long
1⅔ cups granulated sugar blended with 4 tablespoons all-purpose flour, ¼ teaspoon ground ginger, ¾ teaspoon ground cinnamon, and the grated rind of 1 large orange
2 tablespoons butter, cut into small cubes
cold water and granulated sugar, to glaze the pie

1. Up to 3 days in advance (if you want to refrigerate the pastry dough) or longer (up to 1 month if you want to freeze the dough), prepare this shortcrust pastry: Sift 1½ cups

flour (preferably unbleached) with a large pinch of salt into a mixing bowl. Combine 1 egg yolk and 3 tablespoons cold water in a small mixing bowl and keep this refrigerated until later on. Cut 7 tablespoons cold butter and 2 tablespoons *cold* solid shortening into rough cubes. Drop the cubes over the flour. With a round-bladed knife, blend the butter and shortening into the flour until it is broken up into very small bits. With your fingertips only, further break up the fat by dipping down into the flour mixture and up, lightly crumbling it between your fingertips until the butter and shortening turn the flour mixture into what looks like a very coarse meal. Sprinkle over 1 tablespoon granulated sugar and blend it in with a few swift strokes of a fork. Make a well in the center of the flour mixture, and pour in the cold egg yolk and water blend. Quickly mix the two together with a fork, using light strokes, until a dough is formed. Add extra droplets of ice cold water if necessary to form a pliant cake of dough, one that is *not* sticky. Press the dough into a rough cake on a lightly floured working surface. Wrap up the dough in a sheet of plastic wrap followed by a sheet of aluminum foil. To freeze, wrap this package in a sheet of freezer paper and seal.

2. The day the pie is to be put together, smear the tablespoon of butter on the inside of a deep oval pie dish that has a rim of about ⅓ inch and measures at least 9 inches across the top.

3. In a large mixing bowl, toss the rhubarb chunks with the sugar-flour-spice blend. Put half of the tossed rhubarb in the baking dish. Distribute half the butter cubes over the fruit and heap on the remaining rhubarb, mounding it slightly. Dot the top with the rest of the butter cubes.

4. Moisten the rim of the dish with a little cold water. On a lightly floured surface, roll out the pastry ¼ inch thick. Cut a few bands of dough from the outside of the sheet of pastry and lay them on the moistened rim of the dish. Cover the top of the fruit with the sheet of dough. Press the edges down on the pastry rim and trim off the excess with a sharp paring knife.

5. Cut several slits on the top of the pastry to allow the steam to escape. Chill the pie in the refrigerator for 10 minutes. Brush the top of the pie with cold water and sprinkle on a fine dusting of sugar.

6. Bake the pie in a preheated 425° F oven for 15 minutes, then reduce the heat to 350° F and continue baking an additional 35 minutes, until the top is brown and the fruit is cooked through. (Carefully stick a toothpick or very thin metal testing skewer through one of the steam vent openings to test if the fruit is cooked.)

7. Cool the pie on a rack until serving time, but do serve it warm.

SHOPPING LIST

Fruit: rhubarb, orange
Dairy: butter, egg

Staples: granulated sugar, flour, shortening
Spices: ground ginger, ground cinnamon

STRAWBERRIES MARINATED IN
RED WINE AND HONEY

Not only is this a pleasantly easy and refreshing denouement for one of those warm spring dinners, but it is even more enjoyable to make this a part of an out-of-doors meal in early summer.

You have uncorked, let's say, a nice red wine to go with some pâté, and you'll make this dessert on the spot because you have toted along a basket of sparkling strawberries and the few other requisite ingredients. You toss them around in the honey and spice with enough red wine to soak them well, and while you are feasting on the main course, the strawberries sit out under a warm, sunny sky, marinating. They will be delightful with some rich little sugar or nut cookies.

Use an aromatic honey of some distinction for sweetening the strawberries. I have achieved wonderful results with Black Locust honey from Italy, which is golden in color and very rich; with a light brown-rust cranberry honey from Wisconsin; and with a delicious natural unfiltered honey from Berryville, Virginia. The honey for this preparation must have character, and you should like it enough to use "straight," or directly from jar to hot biscuits, as well as for combining with other raw materials. It must be full-bodied and not resemble watered-down corn syrup.

1 quart plump, juicy strawberries	6 whole cloves
⅓ cup honey, or to taste	1 cinnamon stick
2 cups dry red wine	

1. Wash the strawberries quickly under cold running water and pat them dry. Hull or not, as you prefer, but I think the green stems attractive.

2. Put the berries in a bowl and dribble on enough honey to sweeten. Pour over the red wine, dot the berries with the whole cloves, and bury the cinnamon stick within.

3. Shake the bowl gently to mix the ingredients and begin to dissolve the honey. As the honey blends in, taste for additional honey and add it if you think necessary.

4. Let the strawberries marinate in the wine at room temperature until serving time.

Shopping List
Fruit: strawberries
Staples: honey, dry red wine

Spices: whole cloves, cinnamon stick

STRAWBERRIES AND PINEAPPLE
WITH STRAWBERRY PURÉE SAUCE

Here the strawberries are served with pineapple chunks, and both are presented with a sauce made from extra whole strawberries, crushed and enhanced with a little rum or even some strawberry brandy. The sauce is also good with puddings and custard desserts made in spring or early summer.

For the Strawberry Sauce

1 pint ripe strawberries
⅓ cup superfine sugar, or more to taste
2 teaspoons lemon juice
strawberry brandy (fraise) to taste

For the Fruit

1 quart ripe strawberries
1 large ripe pineapple
2½–3½ tablespoons superfine sugar
juice of 1 lemon
3 tablespoons rum

1. For the sauce, cut the pint of strawberries in half if small or into quarters if large. Purée the strawberries with the ⅓ cup sugar in batches in a blender or in one lot in a food processor. Scrape down the sides of the container, as necessary, to blend in any pieces of fruit that may be clinging to the sides.

2. If you object to the tiny "seeds" that are part of the purée, strain the purée through a nonmetallic sieve to remove them. Stir in the lemon juice and brandy. Taste the purée and readjust the flavoring, as necessary.

3. Wash the quart of strawberries quickly under a spray of cold water, drain, and dry. If you are serving the strawberries whole, hull them, if you like. If you prefer to serve the strawberries cut up, hull them and cut each berry in half. Toss the strawberries in 1½ tablespoons of sugar.

4. With a stainless-steel serrated knife, cut off the top and bottom of the pineapple. Remove the entire shell by slicing it off in long vertical strips, making sure that you trim away all of the "eyes." Cut the pineapple into quarters, and slice each section into thick wedges. Toss the pineapple with the lemon juice and the remaining sugar to taste. Sprinkle on the rum and stir gently.

5. Pile the strawberries in the center of a serving bowl and encircle with the pineapple wedges. Serve a helping of both fruits and spoon a ribbon of purée down the center of each portion.

SHOPPING LIST
Fruit: strawberries, pineapple, lemons   *Staples:* granulated sugar, strawberry brandy, rum

STRAWBERRIES STEEPED IN ORANGE BRANDY

I would have used the word "mulled" for "steeped" in the name of this recipe, except that if you mull things, you heat up the liquid, spices, and other goods, which does not occur here. The connection, I was thinking, is that the strawberries become permeated with the three orange flavors (juice, peel, liqueur), like an idea is mulled over, slowly and thoughtfully, taking its strength from surrounding thoughts—and companion tastes. This is a hastily prepared dessert, best put together before you reheat the main course so that the orange flavorings can linger around the strawberries. Serve the berries with Vanilla Custard Sauce (page 282), or Vanilla Whipped Cream Sauce (page 280) into which you have folded about ⅓ cup of chopped toasted walnuts.

1 quart strawberries	4 tablespoons orange brandy
superfine sugar, to taste	6 strips orange peel, taken from the
½ cup fresh orange juice	oranges, above, before they are juiced

1. Quickly rinse the strawberries in cool water. Drain and dry. Hull the berries if you like or leave the green stems on for color. Put the strawberries into a bowl and sprinkle on enough sugar to sweeten to your taste.

2. Pour in the orange juice and orange brandy, scatter in the pieces of orange peel, mix gently, and leave to mull until serving time.

NOTE: A variation on this kind of preparation would be to prepare a sugar syrup based on the orange flavor used above. For this, dissolve ¾ cup granulated sugar in 1 cup plus 2 tablespoons water over low heat. Add 1 cinnamon stick and bring to the boil. Boil for 5 minutes. Add the juice of 1 lemon and 1 orange and boil for 2 minutes. Add 3 tablespoons Cointreau and ⅓ cup Grand Marnier; boil for 2 minutes. Cool completely before pouring over the strawberries, or make this ahead and refrigerate the syrup for up to 3 days in a covered container. When the strawberries marinate, for about 1 hour or longer, I sometimes add long slivers of orange peel.

SHOPPING LIST
Fruit: strawberries, oranges   *Staples:* superfine sugar, orange brandy

STRAWBERRIES WITH WARM LEMON-RUM SAUCE

Heavy-laden desserts, such as layers of sponge cake festooned in butter cream and other assorted concomitants, like *pralin,* candied fruit, and nuts, have been etched in myriad forms by many notable cooks and cookbook writers, and, invariably, they are the beloved children of caterers.

I do prefer the custom of serving an iced cake at tea in an at-home afternoon, or if it suits, well after the evening meal, merely because I appreciate the dessert more. But I always enjoy fresh fruit with cheese, dried fruit revivified in different aromatic potions, and fresh berries in a buttery pastry shell with a good pastry cream and a cloud of whipped cream, or with a warm sauce, light and airy.

This lemon-rum sauce is a valuable one to know. It is excellent over most types of fresh fruit, especially berries, and quite seductive with fruit *beignets,* a smooth foil for the crisp fritters, if you ever find yourself with a warm basket of them. Here is the method for the sauce, and since spring means masses of strawberries, I combine the two here.

5 egg yolks	finely grated rind of 2 lemons
⅓ cup superfine sugar	8 tablespoons light rum
juice of 1 lemon	1 quart strawberries

1. Put the egg yolks and sugar in a large bowl or in the top saucepan of a double boiler. Blend the two together and let stand while you combine the lemon rind and juice in a small bowl, pour the light rum in a container, and wash the strawberries under a spray of cold water (drain them quickly on paper toweling).

2. Now beat the egg yolks and sugar until thick with a hand beater and set over barely simmering water. The bottom of the bowl or double boiler must not touch the simmering water. Begin to beat the egg yolks and sugar on moderate speed.

3. When the egg yolks and sugar start gaining volume, beat in the lemon juice and rind in two additions. Beat for 2 minutes. Beat in the rum, a tablespoon at a time. By the time you have added the last tablespoon of rum, the mixture should be very thick and form cascading ribbony patterns when the beaters are lifted. Turn the sauce into a bowl and serve while still warm along with the strawberries.

SHOPPING LIST
Fruit: strawberries, lemons   *Staples:* superfine sugar, light rum
Dairy: eggs

STRAWBERRY, MELON, AND KIWI BOWL
WITH GINGER AND PORT

Serve this fruit mélange in a clear bowl, not too shallow, to show off the pretty colors. For a special delight, you could add an accompanying warm sauce, in the style of the Lemon-Rum Sauce I use with strawberries in the preceding recipe. Use these proportions: 4 egg yolks, 5 tablespoons superfine sugar, grated rind of 1 orange, and ½ cup port.

1 cup granulated sugar
1¼ cups water
3 pieces of preserved ginger, chopped
3-inch piece of cinnamon stick
4 whole cloves
5 strips of lemon peel
½ cup port

To Serve

1 small ripe melon, peeled and cubed
2 pints perfectly ripe strawberries
3 kiwi fruit, peeled and sliced
¼ cup chopped pistachio nuts

To prepare the syrup, put the sugar, water, ginger, cinnamon stick, cloves, and lemon peel in a saucepan. Cover and place over a low flame. Heat until the sugar has melted completely. Uncover the saucepan, raise the heat to moderately high, and boil the syrup for 4 minutes. Pour in the port and boil for 3 minutes longer.

To Store   Cool the syrup to room temperature. Discard the cloves and lemon peel. Pour the syrup into a storage container, cover, and refrigerate for up to 1 week.

To Serve   Marinate the fruits separately, each in a third of the syrup. Let stand while you put together the rest of the meal. Layer the fruit in a serving bowl, discarding the cinnamon stick, and sprinkle the chopped nuts on top.

Shopping List
Fruit: melon, strawberries, kiwis, lemon
Staples: granulated sugar, preserved ginger, port, pis-
tachio nuts
Spices: cinnamon stick, whole cloves

FROZEN VANILLA CREAM

This is a regal, rich dessert based on the minuscule seeds of the vanilla bean. The vanilla pod is a deep black-brown and the surface is smooth: once you run a sharp knife down the belly of the bean, the full aroma comes forth. And that is what makes this cream so special —the intensity cannot be duplicated even by the purest of extracts.

⅞ cup granulated sugar
½ cup less 1 tablespoon cold water
1½ teaspoons white corn syrup
5 egg yolks, taken from extra-large eggs
pinch of salt
3-inch piece of vanilla bean, split down the center
4 egg whites

2 cups heavy cream (preferably the kind that is not ultrasterilized), well chilled

To Serve

1 cup heavy cream, whipped (optional) and/or ¼ cup chocolate candy coffee beans

1. Put the sugar, water, and corn syrup in a heavy 1-quart saucepan (enameled cast iron works best here). Heat this mixture over a very low flame until all of the sugar has dissolved.

2. Once the sugar has dissolved, raise the heat to moderately high and boil the liquid until it reaches 240° F on a candy thermometer.

3. While the sugar syrup cooks, beat the egg yolks with a pinch of salt in a large mixing bowl and scrape in the tiny seeds of the vanilla bean. Beat until thick and pasty. When the syrup reaches 240° F, quickly remove the thermometer and pour the syrup into the egg yolks, beating constantly with a hand-held mixer.

4. Continue to beat the mixture until it has cooled off. To speed up this process, put the mixing bowl in a larger bowl filled with ice water. The mixture must be thoroughly cooled before the egg whites and whipped cream are added.

5. Beat the egg whites until soft peaks are formed, adding a pinch of salt or cream of tartar as the whites begin to mound. *Stir* one-fourth of the egg whites into the egg yolk base and fold in the remaining whites. Whip the cream until soft peaks are formed and fold into the egg yolk-white mixture, gently, lightly, and thoroughly.

To Store   Turn the cream into a 7-cup serving bowl; level the top with a spatula. Place the bowl in a very large storage container, cover, and freeze overnight.

To Serve   Decorate the top of the cream with a ring of whipped cream and chocolate coffee beans. Or use just the coffee beans.

SHOPPING LIST
Dairy: eggs, heavy cream
Staples: granulated sugar, white corn syrup

Flavoring: vanilla bean
Decoration: chocolate candy coffee beans

TABLE OF METRIC EQUIVALENTS
(Volume and Weight)

Volume (common units)

1 ounce	28.35 grams
1 pound	53.59 grams
1 gram	0.035 ounces
1 kilogram	2.21 pounds

Weight (common units)

1 cup	16 tablespoons
	8 fluid ounces
	236.6 milliliters
1 tablespoon	3 teaspoons
	0.5 fluid ounce
	14.8 milliliters
1 teaspoon	4.9 milliliters
1 liter	1,000 milliliters
	1.06 quarts
1 bushel	4 pecks
1 peck	8 quarts
1 gallon	4 quarts
1 quart	2 pints
1 pint	2 cups
	473.2 milliliters

INDEX

Italic numbers in parentheses indicate pages with menu suggestions for the dish.